Judy

dd

MM

Latinised Hymns

Mark Mortimer

NEWTON PUBLICATIONS

© 2005 Mark Mortimer
Latinised Hymns

ISBN 0-9549101-0-9

Published by:
Newton Publications
Old Rectory,
Newton Reigny
Penrith
Cumbria
CA11 0AY

A CIP catalogue record of this book
can be obtained from the British Library.

Design & production co-ordinated by:
The Better Book Company Ltd
Havant
Hampshire
PO9 2XH

Printed in England.

Cover design by MusicPrint

a.m.D.g.

LATIN VERSIONS OF ENGLISH HYMNS

retaining the metre and rhyme-scheme of the originals

(and singable to the same tunes)

Note: To say the same thing generally requires more syllables (though fewer words) of Latin than of English. Since metre is counted in syllables, some compression, therefore, indeed some omission, has been inevitable. But I hope these "versions" (precis? paraphrases?) are recognisable as such. They are presented in *alphabetical order (of English first lines)*. If many "old favourites" are missing, it is either because they are themselves translations from Latin or because they are short on rhymes – and so insufficiently challenging!

Mark Mortimer   September 2003

Technical Notes

1   **Pronunciation**: Ecclesiastical? (ae rhymes with e)

2   **Rhymes**: I have not followed the mediaeval custom of rhyming, eg glor*ia* and grat*ia*, fort*ibus* and omn*ibus*, but rather the English one, rhyming eg rog*as* and grat*ias*, erig*it* and defu*it*, dec*em* and totid*em*.

3   **Vocabulary**: No particular period; and I have felt free occasionally to coin (morphologically plausible) words, e.g. creamen, omnipollens.

4.   **Elision**: h (mostly) and m are treated as ordinary consonants. Only short vowels are elided.

INDEX

A charge to keep I have,
A God to glorify,
A never-dying soul to save,
And fit it for the sky.

To serve the present age,
My calling to fulfil,
O may it all my powers engage
To do my Master's will.

Arm me with jealous care,
As in thy sight to live,
And O, thy servant, Lord, prepare
A good account to give.

Help me to watch and pray,
And on thyself rely;
And let me ne'er my trust betray,
But press to realms on high.

C. Wesley

Mandatum teneam
dans gloriam Deo;
meamque aeternam animam
accommodem polo.

Dum vivam, serviens
vocatus adsequar
totasque vires admovens,
Deo cum iubear.

Vitamque, ut teste te,
fac acer transeam
et rationem reddere
da Christe, me bonam.

Fac orans vigilem
tuisque viribus
firmatus teneam fidem
et caeli cupidus.

MM 28.1-1.2.00

A safe stronghold our God is still,
A trusty shield and weapon;
He'll help us clear from all the ill
That hath us now o'ertaken.
The ancient prince of hell
Hath risen with purpose fell;
Strong mail of craft and power
He weareth in this hour;
On earth is not his fellow.

With force of arms we nothing can;
Full soon were we down-ridden;
But for us fights the proper Man,
Whom God himself hath bidden.
Ask ye, who is this same?
Christ Jesus is his name,
The Lord Sabaoth's Son;
He, and no other one,
Shall conquer in the battle.

And were this world all devils o'er,
And watching to devour us,
Lay it not to heart so sore;
Nor can they overpower us.
And let the prince of ill
Look grim as e'er he will,
He harms us not a whit:
For why, his doom is writ;
A word shall quickly slay him.

God's word, for all their craft and force,
One moment will not linger,
But, spite of hell, shall have its course;
'Tis written by his finger.
And though they take our life,
Goods, honour, children, wife,
Yet is their profit small;
These things shall vanish all;
The city of God remaineth.

Luther/Carlyle

Scutum Deus cum gladio
et forte munimentum,
omnique expediet malo
quod nobis est intenturn.
Rex infernorum stat,
qui dira cogitat,
vi cinctus et dolis:
est nemo similis
terrestri gente natus.

Per arma nihil possumus,
nam pessum sic iremus;
sed nobis a Deo datus
est hominum supremus:
si nomen quaeritis,
est Jesus Christus is,
Conductor Agminum:
nurn scitis alium
in proelio victorem?

Si mille nos diaboli
vorare destinabunt,
non erimus perterriti,
nec illi nos domabunt;
non rex malitiae
ferus formidine
nocere poterit:
iam se damnatum scit,
quem verbulum prosternet.

Non possunt Verbum laedere,
et opus est ingratum:
Divinum nos in acie
recipirnus afflatum.
Despolient bonis,
uxore, liberis;
cum vita, tum decus
cedatur hostibus:
e Regno non pellemur.

MM 8—13.4.98

Abide with me; fast falls the eventide:
The darkness deepens; Lord, with me abide:
When other helpers fail, and comforts flee,
Help of the helpless, O abide with me.

Swift to its close ebbs out life's little day;
Earth's joys grow dim, its glories pass away;
Change and decay in all around I see:
O thou who changest not, abide with me.

I need thy presence every passing hour;
What but thy grace can foil the tempter's power?
Who like thyself my guide and stay can be?
Through cloud and sunshine, Lord, abide with me.

I fear no foe with thee at hand to. bless;
Ills have no weight, and tears no bitterness.
Where is death's sting? Where, grave, thy victory?
I triumph still, if thou abide with me.

Hold thou thy Cross before my closing eyes;
Shine through the gloom, and point me to the skies:
Heaven's morning breaks, and earth's vain shadows flee;
In life, in death, O Lord, abide with me.

H.F.Lyte

Me protege: crescentes tenebras
nox circumvolvit. O me protegas!
Sum cassus alio solamine:
qui tales adiuvas, O protege.

Lux fugitiva vitae defluit;
terrena laus decusque praeterit.
Est omne circum me mutabile:
qui non mutaris; O me protege.

Praesens quot horae sint appareas:
non aliter vincetur Satanas.
Me nemo sustinebit praeter te:
caelo sub qualicumque protege.

Te coram hostem nullum metuo;
nil opprimit, nec anxius fleo.
Est hebetata mortis acies.
Sum victor usque, dum tu proteges.

Da crucem dormiturus videam
caelestem et per umbras patriam.
Terrestres en! fugantur tenebrae.
Vivum me mortuumque protege.

MM 25.2-04.3.97

Accept, O Lord, we pray,
The humble prayers we bring,
As on this joyful day
We laud our Founder King.
Our lives so guide,
That all our days
May in thy praise
Be glorified.

Laudationes has
ausculta, Domine,
pro Fundatore quas
hac ferimus die.
Laudantibus
illumines
nostros dies,
dum vivimus.

All ye, whose days were few
Upon this earthly scene,
With him give praises due
For all that since hath been.
That purpose bold,
Which once did seem
Mere boyhood's dream,
We now uphold.

Vitae quibus fuit
hic spatium breve,
quid post evenerit,
cum eo canite.
Quod somnium
visumst leve
puertiae
fit hic ratum.

To thee we now draw near,
and for our comrades, Lord,
Who loved and served thee here
Our thankful praise accord.
May we fulfil
From age to age
Our heritage,
As thou dost will.

Te prope, Domine,
nos pro sodalibus,
qui coluere te
hic, grates agimus.
Et tradita
quae liquerint,
probata sint
per saecula.

To thank our Founder King,
With grateful hearts we raise
Our anthems, echoing
Thy glory and thy praise.
Assembled here
His school★ doth own
In frailty shown
That vision clear.

Tibi ut sacramus hunc
canorem, Domine,
sic Fundatori nunc
agantur gratiae.
Testes sumus
quod fuit is
ut fragilis
sic providus.

J.M.Peterson

MM   9 – 28.12.99

★ Shrewsbury

All creation groans and travails:
Thou, O God, shalt hear its groan:
For of man and all creation
Thou alike art God alone.

Pity then thy guiltless creatures,
Who not less man's sufferings share:
For our sins it is they perish:
Let them profit by our prayer.

Cast thine eyes of love and mercy
On the misery of the land:
Say to the destroying Angel,
"'Tis enough: stay now thine hand."

In our homesteads, in our valleys,
Through our pasture-lands give peace:
Through the Goshen of thine Israel
Bid the grievous murrain cease.

But with deeper, tenderer pity,
Call to mind, O Son of God,
Those in thine own image fashioned,
Ransomed with thy precious blood:

Hear and grant the supplications₁
Like a cloud of incense borne
Up toward thy Seat of Mercy
From thy people's hearts forlorn.

For the widow and the orphan,
For the helpless and the poor;
Helpless, hopeless, if thou spare not
Of their basket and their store,

So – while these her earnest accents
Day by day thy Church repeats, –
That our sheep may bring forth thousands
And ten thousands in our streets;

Gemit mundus et laborat;
laborantem tu vides:
quippe hominum et mundi
Deus aeque solus es.

Parce nobiscum dolenti
nec culpando pecori:
culpa nostra pereunti
prosit nostra prex ei.

Nostrum rus adflictum clemens
atque amans inspexeris
angeloque perditori
"Ohe! iam" dic "est satis!"

Ut casis convallibusque,
pascuis sit otium;
nostrum, sicut in Aegypto,
peste libera solum.

Sed in primis miserescens,
Deo Nate, respice
specie tua creatos,
emptos tuo sanguine.

Cum favore votum audi
surgens turi simile
desperante tua plebe
ad Thronum Clementiae,

viduis favens et orbis,
quis nec ops nec sunt opes:
nec ops, nisi quid tu parces
calathis, nec ulla spes,

ut, ex corde tui cantum
dum cultores iterant,
nostrae per vias bidentes
milliens parturiant;

That our oxen, strong to labour,	*sani boves et securi*
May not know nor fear decay:	*tollant fortes onera,*
That there be no more complaining,	*neve sit quod tum queramur*
And the plague have passed away.	*dempta pestilentia;*
And at last, to all thy servants,	*et tuis cum pace terrae*
When earth's troubles shall be o'er,	*universis denique*
Give, O Triune God, a portion	*dona tecum sempiternam*
With thyself for evermore.	*partem, Trine at Unice.*

J. M. Neale (1866)   MM 29.3.—10.4.01

All hail the power of Jesus' name!	*Ab angelis Jesus potens*
Let angels prostrate fall;	*laudetur editus;*
Bring forth the royal diadem	*regalem apicem gerens*
And crown him Lord of all.	*is praestet omnibus.*
Crown him, ye morning stars of light,	*Quin, stellae, hunc extollitis,*
Who fixed this floating ball;	*unde orbis est situs?*
Now hail the Strength of Israel's might,	*Illa Israel laudanda Vis*
And crown him Lord of all.	*iam praestet omnibus.*
Crown him, ye martyrs of your God,	*Prope aram martyres suam*
Who from his altar call;	*quos audiit Deus,*
Extol the Stem of Jesse's Rod,	*laudate Virgam Jessicam,*
And crown him Lord of all.	*quae praestet omnibus.*
Ye seed of Israel's chosen race,	*Vos Israel prosapiae,*
Ye ransomed of the fall,	*quos emit Dominus,*
Hail him who saves you by his grace,	*iam Salvatori plaudite:*
And crown him Lord of all.	*is praestet omnibus.*
Sinners, whose love can ne'er forget	*Scelesti, vestrum memores*
The wormwood and the gall,	*quem laeserit scelus,*
Go spread your trophies at his feet,	*nunc ferte praedam ad pedes:*
And crown him lord of all.	*is praestet omnibus.*
Let every tribe and every tongue	*A vobis, gentes variae,*
Before him prostrate fall,	*noscatur Dominus;*
And shout in universal song	*hunc universi canite,*
The crowned Lord of all.	*qui praestat omnibus.*

E. Perronet   MM 15—21.5.99

Latinised Hymns

All my hope on God is founded;
He doth still my trust renew.
Me through change and chance he guideth,
Only good and only true.
God unknown,
He alone
Calls my heart to be his own.

In Deo mea stat omnis
spes, novatur et fides;
iustus unus is meusque
dux per varias vices,
ut suus
sim, Deus
me vocat incognitus.

Pride of man and earthly glory,
Sword and crown betray his trust;
What with care and toil he buildeth,
Tower and temple, fall to dust.
But God's power,
Hour by hour,
Is my temple and my tower.

Est superbia terrena
male fida, mobilis;
templum aut turris struatur
cum labore, fit cinis:
usque mi
vim Dei
templum, turrim habui.

God's great goodness aye endureth,
Deep his wisdom, passing thought:
Splendour, light and life attend him,
Beauty springeth out of naught.
Evermore
From his store
New-born worlds rise and adore.

Sapientiae stupendae
est, nec virtus deficit;
vitam ducit et nitorem;
pulchrum ex inani fit
et nova
copia
cultorum perpetua.

Daily doth th'Almighty giver
bounteous gifts on us bestow;
His desire our soul delighteth,
Pleasure leads us where we go.
Love doth stand
At his hand;
Joy doth wait on his command.

Largus is potensque Dator,
dona qui diurna dat;
cui parere nos delectat,
ire euntes et iuvat;
ad manum
proximum
praestat amor gaudium.

Still from man to God eternal
Sacrifice of praise be done,
High above all praises praising
For the gift of Christ his Son.
Christ doth call
One and all:
Ye who follow shall not fall.

Sine fine iam laudetur
inter homines Deus,
hoc praecipue laudandus
Filius quod est datus,
qui vocet
quemlibet:
qui sequetur haud cadet.

Neander/Bridges

MM 4—8.11.00

All people that on earth do dwell,
Sing to the Lord with cheerful voice;
Him serve with fear, his praise forth tell,
Come ye before him, and rejoice.

The Lord, ye know, is God indeed;
Without our aid he did us make;
We are his folk, he doth us feed,
And for his sheep he doth us take.

O enter then his gates with praise,
Approach with joy his courts unto;
Praise, laud, and bless his name always,
For it is seemly so to do.

For why? the Lord our God is good;
His mercy is for ever sure;
His truth at all times firmly stood,
And shall from age to age endure.

To Father, Son, and Holy Ghost,
The God whom heaven and earth adore,
From men and from the angel-host
Be praise and glory evermore.

W.Kethe (Ps 100)

Quicumqjue mundum colitis,
cantate laeti Domino;
verendus et laudandus is:
adite eum cum gaudio.

Est vere Deus Dominus,
ultroque fecit ille nos;
nos pascit (grex enim sumus)
ovili suo conditos.

Cum laude intrate limina,
laetantes aulam petite,
multiplicate encomia,
decet quod ita facere.

Nam Domini, qui bonus sit,
perpetua est clementia,
semperque veritas stetit
durabit et per saecula.

Nunc Trinitati, quam colit
superna plebs et infera,
utrinque contributa sit
aeterna laus et gloria.

MM 30.9.—6.10.99

All things bright and beautiful,
All creatures great and small,
All things wise and wonderful,
The Lord God made them all.

Each little flower that opens,
Each little bird that sings,
He made their glowing colours,
He made their tiny wings.

The rich man in his castle,
The poor man at his gate,
God made them, high or lowly,
And ordered their estate.

The purple-headed mountain,
The river running by,
The sunset, and the morning
That brightens up the sky:

The cold wind in the winter,
The pleasant summer sun,
The ripe fruit in the garden,
He made them every one.

The tall trees in the greenwood,
The meadows where we play,
The rushes by the water
We gather every day:

He gave us eyes to see them,
And lips that we might tell
How great is God Almighty,
Who has made all things well.

C.F. Alexander

Lepida lucentia,
et maius at minus,
fecit, sapientia
stupendaque, Deus.

Quot se pandere gemrnae,
quot cantant volucres,
tot his pigmenta fecit
alasque tenues.

In aula locupletem
et extra pauperem
is fecit et utrumque
probavit ordinem.

Purpureumque montem,
quod flumen praemeat
caelumque quod sub noctem
et mane rutilat:

Hiberni qui sunt venti,
aestivus qui tepor,
qui fructus sunt in horto,
is omnium dator.

Is arborem proceram,
ludendo gramina,
ripariasque cannas,
diurna spolia:

Ut facta videamus
is oculos dedit
et voces ut dicamus
quam bene fecerit.

MM 16—21.8.01

Almighty Father, Lord most high,
Who madest all, who fillest all,
Thy name we praise and magnify,
For all our needs on thee we call.

We offer to thee of thine own
Ourselves and all that we can bring,
In Bread and Cup before thee shown,
Our universal offering.

A11 that we have we bring to thee,
Yet all is naught when all is done,
Save that in it thy love can see
The Sacrifice of thy dear Son.

By his command in Bread and Cup
His Body and his Blood we plead:
That on the Cross he offered up
is here our Sacrifice indeed.

For all thy gifts of life and grace,
Here we thy servants humbly pray
That thou would'st look upon the face
of thine anointed Son to-day.

V.S.S. Coles

Omnipotens Pater Deus,
ut nos creasti, sic reples;
tibi, quem laude tollimus,
egeni fundimus preces.

Offerimus tibi tuum,
nos et quod ferre possumus
tuum(st) cum Pane Poculum
oblatum hic ab omnibus.

Quodcumque nostrum est habes
sed id valebit minimum
et solum quatenus vides
Mactatum ibi Filium.

Panem Vinumque porgere,
Corpus Cruorem, docuit
is ipse qui cum in Cruce
tum hic se Victimam dedit.

Qui vitam gratiamque das,
nos nunc satellites tui
oramus ut inspicias
hic uncti vultum Filii.

MM 14—18.7.01

Latinised Hymns

Almighty Father, who dost give
The gift of life to all who live,
Look down on all earth's sin and strife
And lift us to a nobler life.

Lift up our hearts, O King of Kings,
To brighter hopes and kindlier things,
To visions of a larger good,
And holier dreams of brotherhood.

The world is weary of its pain,
Of selfish greed and fruitless gain,
Of tarnished honour, falsely strong,
And all its ancient deeds of wrong.

Hear thou the prayer thy servants pray
Uprising from all lands to-day,
And, o'er the vanquished powers of sin,
O bring thy great salvation in!

J.H.B. Masterman

Omnipotens Pater Deus,
qui vitam das viventibus,
despiciens sollicitos
ad altiora tolle nos.

In spem, Rex Regum, erigas
et aucta sit benignitas;
bonum noscamus amplius,
ut fratres simus fratribus.

Taedet dolere et esse nos
lucrandi frustra cupidos,
per vim celare dedecus,
qui prava diu gerimus.

Audi surgentes undique
servorum preces hodie;
viresque superans malas
tuam salutem inferas.

MM 14—19.7.00

All unseen the Master walketh
By the toiling servant's side;
Comfortable words he talketh,
While his hands uphold and guide.

Grief nor pain nor any sorrow
Rends thy breast to him unknown;
He today and he tomorrow
Grace sufficient gives his own.

Holy strivings nerve and strengthen,
Long endurance wins the crown;
When the evening shadows lengthen,
Thou shalt lay thy burden down.

T.Mackellar

Erus servo laboranti
comes haud conspectus it,
quem cum voce consolanti
fulcit atque dirigit.

Suis ille, qui dolentem
bene te cognoverit,
gratiam sufficientem
cras ut hodie dabit.

Fortis exercendo fies,
vincitur durantibus;,
vesperascet ubi dies,
tuum depones onus.

MM 15—17.9.98

Amazing grace! How sweet the sound
That saved a wretch like me.
I once was lost, but now am found,
Was blind, but now I see.

'Twas grace that taught my heart to fear,
And grace my fears relieved.
How precious did that grace appear
The hour I first believed.

Through many a danger, toil and snare
I have already come;
'Tis grace hath brought me safe thus far
And grace will lead me home.

When we've been there ten thousand years
Bright shining as the sun,
We've no less days to sing God's praise
Than when we've first begun.

J. Newton

Per quam servatus sum miser
admiror gratiam,
ut perditus recuperer
et caecus videam.

Quae gratia metum dedit,
medetur metui,
et cara gratia fuit,
cum primurn credidi.

Tam multa per discrimina
progressus ego sum;
huc tulit usque gratia
et perferet domum.

Millennia si mille ibi
ut sol nitebimus,
manebit ad laudes Dei
dierum haud minus.

MM 6—11.2.01

And can it be that I should gain
An interest in the Saviour' s blood?
Died he for me, who caused His pain?
For me, who Him to death pursued?
Amazing love! How can it be
That thou, my God, shouldst die for me?

'Tis mystery all – The Immortal dies –
Who can explore His strange design?
In vain the first-born seraph tries
To sound the depths of love divine!
'Tis mercy all - Let earth adore,
Let angel minds inquire no more.

He left his Father's throne above,
So free, so infinite his grace;
Emptied himself of all but love,
And bled for Adam's helpless race.
'Tis mercy all, immense and free;
For, O my God, it found out me.

Long my imprisoned spirit lay
Fast bound in sin and nature's night:
Thine eye diffused a quickening ray;
I woke – the dungeon flamed with light.
My chains fell off, my heart was free;
I rose, went forth, and followed thee.

No condemnation now I dread;
Jesu, and all in him, is mine!
Alive in Him, my living Head,
And clothed in righteousness divine,
Bold I approach the eternal throne,
And claim the crown
            through Christ my own.

C. Wesley

De Salvatoris sanguine
lucrum-ne vere mihi fit?
Ad mortem propellente me
is pro laedente periit?
Mirandus est amor tuus,
o mihi mortue Deus.

Is immortalis, sed perit:
iacturam inscrutabilem!
Quis eius angelorum scit
amoris altitudinem?
Nos adoremus inferi,
nec ultra quaerant angeli.

Paternum liquit apicem
largeque gratiam tulit;
cum fudit lapsis sanguinem,
exhaustus haud amor fuit.
Expertus ipse ego tuam
testor, Deus, clementiam.

Qui sum diu coercitus
umbroso culpae carcere,
tuus mi luxit oculus;
tunc arsit carcer lumine;
vinclis solutus orior,
egrediensque te sequor.

Damnatione liberum
(in Jesu quid non habeo?
Is vivit, ergo vivus sum)
factumque iustum a Deo
me Christus ad thronum vocat,
coronam mihi consecrat.

MM 10—22.11.99

And now, O Father, mindful of the love
That bought us, once for all, on Calvary's Tree
And having with us him that pleads above,
We here present, we here spread forth to thee
That only offering perfect in thine eyes,
The one true, pure, immortal Sacrifice.

Look, Father, look on his anointed face,
And only look on us as found in him;
Look not on our misusings of thy grace,
Our prayer so languid, and our faith so dim:
For lo, between our sins and their reward
We set the Passion of thy Son our Lord.

And then for those, our dearest and our best,
By this prevailing Presence we appeal:
O fold them closer to thy mercy's breast,
O do thine utmost for their souls' true weal;
From tainting mischief keep them white and clear,
And crown thy gifts with strength to persevere.

And so we come: O draw us to thy feet,
Most patient Saviour, who canst love us still
And by this food, so aweful and so sweet,
Deliver us from every touch of ill:
In thine own service make us glad and free,
And grant us never more to part with thee.

W. Bright

Nunc, Pater, haud amoris inscii,
quo pensum est in Cruce pretium,
donamus hic et pandimus tibi,
clientes invocantis ad thronum,
quam solam tu probas ut integram,
aeternam, unam, puram Hostiam.

Illius unctam faciem nota,
videque nos sub eius specie,
perverse tua abusi gratia
si prece, si deficimus fide;
nam scelus inter et supplicium
passum locamus Filium tuum.

Et amicorum pro carissimis
praesentis en! oramus nomine:
qui potes, o tu consulas eis,
clementi foveas in pectore;
da nullum crimen eos polluat,
et, praeter hoc, ne vis deficiat.

Nos te petentes propius trahe,
Salvator, nos amare qui potes;
per hoc nutrimen venerabile
a malo, si quid tangat, liberes,
libenter serviamus ut tibi
nec umquam simus abs te positi.

MM 20.9—1.10.99

And now the wants are told, that brought
Thy children to thy knee;
Here lingering still, we ask for nought,
But simply worship thee.

The hope of heaven's eternal days
Absorbs not all the heart
That gives thee glory, love and praise,
For being what thou art.

For thou art God, the One, the Same,
O'er all things high and bright;
And round us, when we speak thy name,
There spreads a heaven of light.

O wondrous peace, in thought to dwell
On excellence divine;
To know that nought in man can tell
How fair thy beauties shine!

O thou, above all blessing blest,
O'er thanks exalted far,
Thy very greatness is a rest
To weaklings as we are;

For when we feel the praise of thee
A task beyond our powers,
We say, "A perfect God is he,
And he is fully ours."

All glory to the Father be,
All glory to the Son,
All glory, Holy Ghost, to thee,
While endless ages run.

W. Bright

*Id quod petentes venimus
audisti, Domine;
manetur hic diutius
ut veneremur te.*

*Non sola aeternitatis spes
cor nostrum occupat:
ut laudet te qui sis quod es,
huic quoque cor vacat.*

*Es Unus, Immutabilis,
nec quicquam tibi par;
tuique dictu nominis
caeleste fit iubar.*

*Te contemplamur optimum:
(O quae serenitas!),
qui praeter mentes hominum
pulchre refulgeas.*

*O maior et beatior
quam cui sint gratiae,
invalidos tuus vigor
sinit quiescere.*

*Quid laudi si deficimus
(tu nempe tantus es)?
At plane noster es Deus
et integer manes.*

*Sit gloria, Pater, tibi
una cum Filio,
et gloria Spiritui
privata termino.*

MM 30.9—9.10.01

Angels, from the realms of glory,
Wing your flight o'er all the earth;
Ye who sang creation's story,
Now proclaim Messiah's birth:
    Come and worship,
Worship Christ, the new-born King.

Shepherds, in the field abiding,
Watching o'er your flocks by night,
God with man is now residing,
Yonder shines the infant Light:

Sages, leave your contemplations;
Brighter visions beam afar:
Seek the great Desire of Nations:
Ye have seen his natal star:

Saints before the altar bending,
Watching long in hope and fear,
Suddenly the Lord, descending,
In his temple shall appear:

Though an infant now we view him,
He shall fill his Father's throne,
Gather all the nations to him;
Every knee shall then bow down:
    Come and worship, etc.

J. Montgomery

Terram alites lustrate,
ex supernis Angeli,
natum Christum praedicate,
orbis ante nuntii:
    adorate
Regem nuper genitum.

Qui per rura vigilatis
nocte servantes pecus,
Deo nunc cohabitatis:
Infans ecce lucidus!

Satis astra contemplati,
splendor novus emicat:
Gentium Cum Prece Nati★
stella vos, Magi, trahat:

Sancti, sacra coram sede
qui summittitis genu,
aderit repente in aede
exspectatus Is diu:

Sellam Patris occupabit,
quemque parvum vidimus,
gentes ille convocabit
omnipollens agnitus:
    adorate etc.

MM 17-21 Feb 98

★*Gentibus Desiderati*

Angel-voices ever singing
Round thy throne of light,
Angel-harps for ever ringing,
Rest not day nor night;
Thousands only live to bless thee
And confess thee
Lord of might.

Thou who art beyond the farthest
Mortal eye can scan,
Can it be that thou regardest
Songs of sinful man?
Can we know that thou art near us,
And wilt hear us?
Yea, we can.

Yea, we know that thou rejoicest
O'er each work of thine;
Thou didst ears and hands and voices
For thy praise design;
Craftsman's art and music's measure
For thy pleasure
All combine.

In thy house, great God, we offer
Of thine own to thee;
And for thine acceptance proffer
All unworthily
Hearts and minds and hands and voices
In our choicest
Psalmody.

Honour, glory, might and merit
Thine shall ever be,
Father, Son, and Holy spirit,
Blessed Trinity!
Of the best that thou hast given
Earth and heaven
Render thee.

F.Pott

Cingunt angeli canentes
thronum lucidum,
chordis, ut diem, replentes
noctis spatium;
mille vivunt ut beent te
et vocent te
Dominum.

Qui nostrorum oculorum
expers habitas,
canticum-ne peccatorum
est ut audias?
Vere prope nos te stare
et notare
indicas.

Quae creasti, certe gaudes,
scimus, omnibus;
ad tuas directa laudes
auris, vox, manus:
iunctum tibi cantatorum
et fabrorum
est opus.

Apud te qui tibi damus
de tuis, Deus,
accepturum te speramus
quod offerimus,
voces, manus, corda, mentes,
contendentes
cantibus.

Fas honoribus coli te
semper, quodque das,
Pater, Fili, Paraclite,
sancta Trinitas,
terra caelis usurpatum
rursus datum
habeas.

MM 5–13.10.99

Approach, my soul, the mercy–seat,
 Where Jesus answers prayer;
Then humbly fall before his feet,
 For none can perish there.

Thy promise is my only plea,
 With this I venture nigh:
Thou callest burdened souls to thee,
 And such, O Lord, am I.

Bowed down beneath a load of sin,
 By Satan sorely pressed,
By war without and fears within,
 I come to thee for rest.

Be thou my shield and hiding-place,
 That, sheltered near thy side,
I may my fierce accuser face,
 And tell him thou hast died.

O wondrous love, to bleed and die,
 To bear the Cross and shame,
That guilty sinners, such as I,
 Might plead thy gracious name!

J. Newton

Ad Iesum (est orabilis
favetque supplici)
quin, anima, te proicis?
Est nulla rnors ibi.

Id promisisti quod peto
te veniens prope,
onustos, qualis en! ego,
 vocantem, Domine.

Premunt gravi Diabolus
me culpae subditum
extraque bella, intra metus:
tu da mihi otium.

Habere te scutum volo;
te juxta lateam;
saevoque te adversario
mactatum proferam.

Ut nos amasti, proditus
in cruce moriens,
testandum nomen sontibus
mihique porrigens!
(ut mihi)

MM 26—31 Jan 98

Around the throne of God a band
Of glorious angels ever stand;
Bright things they see, sweet harps they hold,
And on their heads are crowns of gold.

Some wait around him, ready still
To sing his praise and do his will;
And some, when he commands them, go
To guard his servants here below.

Lord, give thy angels every day
Command to guide us on our way,
And bid them every evening keep
Their watch around us while we sleep.

So shall no wicked thing draw near,
To do us harm or cause us fear;
And we shall dwell, when life is past,
With angels round thy throne at last.

J.M. Neale

Cingentes solium Dei
videntur semper angeli;
habent manu psalteria
et fronte diademata.

Hi circum eum haesitant
dum laudent aut oboediant;
descendunt, id si iussit, hi
nos hic tuendo dediti.

Fac hos ministros, Domine,
nos per diem dirigere,
et idem nocte fac eos
invigilare circum nos.

Sic nihil nobis accidet
quod terreat seu vulneret,
vitaque cingemus thronum
functi cum angelis tuum.

MM 9—11.2.99

As with gladness men of old
Did the guiding star behold,
As with joy they hailed its light,
Leading onward, beaming bright;
So, most gracious Lord, may we
Evermore be led to thee.

As with joyful steps they sped,
Saviour, to thy lowly bed,
There to bend the knee before
Thee whom heaven and earth adore;
So may we with willing feet
Ever seek thy mercy-seat.

As they offered gifts most rare
At thy cradle rude and bare,
So may we with holy joy,
Pure and free from sin's alloy,
All our costliest treasures bring,
Christ, to thee our heavenly King.

Holy Jesus, every day
Keep us in the narrow way,
And when earthly things are past,
Bring our ransomed souls at last
Where they need no star to guide,
Where no clouds thy glory hide.

In the heavenly country bright
Need they no created light;
Thou its light, its joy, its crown,
Thou its sun which goes not down;
There for ever may we sing
Alleluias to our King.

W. Chatterton Dix

Sicut placuit Magis
ductus ohm sideris
lumen, ibat ut prius,
laete salutantibus,
sic ducamur, Domine,
propiores usque te.

Ut gaudentes ad tuum
festinarunt lectulum,
terris et caelo pares
facti tibi supplices,
properemus ad tuae
sedem nos clementiae.

Cunis ut insignia
obtulerunt munera,
sic laetantes et pii,
dempta labe nos tibi
quod habemus optimum
demus ante solium.

Recta nos cotidie
via, Iesu, dirige,
deinde post terrestria
illuc emptos tolle, qua ★
non opus stellae ducis, ★
nec tu nube conderis. ★

Num caelorum incolae
lucis egent additae?
Ibi totum tu decus
tuque sol perpetuus;
quo canamus in loco
Alleluia nos Deo.

MM 30.12.98—5.1.99

★illuc emptos subleva
ubi stellae non opus
nec lates sub nubibus.

Latinised Hymns

At even, ere the sun was set,
　　The sick, O Lord, around thee lay;
O in what divers pains they met!
　　O with what joy they went away!

Once more 'tis eventide, and we
　　Oppressed with various ills draw near;
What if thy form we cannot see?
　　We know and feel that thou art here.

O Saviour Christ, our woes dispel;
　　For some are sick, and some are sad,
And some have never loved thee well,
　　And some have lost the love they had;

And some have found the world is vain,
　　Yet from the world they break not free;
And some have friends who give them pain,
　　Yet have not sought a friend in thee;

And none, O Lord, have perfect rest,
　　For none are wholly free from sin;
And they who fain would serve thee best
　　Are conscious most of wrong within.

O Saviour Christ, thou too art Man;
　　Thou hast been troubled, tempted, tried;
Thy kind but searching glance can scan
　　The very wounds that shame would hide;

Thy touch has still its ancient power;
　　No word from thee can fruitless fall:
Hear in this solemn evening hour,
　　And in thy mercy heal us all.

H. Twells

Sub noctem tibi proximi
　　iacebant aegri homines:
qui convenere miseri,
　　max dimittuntur hilares.

Nos quoque nunc, ut lux abit
　　venimus cum doloribus,
et, forma cum celata sit,
　　adesse te cognovimus.

Seu corpus dolet sive cor,
　　dolores, Jesu, dissipa,
seu tui nullus est amor,
　　seu dest qui fuit antea.

His nota mundi vanitas
　　est, nec tamen reiciunt:
hi plorant amicitias,
　　ut laesi, nec tuam petunt.

Nec ulli pura requies
　　(sunt omnes culpae conscii)
fidissimos satellites
　　heu! maxime pudet sui.

Ut nos homo, Salvator, es,
　　et passus es temptamina
tu perspicaciter vides
　　quae celat pudor vulnera.

Quod olim, tactus is facit,
　　nec umquam frustra loqueris;
nos audiens, ut nox adit,
　　medere clemens sauciis.

MM   2—18.9.99

Author of life divine,	*Vivificans Deus,*
Who hast a table spread,	*durabilem cibum*
Furnished with mystic Wine	*praebens hospitibus*
And everlasting Bread,	*vinumque mysticum,*
Preserve the life thyself hast given,	*vitam dedisti: sustine;*
And feed and train us up for heaven.	*futuros caelites ale.*

Our needy souls sustain	*Egentes repleas*
With fresh supplies of love,	*amoris fontibus;*
Till all thy life we gain,	*vivosque facias*
And all thy fulness prove,	*sisque omnis agnitus;*
And, strengthened by thy perfect grace,	*sis gratiosus, atque des*
Behold without a veil thy face.	*ut videare qualis es.*

J. Wesley	*MM 20—25.6.01*

Awake, awake, put on thy stength, O Zion,
    God's purpose tarries but his will stands fast;
Of Judah's tribe is born the mighty Lion,
    And Man shall bruise the serpent's head at last.
Promise and covenant God surely keeps;
He watching o'er us slumbers not nor sleeps.

Ho, ye that thirst, the pleasant fountains wait you;
    Ye that are poor, ye shall be freely fed;
Why give ye gold for wine that cannot sate you?
    Why strive your hands for that which is not bread?

For now the low estate of his handmaiden
    God hath regarded and she shall be blest;
Hear him that saith "Come, all ye heavy laden,
    Come unto me and I will give you rest."

Scornful we looked, and lo! his face was stained,
    His visage marred beyond the sons of men;
Yet those his stripes our life and peace regained,
    Those hands shall heal us that were pierced then.

Arise and shine, thy battlements are shining,
  Upon thee breaks the glory of the Lord;
And from the east, thy royalty divining,
  The Gentiles come to see thy peace restored.

C.A.Alington & R.A.Knox

Praecide, Sion, hibernationem. ★
  Dei morantis stat propositum.
Iudaea stirps progenuit Leonem;
  premetque calx humana colubrum.
  Certa fides ea quam Deus dat;
  is super nobis usque vigilat.

Vos, sitientes, rore fons rigabit,
  et pauperes pascentur gratiis.
Vinum cur emitis quod non iuvabit,
  nugas neglecto pane prenditis?

Ancillam vidit ecce! servientem
  Deus et exaltabit humilem.
Audite qui gravantur arcessentem:
  fessis promittit ille requiem.

Prae ceteris cui facies foedata,
  contemptus est. At eius sanguine
est vita nostra et pax redintegrata.
  Punctae manus sunt nobis commodae.

Pellucidis exsurge munimentis
  splendore circumfulsa Domini,
ut regiam mirentur Orientis
  te restituta pace populi.

MM 22—7.11.96

★ *v.1. Festina, Sion, experrectionem.*

Awake, my soul, and with the sun
Thy daily stage of duty run;
Shake off dull sloth, and joyful rise
To pay thy morning sacrifice.

Redeem thy mis-spent time that's past,
And live this day as if thy last;
Improve thy talent with due care;
For the great day thyself prepare.

Let all thy converse be sincere,
Thy conscience as the noon-day clear;
Think how all-seeing God thy ways
And all thy secret thoughts surveys.

Wake, and lift up thyself, my heart,
And with the angels bear thy part,
Who all night long unwearied sing
High praise to the eternal King.

Glory to thee, who safe hast kept
And hast refreshed me whilst I slept;
Grant, Lord, when I from death shall wake,
I may of endless light partake.

Lord, I my vows to thee renew.;
Disperse my sins as morning dew;
Guard my first springs of thought and will,
And with thyself my spirit fill.

Direct, control, suggest, this day,
All I design or do or say;
That all my powers, with all their might,
In thy sole glory may unite.

Praise God, from whom all blessings flow,
Praise him, all creatures here below,
Praise him above, angelic host,
Praise Father, Son, and Holy Ghost.

Bp Ken

Cum sole surgens, anima,
diurna sume officia,
et impigre Deo datum
sit mane sacrificium.

Delicta prisca dissipes,
quasi ultimus sit hic dies;
te naviter instruxeris
ut Judici paratus sis.

Candore sermo ne carens
sit neu serenitate mens;
nam Deus, omne cui patet,
arcana pectoris videt.

Exoriare, cor meum;
supernum augeas chorum,
quem nulla nox debilitat
quin Regis laudem concinat.

Laus tibi, qui me tutus sis
sopitum et refeceris;
morte experrecto, Domine,
sit lucis pars perpetuae.

Nunc vota renovo mea;
ut ros fugentur scelera;
nihil temptarim sine te;
te spiritum meum reple.

Quodcumque hodie geram,
id te ducente faciam,
et quicquid est potentiae
dicetur gloriae tuae.

Quot estis animalia,
laudate eum qui dat bona;
neu segnius, caelicolae,
vos Trinitatem psallite.

MM 24.8—3.9.99

Be thou my guardian and my guide,
And hear me when I call;
Let not my slippery footsteps slide,
And hold me lest I fall.

The world, the flesh, and Satan dwell
Around the path I tread;
O save me from the snares of hell,
Thou quickener of the dead.

And if I tempted am to sin,
And outward things are strong,
Do thou, O Lord, keep watch within,
And save my soul from wrong.

Still let me ever watch and pray,
And feel that I am frail;
That if the tempter cross my way,
Yet he may not prevail.

I. Williams

Tu dux et custos mihi sis
vocantemque audias;
labentem ne neglexeris,
casurum teneas.

Circumvenit illecebris
euntem Satanas;
Orci me solve laqueis,
qui mortuos levas.

Cum valeant extrinsecus
in me temptamina,
intus tu vigila, Deus,
ne peccet anima.

Sic vigil et cum precibus
imbellem me sciam,
ne temptatori obvius
temptatus occidam.

MM 30—31.7.98

Before Jehovah's awful throne,
    Ye nations, bow with sacred joy;
Know that the Lord is God alone:
    He can create, and he destroy.

His sovereign power, without our aid,
    Made us of clay, and formed us men;
And, when like wandering sheep we strayed,
    He brought us to his fold again.

We'll crowd thy gates with thankful songs,
    High as the heavens our voices raise;
And earth, with her ten thousand tongues,
    Shall fill thy courts with sounding praise

Wide as the world is thy command,
    Vast as eternity thy love;
Firm as a rock thy truth shall stand
    When rolling years shall cease to move.

I. Watts (Psalm 100)

Jehovae iuxta solium
    gavisae, gentes, cumbite;
Deum sciatis unicum
creare posse et perdere.

Nos impotentes is potens
    humanos fecit e luto,
ut pastor et vagos tuens
    ovili reddidit suo.

Ad portas te cantabimus:
    tolletur vox ad aethera;
de terra mille laudibus
    palatia sonent tua!

Orbi terrarum imperas,
    aeternus est amor tuus,
et stabit ista veritas
    annis deficientibus.

MM 30.11.—9.12.97

Latinised Hymns

"Behold, the Bridegroom draweth nigh!"
Hear ye the oft-repeated cry?
Go forth into the midnight dim;
For blest are they whom he shall find
With ready heart and watchful mind;
Go forth, my soul, to him.

"Behold, the Bridegroom cometh by!"
The call is echoed from the sky:
Go forth, ye servants, watch and wait;
The slothful cannot join his train
No careless one may entrance gain:
Awake, my soul, 'tis late.

The wise will plead with one accord,
"O Holy, Holy, Holy Lord,
On us thy quickening grace bestow,
That none may reach the door too late,
When thou shalt enter at the gate
And to thy Kingdom go."

'Behold, the Bridegroom draweth near!"
The warning falls on every ear:
That night of dread shall come to all:
Behold, my soul, thy lamp so dim,
Rise, rise the smoking flax to trim;
Soon shalt thou hear his call.

R.M. Moorsom (from Greek)

"Maritus en adest propel"
vox clamitat. Attendite!
Exite nocte media.
Beati quos paratos et
quos vigiles inveniet;
i coram, anima.

"Maritus ecce praeterit!"
hunc sonum aether reicit;
i vigilans familia!
Ignavus nequit hunc sequi
iners aut ullus accipi:
festines, anima!

En! preces sapientium
Ter Sanctum erga Dominum:
"quin gratia vivificas,
ne sero quis petat fores,
tu quando portam penetres,
ut regnum ineas?"

"Maritus ecce proximusl"
cunctorum sonat auribus,
cunctis minatur ista nox
heus! paene extinctam, anima,
fumantem taedam suscita;
iam poscet illa vox.

MM   13—16.20.01

Behold, the great Creator makes
    Himself a house of clay,
A robe of virgin flesh he takes
    Which he will wear for aye.

Hark! hark! the wise eternal Word
    Like a weak infant cries;
In form of servant is the Lord,
    And God in cradle lies.

This wonder struck the world amazed,
    It shook the starry frame;
Squadrons of spirits stood and gazed,
    Then down in troops they came.

Glad shepherds ran to view this sight;
    A choir of angels sings,
And eastern sages with delight
    Adore the King of Kings.

Join then, all hearts that are not stone,
    And all our voices prove:
To celebrate this Holy One,
    The God of peace and love.

T.Pestel

Mundi Creator en! facit
    sibi ex luto domum
et carnis tegmen induit
    purae perpetuum.

En! Verbum parvuli modo
    debiliter sonat,
nec dispar Deus famulo
    in cunis recubat.

Portento mundus stupuit,
    sunt quassa sidera;
idque angelorum detulit
    ad terram agmina.

Visum, dum cantant angeli,
    pastores corruunt,
et Regum ad Regem magi
    sese proiciunt.

Vos, quot sentitis, pectora,
    negate ne sonum,
amoris celebrantia
    et pacis hunc Deum.

MM 21—4.12.98

Blessed assurance, Jesus is mine:
O what a foretaste of glory divine!
Heir of salvation, purchase of God;
Born of his Spirit, washed in his blood.
THIS IS MY STORY, THIS IS MY SONG,
PRAISING MY SAVIOUR ALL THE DAY LONG.

Perfect submission, perfect delight,
Visions of rapture burst on my sight;
Angels descending, bring from above
Echoes of mercy, whispers of love.

Perfect submission, all is at rest,
I in my Saviour am happy and blest;
Watching and waiting, looking above,
Filled with his goodness, lost in his love.

F van Alstyne

Pignus amandum, Jesu meus,
anticipatur caeleste decus;
capto salutem quam mihi das;
sanguine purgans vivificas.
HOC TIBI DICENS HOCCE CANO,
PERQUE DIEM TE LAUDE COLO.

Pareo totus, et placuit;
meque voluptas visa rapit;
dona chorus fert superior:
venia sonat, mussat amor.

Pareo totus; fit requies;
quippe beator, Salutifer, es
teque supernum opperior;
bonitas implet, mergit amor.

MM   3—5.11.01

Blow, winds of God, awake and blow
    The mists of earth away:
Shine out, O Light divine, and show
    How wide and far we stray.

The letter fails, and systems fall,
    And every symbol wanes;
The Spirit overbrooding all
    Eternal Love remains.

In joy of inward peace, or sense
    Of sorrow over sin,
He is his own best evidence,
    His witness is within.

J.G. Whittier

Fugate terrae nebulas,
    O flamina Dei;
et, Lux divina, detegas
    quam simus avii.

Caelata lex, ut littera
    est tempore minor;
sed spirans super omnia
    aeternus est Amor.

Interni dator otii
    et paenitentiae,
se testem optimum sui
    praesentat animae.

MM 11—14.9.00

Bread of heaven, on thee we feed,
For thy flesh is meat indeed;
Ever may our souls be fed
With this true and living bread;
Day by day with strength supplied
Through the life of him who died.

Vine of heaven, thy blood supplies
This blest Cup of Sacrifice;
Lord, thy wounds our healing give,
To thy Cross we look and live:
Jesus, may we ever be
Grafted, rooted, built in thee.

J . Conder

Te, caelestis o cibe,
pascimur nutrimine;
animae perpetuo
nutriantur hoc cibo;
firmet nos cotidie
caesi vita victimae.

Vitis o superna, dans
Poclum hoc Sacrificans,
tua sanant vulnera,
Crux vivificat tua:
sis fundamen, et tibi
usque simus insiti.

MM 15—21.8.99

Latinised Hymns

Bread of the world in mercy broken,	*O fracte Panis, orbi clemens,*
Wine of the soul in mercy shed,	*O Vinum spargens animas,*
By whom the words of life were spoken,	*peccata nostra morte demens,*
And in whose Death our sins are dead;	*qui vera nobis praedicas,*
Look on the heart by sorrow broken,	*vide dolore nos gravatos*
Look on the tears by sinners shed;	*et peccatorum lacrimas*
And be thy feast to us the token	*tuaque gratia cibatos*
That by thy grace our souls are fed.	*has indica per epulas.*
Bishop R. Heber	*MM 15.1.97*

Bright the vision that delighted	*Placuit Iudaeo vati*
Once the sight of Judah's seer;	*visio pellucida,*
Sweet the countless tongues united	*et fuere voluptati*
To entrance the prophet's ear.	*mille vocum carmina.*
Round the Lord in glory seated	*Adsidebat et decorus,*
Cherubim and Seraphim	*circumfusus Daminum,*
Filled his temple, and repeated	*duplex angelorum chorus*
Each to each the alternate hymn:	*dividebat canticum:*
"Lord, thy glory fills the heaven;	*"Plenus aether et repletur*
Earth is with its fulness stored;	*tuae terra glariae.*
Unto thee be glory given,	*Honos tibi, Sancte, detur,*
Holy, Holy, Holy, Lord."	*Sancte, Sancte Domine!"*
Heaven is still with glory ringing,	*Sic superni, neque muta*
Earth takes up the angels' cry,	*captat terra canticum,*
"Holy, Holy, Holy," singing,	*"Sancte", bis et ter locuta,*
"Lord of Hosts, the Lord most high."	*"Salve, Rector Agminum!"*
With his seraph train before him,	*Nos caelestibus coniuncti*
With his holy Church below,	*sanctis et terrestribus*
Thus unite we to adore him,	*carmen rituale cuncti*
Bid we thus our anthem flow:	*una voce tollimus:*
"Lord, thy glory ...	*"Plenus aether ...*
Bishop R. Mant	*MM 15-16 Nov 96*

Brightest and best of the sons of the morning,
Dawn on our darkness, and lend us thine aid;
Star of the east, the horizon adorning,
Guide where our infant Redeemer is laid.

Cold on his cradle the dew-drops are shining;
Low lies his head with the beasts of the stall;
Angels adore him in slumber reclining,
Maker and Monarch and Saviour of all.

Say, shall we yield him, in costly devotion,
Odours of Edom, and offerings divine,
Gems of the mountain, and pearls of the ocean,
Myrrh from the forest, or gold from the mine?

Vainly we offer each ample oblation,
Vainly with gifts would his favour secure:
Richer by far is the heart's adoration,
Dearer to God are the prayers of the poor.

Bishop Heber

Optima splendida lux matutina,
pelle tenebras et alma nite,
solis et ortui stella vicina,
parvus ubi cubet ille doce.

Roscida frigora gutta iacenti.
inter ovesque bovesque tulit
laudem angelicam accipienti,
qui creat et regit et redimit.

Dicite, balsamum orientale,
gemma de colle vel oceano,
gaza metallica, tus nemorale,
dentur idonea dona Deo?

Nec tamen haec satis ampla tributa,
neque favoris erunt pretium
grata Deo veneratio muta.
et placuere preces inopum.

MM 18—21.4.98

Brothers, joining hand to hand
In one bond united,
Pressing onward to that land
Where all wrongs are righted:
Let your words and actions be
Worthy your vocation;
Chosen of the Lord, and free,
Heirs of Christ's salvation.

Christ, the Way, the Truth, the Life,
Who hath gone before you
Through the turmoil and the strife,
Holds his banner o'er you:
All who see the sacred sign
Press towards heaven's portal,
Fired by hope that is divine,
Love that is immortal.

They who follow fear no foe,
Care not who assail them;
Where the Master leads they go,
He will never fail them.
Courage, brothers! we are one,
In the love that sought us;
Soon the warfare shall be done,
Through the grace he brought us.

J.A. Warner

Nexione manuum
una vos ligantes,
rectionis ad locum
prorsum properantes:
dignos Vocatore vos
esse monstraritis,
lectos Christi, liberos,
qui redempti sitis.

Vita, Veritas, Via,
ante vos qui prodit
cuncta per pericula,
Cruce vos custodit:
quam qui vident homines
caelum apprehendunt,
quos divina aeterna spes
atque amor incendunt.

Qui sequuntur haud tremunt,
quisquis oppugnabit;
quos Erus, quem post eunt,
usque vindicabit.
Sumus, quos amans Deus
petiit, uniti,
cuius debellabimus
gratia potiti.

MM   22—25.8.01

Children of the heavenly King,
As ye journey, sweetly sing;
Sing your Saviour's worthy praise,
Glorious in his works and ways.

We are travelling home to God
In the way the fathers. trod;
They are happy now, and we
Soon their happiness shall see.

Lift your eyes, ye sons of light!
Sion' s city is in sight;
There our endless home shall be,
Where our Lord we soon shall see.

Fear not, brethren! joyful stand
On the borders of your land;
Jesus Christ, your Father's Son,
Bids you undismayed go on.

Lord, obedient we would go,
Gladly leaving all below;
Only thou our leader be,
And we still will follow thee.

? Cennick

Stirpis proles Regiae,
dulce euntes canite;
laus Salvanti digna sit,
mira mire qui facit.

Nos redimus ad Deum
in vestigiis patrum;
gaudent ei, nec minus
mox felices erimus.

Ecce! Lucis filii,
Sion conspicamini;
ibi aeterna erit domus
et videbitur Deus.

Fratres, ne timete! Iam
state iuxta patriam;
non, quem idem genuit,
absterreri vos sinit.

Tibi nos parebimus
spretis saecularibus:
duxeris, ducemque te
nos sequemur, Domine.

MM 22—5.1.99

Christ is gone up; yet ere he passed
From earth, in heaven to reign,
He formed one holy Church to last
Till he should come again.

His twelve Apostles first he made
His ministers of grace;
And they their hands on others laid,
To fill in turn their place.

So age by age, and year by year,
His grace was handed on:
And still the holy Church is here,
Although her Lord is gone.

Let those find pardon, Lord, from thee,
Whose love to her is cold:
Bring wanderers in, and let there be
One Shepherd and one fold.

J.M.Neale

Caelestem Christus regiam
iam dudum petiit,
at rediturus unicam
Ecclesiain dedit.

Praefecit primum gratiae
bis sex Apostolos,
legerunt qui sua vice
heredes posteros.

Sic Gratia stat tradita
a saeclo saeculo,
nec minus haec Ecclesia
absente Domino.

Ignosce tu palantibus,
in eam frigidis;
collecti Pastor unicus
sit unius gregis.

MM   19—22.9.98

Christ the Lord is risen again!	*Fregit, ortus iterum,*
Christ hath. broken every chain!	*Christus omne vinculum;*
Hark! angelic voices cry,	*audiuntur en! supra*
Singing evermore on high,	*angelorum cantica,*
Alleluia!	*"Alleluia!"*
He who gave for us his life,	*Qui pro nobis periit*
Who for us endured the strife,	*nec certare timuit,*
Is our Paschal Lamb today;	*est Paschalis hodie*
We too sing for joy, and say …	*Agnus; ergo canite …*
He who bore all pain and loss	*Is carens solamine*
Comfortless upon the Cross,	*omne passus in Cruce*
Lives in glory now on high,	*vivit semper eminens*
Pleads for us, and hears our cry:	*intercessor audiens.*
He whose path no records tell,	*Haud narrata qui via*
Who descended into hell,	*vectus est ad infera,*
Who the strong man armed hath bound,	*vincto nunc armigero*
Now in highest heaven is crowned.	*summo regnat in loco.*
He who slumbered in the grave	*Qui sepultus dormiit*
Is exalted now to save;	*nos elatus expedit;*
Now through Christendom it rings	*"Rex", Ecclesia sonat,*
That the Lamb is King of Kings.	*"Regum Agnus imperat."*
Now he bids us tell abroad	*Iubet nuntiare nos*
How the lost may be restored,	*posse reddi perditos,*
How the penitent forgiven,	*quod paenituit lui,*
How we too may enter heaven.	*caelum nos quoque ingredi.*
Thou, our Paschal Lamb indeed,	*Ut Paschalis Agnus es,*
Christ, thy ransomed people feed;	*emptos nonne nos ales?*
Take our sins and guilt away:	*Culpam omnem amove,*
Let us sing by night and day	*ut sonet, nocte et die,*
Alleluia!	*Alleluia!*

Weisse/Winkworth   *MM 26.4—4.5.00*

Christ triumphant ever reigning,
Saviour, Master, King,
Lord of heav'n, our lives sustaining,
Hear us as we sing:
Yours the glory and the crown,
the high renown,
the eternal name.

Word incarnate, truth revealing,
Son of Man on earth!
Power and majesty concealing
By your humble birth:

Suffering servant, scorned, ill-treated,
Victim crucified!
Death is through the Cross defeated,
Sinners justified:

Priestly King, enthroned for ever
High in heaven above!
Sin and death and hell shall never
Stifle hymns of love:

So, our hearts and voices raising
Through the ages long,
Ceaselessly upon you gazing,
This shall be our song:

M Saward

Tibi, Christe, praevalenti,
Ere, Rex, Salus,
vitam nostram sustinenti
(audi) canimus:
Regnum et decus tuum
Altissimum
Est et erit.

Vera Verbum O revelans,
factum hic caro,
magnitudinemque celans
humili domo,

Serve sprete, condemnate,
Cruce te sacrans,
victor mortis ibi date,
reos vindicans,

Rex Sacerdos, sede numquam
non sedes supra;
neque amor tacebit umquam
pressus Satana.

Vocem, corda sic tollentes
aevis omnibus,
te perpetuo videntes
hoc cantabimus:

MM 6—13.11.01

Christ, who knows all his sheep,
Will all in safety keep:
He will not lose one soul,
Nor ever fail us:
Nor we the promised goal,
Whate'er assail us.

We know our God is just;
To him we wholly trust;
All that we have and claim,
And all we hope for:
All's sure and seen to him,
Which here we grope for.

Fear not the world of light,
Though out of mortal sight;
There shall we know God more,
Where all is holy:
There is no grief or care,
No sin or folly.

O blessed company,
there all in harmony
God's joyous praises sing,
In love unceasing;
and all obey their King,
With perfect pleasing.

R. Baxter

Oves qui bene scit
omnes servaverit;
neque deficiet
gregem capessens;
nil nobis obstruet
metam lacessens.

Est iustus Dominus,
eique credimus
quod nobis propriumst
et quod sectamur;
illi perspicuumst
quod hic scrutamur.

Quod parum videas,
ne lucida tremas;
qua sancta sunt, magis
Deum cognoris:
nil ibi sceleris,
nil est doloris.

Est beatissima
ea concordia,
qua Dominum canunt
semper colentes
et iussa faciunt
valde placentes.

MM 24.12.01—7.1.02

Christ, whose glory fills the skies,
Christ, the true, the only light,
Sun of Righteousness, arise,
Triumph o'er the shades of night;
Dayspring from on high, be near;
Daystar, in my heart appear.

Dark and cheerless is the morn
Unaccompanied by thee;
Joyless is the day's return,
Till thy mercy's beams I see,
Till they inward light impart,
Glad my eyes, and warm my heart.

Visit then this soul of mine,
Pierce the gloom of sin and grief;
Fill me, radiancy divine,
Scatter all my unbelief;
More and more thyself display,
Shining to the perfect day.

C. Wesley

*Unus caelum, Domine,
vera luce illuminas;
surge, Sol Iustitiae;
pelle noctis tenebras;
corda Phosphorus* mea
matutinus occupa!*

*Tristis en! aurora fit
et molesta sine te;
lugubris dies redit
expers tuae gratiae,
donec illa intus micet,
oculos et cor iuvet.*

*Dissipa caliginem;
anima te capiat
mea, quam, ne dubitem,
lux divina repleat.
Ortus ut crescet dies,
manifestior ades.*

MM   7—9.2.98

*   *radians?*

"Christian, seek not yet repose,"
Hear thy guardian angel say;
"Thou art in the midst of foes:
    Watch and pray!"

Principalities and powers,
Mustering their unseen array,
Wait for thine unguarded hours:
    Watch and pray!

Gird thy heavenly armour on,
Wear it ever night and day;
Ambushed lurks the evil one:
Watch and pray!

Hear the victors who o'ercame;
Still they mark each warrior's way
All with one sweet voice exclaim:
    "Watch and pray!"

Hear, above all, hear thy Lord,
Him thou lovest to obey;
Hide within thy heart his word:
    "Watch and pray!"

Watch, as if on that alone
Hung the issue of the day;
Pray, that help may be sent down:
    Watch and pray!

C.Elliott

"Cincte multis hostibus,
differ" tuus "otia;"
custos inquit angelus,
    "vigila!"

Qui in mundo praevalent
caeca te concilia,
dum neglexeris, manent:
vigila!

Arma nocte tu geras
et die caelestia;
latet enim Satanas:
    vigila!

Quemque militem notant
qui vicerunt antea;
dulci voce consonant:
    "vigila!"

Audiatur Dominus,
cuius grata imperia;
dictum conde intrinsecus:
    "vigila!"

Solo vigila quasi
staret hoc victoria;
ora, detur ops tibi;
vigila!

MM 17—24.9.99

Christians, awake, salute the happy morn
whereon the Saviour of the world was born;
rise to adore the mystery of love,
which hosts of angels chanted from above;
with them the joyful tidings first begun
of God Incarnate and the Virgin's Son.

Then to the watchful shepherds it was told,
who heard the angelic herald's voice: "Behold,
I bring good tidings of a Saviour's birth,
to you and all the nations on the earth:
this day hath God fulfilled his promised word,
this day is born a Saviour, Christ the Lord."

He spake, and straightway the celestial choir
in hymns of joy, unknown before, conspire;
the praises of redeeming love they sang,
and heaven's whole orb with alleluias rang;
God's highest glory was their anthem still,
peace on the earth, and unto men good will.

To Bethlehem straight the enlightened shepherds ran
to see the wonder God had wrought for man,
and found, with Joseph and the blessèd Maid,
her Son, the Saviour, in a manger laid;
then to their flocks, still praising God, return,
and their glad hearts with holy rapture burn.

O may we keep and ponder in our mind
God's wondrous love in saving lost mankind;
trace we the Babe, who hath retrieved our loss,
from his poor manger to his bitter cross;
treading his steps, assisted by his grace,
till man's first heavenly state again takes place.

Then may we hope, the angelic thrones among,
to sing, redeemed, a glad triumphal song;
he that was born upon this joyful day
around us all his glory shall display;
saved by his love, incessant we shall sing
eternal praise to heaven's almighty King.

J. Byrom

Latinised Hymns

Heus! Christiani, lucem hodie
natumque Salvatorem plaudite,
mirumque amorem veneramini
crebri quem cantaverunt angeli;
haec unde primum laeta vox iit:
"in carne Deum Virgo peperit."

Qu0d est bubulcis inde traditum;
praeconem audiverunt angelum:
"Sum Salvatoris ego nuntius
vobis et quot sunt nationibus;
hac die Deus fidem praestitit
Christumque Salvatorem genuit."

Cacli chorus, locuto sic eo,
gavisus hymno concinit novo:
amorem redimentem celebrat,
et alleluiis aether resonat;
Deique summus canitur decor,
in terra pax et erga nos favor.

Id qui miraculum visuriunt,
recta bubulci Bethlehem petunt,
videntque cum Josepho Virginem
et in praesepio Progeniem;
ardente dein laetantes animo
greges revisunt cum elogio.

Ne mente cedat amor ille, nos
qui vindicavit ante perditos,
et salutarem hanc Propaginem
a stabulo sequamur ad Crucem,
euntibus ut eius semita
detur primalis innocentia.

Spes est triumphaturos esse nos,
quos is redemit, inter angelos;
nos ille laeta natus hac die
circumnitebit toto lumine,
salvante semper quo laudabimus
eum qui regnat cacli Dominus.

MM 25.12.00—10.1.01

City of God, how broad and far	Urbs o Dei, latissime
Outspread thy walls sublime!	tu muros explicas,
The true thy chartered freemen are	fideliumque es ubique
Of every age and clime:	et usque civitas.

One holy Church, one army strong,	Ecclesia una, exercitus
One steadfast, high intent;	est unus, una mens;
One working band, one harvest-song,	est una messorum manus
One King omnipotent.	et Rex omnipotens.

How purely hath thy speech come down	Quam pura vax sonat tua
From man's primeval youth!	Usque a primigenis!
How grandly hath thine empire grown	Ut usque amans et libera
Of freedom, love, and truth!	et sapiens regis!

How gleam thy watch-fires through the night	Ut ignes tui rutilant
With never-fainting ray!	per noctem vigiles,
How rise thy towers, serene and bright,	serenae turres se levant,
To meet the dawning day!	cum rediit dies!

In vain the surge's angry shock,	Lacessat undarum furor,
In vain the drifting sands:	harena mobilis:
Unharmed upon the eternal rock	in firma rupe firmior
The eternal city stands.	stat Urbs incolumis.

S.Johnson

MM 15—19.4.99

Come down, O Love divine,
Seek thou this soul of mine,
And visit it with thine own ardour glowing;
O Comforter, draw near,
Within my heart appear,
And kindle it, thy holy flame bestowing.

O let it freely burn,
Till earthly passions turn
To dust and ashes in its heat consuming;
And let thy glorious light
Shine ever on my sight,
And clothe me round, the while my path illuming.

Latinised Hymns

Let holy charity
My outward vesture be,
And lowliness become mine inner clothing:
True lowliness of heart,
Which takes the humbler part,
And o'er its own shortcomings weeps with loathing.

And so the yearning strong,
With which the soul will long,
Shall far outpass the power of human telling;
For none can guess its grace,
Till he become the place
Wherein the Holy Spirit makes his dwelling.

Bianco da Siena/R.F. Littledale

Divine Amor, meam
visurus animam
cum propriis ardoribus descendas;
tu mea pectora,
Solator, occupa,
et sanctis ignibus tuis incendas.

Libenter hi flagrent
terrestrem ut crement
sensum suo calore incinerantes;
lucisque radii
appareant mihi
cingentes me viamque illuminantes.

Cum partes caritas
tegat mihi exteras,
humilitas sit intestina vestis,
summissa quae fleat,
ex corde quae gemat
suisque maledicat male gestis.

Sic desiderium,
quod urget animum,
humanam dictionem superabit;
nec est qui gratiam
cognoscat antequam
Paraclitus in eo habitabit.

MM 25—30.5.99

Come, gracious Spirit, heavenly Dove, | *Veni, Columba Spiritus,*
With light and comfort from above; | *huc donis cum caelestibus;*
Be thou our guardian, thou our guide, | *custos et dux, Paraclite,*
O'er every thought and step preside. | *mentes gradusque dirige.*

The light of truth to us display, | *Nos veritas illuminet;*
And make us know and choose thy way; | *noscatur iter, et iuvet;*
Plant holy fear in every heart, | *timor sit sanctus omnibus:*
That we from God may ne'er depart. | *sic Deo non abibimus.*

Lead us to Christ, the living Way, | *Ad Christum veram duc viam,*
Nor let us from his pastures stray; | *nec a pascente perperam;*
Lead us to holiness, the road | *duc sanctitatis semita*
That we must take to dwell with God. | *divina nos ad atria.*

Lead us to heaven, that we may share | *Ad caelum duc: ibi loces*
Fulness of joy for ever there; | *nos gaudii participes;*
Lead us to God, our final rest, | *duc ad Deum nos ultimo*
To be with him for ever blest. | *beandos semper otio.*

S. Browne | *MM 15—20.2.00*

Come, let us join our cheerful songs | *Quin angelis concinimus*
With angels round the throne; | *adstantibus throno,*
Ten thousand thousand are their tongues, | *tot linguas exercentibus*
But all their joys are one. | *in uno gaudio?*

"Worthy the Lamb that died," they cry, | *"Sic Agnus" illi "mortuus*
To be exalted thus;" | *est exaltabilis"*
"Worthy the Lamb," our lips reply, | *canunt. "Pro nobis" addimus*
"For he was slain for us." | *"quod est mactatus is."*

Jesus is worthy to receive | *Sit ea, Iesu, quae Deo,*
Honour and power divine; | *tibi potentia,*
And blessings, more than we can give, | *nec sola benedictio*
Be, Lord, for ever thine. | *haec nostra sit tua.*

Let all creation join in one | *Uno, quot fecit, animo*
To bless the sacred name | *coniuncta celebrent*
Ot him that sits upon the throne, | *nomen sedentis in throno*
And to adore the Lamb. | *et Agnum invocent.*

I. Watts | *MM 31.3—3.4.00*

44

Come, let us join our friends above
That have obtained the prize,
And on the eagle wings of love
To joy celestial rise.

E'en now by faith we join our hands
With those that went before,
And greet our Captain's ransomed bands
On the eternal shore.

C. Wesley

Caris iungamur superis
nactisque praemium,
surgentes aquilae modis
beatum ad polum.

Iam praegressorum manibus
arreptis in fide
redemptos Duce noscimus
aeterno litore.

MM   3—9.6.00

Come, my soul, thy suit prepare:
Jesus loves to answer prayer;
He himself has bid thee pray,
Therefore will not say thee nay.

Thou art coming to a King:
Large petitions with thee bring;
For his grace and power are such
None can ever ask too much.

With my burden I begin:
Lord, remove this load of sin;
Let thy Blood, for sinners spilt,
Set my conscience free from guilt.

Lord, I come to thee for rest;
Take possession of my breast;
There thy blood-bought right maintain,
And without a rival reign.

While I am a pilgrim here,
Let thy love my spirit cheer;
Be my guide, my guard, my friend,
Lead me to my journey's end.

J. Newton

Anima, preceris, et
sponte Christus adnuet;
nec preces respuerit,
qui precari docuit.

Parva dona ne petas,
quae ad Regem venias:
eius opes gratiae
possit nemo vincere.

Primum, Domine, precor:
tolle culpam qua gravor,
perque tua vulnera
solve noxae vincula.

Praebiturus otium
pectus occupa meum,
iusque partum sanguine
ibi solus exige.

Dum viator hic eam
te iuvare sentiam:
custos, dux, amicus sis,
adque metam vexeris.

MM 17—21.9.97

Come, O come, in pious lays
Sound we God Almighty's praise:
Hither bring, in one concent,
Heart and voice and instrument.
Let those things which do not live
In still music praises give;
Nor a creature dumb be found,
That hath either voice or sound.

Come, ye sons of human race,
In this chorus take your place;
And amid the mortal throng
Be ye masters of the song.
Let, in praise of God, the sound
Run a never-ending round,
That our song of praise may be
Everlasting, as is he.

So this huge, wide orb we see
Shall one choir, one temple be,
And our song shall overclimb
All the bounds of space and time,
And ascend from sphere to sphere
To the great Almighty's ear.
Then, O come, in pious lays
Sound we God Almighty's praise!

G. Wither

Ite! Quin concinimus
piis Dei laudibus?
Adsint in harmonia
corda, voces, organa.
Si quid anima caret,
sileat, sed celebret;
reve quicquam taceat,
cui sonum natura dat.

Vosque, hominum genus,
vos includat hic chorus:
inter animalia
dirigatis cantica.
Circumito, quo Deus
usque laudetur, sonus
ut aeterna sit Dei
nostra laus perpetui.

Orbis, quem conspicimus,
templum fiat et chorus;
et transcendat canticum
tempus atque spatium,
se per globos erigens;
audiatque Omnipotens.
Ergo quin concinimus
piis Dei laudibus?

MM 8—13.9.00

Come, O thou Traveller unknown,
Whom still I hold, but cannot see;
My company before is gone,
And I am left alone with thee;
With thee all night I mean to stay,
And wrestle till the break of day.

I need not tell thee who I am,
My misery or sin declare;
Thyself hast called me by my name;
Look on my hands, and read it there!
But who, I ask thee, who art thou?
Tell me thy Name, and tell me now.

In vain thou strugglest to get free;
I never will unloose my hold.
Art thou the Man that died for me?
The secret of thy love unfold:
Wrestling, I will not let thee go,
Till I thy Name, thy nature know.

Yield to me now, for I am weak,
But confident in self-despair;
Speak to my heart, in blessings speak,
Be conquered by my instant prayer.
Speak, or thou never hence shalt move,
And tell me if thy Name is Love?

'Tis Love! 'tis Love! thou diedst for me!
I hear thy whisper in my heart!
The morning breaks, the shadows flee;
Pure universal Love thou art;
To me. to all, thy mercies move;
Thy nature and thy Name is Love.

C. Wesley
(see Genesis 32.24—30)

Viator parum cognite,
quem prensum male video,
misso meorum agmine
tecum relictus en! ego,
hic pernoctare destinans,
ad lucem usque dimicans.

Num quis sim dicere est opus,
luctum culpamque pandere?
Legas meis in manibus;
tu me vocasti nomine.
Tuum sed nomen nuncupa.
Quis es tu? Dic, neu sit mora.

Frustra conere solui:
non me laxare facias.
Tune ille mortuus mihi?
Arcana amoris detegas.
Luctabor, neque desinam
dum quis et qualis es sciam.

Concede: ego sum aeger, at
fert desperatio fidem;
cor te beantem audiat,
et, te precatus, impetrem.
Hic usque ni mansurus es,
dicas: Amor-ne tu clues?

Amor clues! Cordique te
susurras mihi mortuum.
Fit lux, fugantur tenebrae.
Quot sunt Amator hominum,
mihi cunctisque mitis es;
Amor tu, quod et es, clues.

MM   24.5—3.6.00

Come, thou long-expected Jesus,	*Veni, Jesus expectate*
Born to set thy people free;	*liberator hominum!*
From our fears and sins release us;	*Culpa solve nos, et a te*
Let us find our rest in thee.	*detur nobis otium.*

Israel's strength and consolation,	*Firmas Iacob et solaris,*
Hope of all the earth thou art;	*unus orbi spem parans;*
Dear Desire of every nation,	*gentibus desideraris,*
Joy of every longing heart.	*supplices laetificans.*

Born thy people to deliver;	*Nate populi salvator*
Born a Child and yet a King;	*idem rector et puer,*
Born to reign in us for ever;	*sempiterne moderator,*
Now thy gracious kingdom bring.	*iura nobis alma fer.*

By thy own eternal spirit,	*Semper inspirare volens*
Rule in all our hearts alone:	*solus intra nos rege,*
By thy all-sufficient merit,	*daque nobis omnipollens*
Raise us to thy glorious throne.	*iuxta te considere.*

C. Wesley   *MM 20—30 Dec 97*

Come, ye thankful people, come,	*Gratus ito populus*
Raise the song of harvest-home:	*celebrandis messibus:*
All is safely gathered in,	*vitat hibernas nives*
Ere the winter storms begin;	*tuta sub tectis seges;*
God, our Maker, doth provide	*neve quis esuriat,*
For our wants to be supplied:	*qui creavit, ipse dat:*
Come to God's own temple, come,	*aede laudetur Deus*
Raise the song of harvest-home.	*messem celebrantibus.*
All this world is God's own field,	*Dei mundus est ager,*
Fruit unto his praise to yield;	*laudum eius fructifer:*
Wheat and tares therein are sown,	*fruge et loliis satus*
Unto joy or sorrow grown;	*laeta fert cum tristibus;*
Ripening with a wondrous power	*miro more sol coquit*
Till the final harvest-hour:	*messor dum secaverit:*
Grant, O Lord of life, that we	*ut aristas redde nos*
Holy grain and pure may be.	*puros, Deus, et probos.*
For we know that thou wilt come,	*Namque scimus te domum*
And wilt take thy people home;	*portaturum populum,*
From thy field wilt purge away	*quo dempturum esse te*
All that doth offend, that day;	*omne noxium die;*
And thine angels charge at last	*loliumque tum dabis*
In the fire the tares to cast,	*comburendum angelis,*
But the fruitful ears to store	*far tamen perpetuo*
In thy garner evermore.	*conservandum horreo.*
Come then, Lord of mercy, come,	*Messem, clemens Domine,*
Bid us sing thy harvest-home:	*celebrare nos iube;*
Let thy saints be gathered in,	*cumulari fac tuos*
Free from sorrow, free from sin;	*labe et luctu liberos;*
All upon the golden floor	*areaque in aurea*
Praising thee for evermore:	*usque sint encomia;*
Come, with all thine angels come,	*"Messem" et cum angelis*
Bid us sing thy harvest-home.	*"celebrate" dic tuis.*
H. Alford	*MM 26—30.7.00*

Creator of the earth and skies,
To whom all truth and power belong,
Grant us your truth to make us wise;
Grant us your power to make us strong.

We have not known you: to the skies
Our monuments of folly soar,
And all our self-wrought miseries
Have made us trust ourselves the more.

We have not loved you: far and wide
The wreckage of our hatred spreads,
And evils wrought by human pride
Recoil on unrepentant heads.

We long to end this worldwide strife:
How shall we follow in your way?
Speak to mankind your words of life,
Until our darkness turns to day.

D.W. Hughes

Creasti terram et polos;
est tua vis et veritas:
prudentes veritate nos
et vi valentes facias.

Nesciris; heu! dementiae
tolluntur sursum culmina,
nostroque ipsorum vulnere
est aucta pertinacia.

Te non amavimus; loca
fragmentis odium replet;
nec, nostra quos superbia
punivit, illius pudet.

Sit pax per orbem quaesumus,
euntem ut sequamur te;
salutem dic hominibus
cedantque luci tenebrae.

MM 8-12 1 02

Crown him with many crowns,
The Lamb upon his throne;
Hark! how the heavenly anthem drowns
All music but its own:
Awake, my soul, and sing
Of him who died for thee,
And hail him as thy matchless King
Through all eternity.

Crown him the Virgin's Son,
The God incarnate born,
Whose arm those crimson trophies won
Which now his brow adorn:
Fruit of the mystic Rose,
As of that Rose the Stem;
The Root whence mercy ever flows,
The Babe of Bethlehem.

Cingite Victimam,
qui nactus est thronum.
Ut mergit omnem musicam
caeleste canticum!
Hic pro te mortuus,
cantetur, anima:
laudetur Rex egregius
per quot sunt saecula.

Cingite nunc Deum
quem Virgo genuit;
paravit ei brachium,
quae signa frons gerit:
is Fructus est Rosae,
et Stamen itidem,
est Radix is clementiae,
is Infans Bethlehem.

Crown him the Lord of love;
Behold his hands and side,
Those wounds yet visible above
In beauty glorified:
No angel in the sky
Can fully bear that sight,
But downward bends his burning eye
At mysteries so bright.

Crown him the Lord of peace,
Whose power a sceptre sways
From pole to pole, that wars may cease,
And all be prayer and praise:
His reign shall know no end,
And round his pierced feet
Fair flowers of Paradise extend
Their fragrance ever sweet.

Crown him the Lord of years,
The Potentate of time,
Creator of the rolling spheres,
Ineffably sublime:
All hail, Redeemer, hail!
For thou hast died for me;
Thy praise shall never, never fail
Throughout eternity.

M. Bridges

Cingite, cui amor
inflixit vulnera;
nunc latus et manus decor
distinguit en! supra;
quam claritudinem
vix angeli ferunt,
suamque deorsum aciem
candentem dirigunt.

Cingitor otii
Princeps polum polo
ligans, dum iuncta laus preci
pugnae stet in loco:
regnabit semper is;
punctos pedes ei
odoribus ambrosiis
perfundent flosculi.

Cingite temporis
potentem Dominum;
Creator est globorum is
supra volventium.
Ave, Redemptor, qui
es pro me mortuus.
Addetur usque laus tibi
saeclis in omnibus.

MM 4—10.5.99

Dear Lord and Father of mankind,
Forgive our foolish ways!
Re-clothe us in our rightful mind,
In purer lives thy service find,
In deeper reverence praise.

In simple trust like theirs who heard,
Beside the Syrian sea,
The gracious calling of the Lord,
Let us, like them, without a word
Rise up and follow thee.

O Sabbath rest by Galilee!
O calm of hills above,
Where Jesus knelt to share with thee
The silence of eternity,
Interpreted by love!

Drop thy still dews of quietness,
Till all our strivings cease;
Take from our souls the strain and stress,
And let our ordered lives confess
The beauty of thy peace.

Breathe through the heats of our desire
Thy coolness and thy balm;
Let sense be dumb, let flesh retire;
Speak through the earthquake, wind and fire,
O still small voice of calm!

J.G. Whittier

O care, quod stulti sumus,
ignosce, Domine;
pravis medere mentibus,
laudare fac sincerius,
ex corde colere.

Ut litore Syriaco
qui sunt arcessiti,
tuo fidentes Filio,
et nos eodem fac modo
te tacitos sequi.

Quod Galilaeum Sabbatum
collisque placidus!
Aeternum quod silentium,
Iesu tibique mutuum
ut diligentibus!

Silentio rorata eo
cedant certamina;
angore tum deposito
sit vita testimonio
quam pulchra pax tua.

Frigus calentes temperet
tuum cupidines,
locum quod est carnale det;
procellam tua personet
tranquilla vax, quies!

MM 17—20.10.00

Latinised Hymns

Eternal Father, strong to save,	Aeterne Peter et Salus,
Whose arm hath bound the restless wave,	undarum cogens impetus
Who bidd'st the mighty ocean deep	altumque cohibens fretum
Its own appointed limits keep:	intra permissum terminum,
O hear us when we cry to thee	mandari sentias tibi
For those in peril on the sea.	periclitantes in mari.

O Christ, whose voice the waters heard
And hushed their raging at thy word,
Who walkedst on the foaming deep,
And calm amid the storm didst sleep:
O hear us when we cry to thee
For those in peril on the sea.

Tu, quem tempestas audiit
et te iubente tacuit,
pressisti qui fluctus pedes,
per flabra cui fuit quies,
mandari sentias tibi
periclitantes in mari.

O Holy Spirit, who didst brood
Upon the waters dark and rude,
And bid their angry tumult cease,
And give, for wild confusion, peace:
O hear us when we cry to thee
For those in peril on the sea.

Incubuisti, Spiritus,
aquis super deformibus,
tumultuari prohibens
saevitiamque molliens:
mandari sentias tibi
periclitantes in mari.

O Trinity of love and power,
Our brethren shield in danger's hour;
From rock and tempest, fire and foe,
Protect them wheresoe'er they go:
Thus evermore shall rise to thee
Glad hymns of praise from land and sea.

Potens et alma Trinitas,
periclitantes protegas; ★
per saxa et flabra et hosticos
ignes defende ubique eos.
Sic surget laeta laus tibi
et a tellure et a mari.

W. Whiting

MM   13-15 Feb 98

★periclo nostros eximas;

Eternal Ruler of the ceaseless round
Of circling planets singing on their way;
Guide of the nations from the night profound
Into the glory of the perfect day;
Rule in our hearts, that we may ever be
Guided and strengthened and upheld by thee.

We are of thee, the children of thy love,
The brothers of thy well-beloved Son;
Descend, O Holy Spirit, like a dove,
Into our hearts, that we may be as one:
As one with thee, to whom we ever tend;
As one with him, our Brother and our Friend.

We would be one in hatred of all wrong,
One in our love of all things sweet and fair,
One with the joy that breaketh into song,
One with the grief that trembles into prayer,
One in the power that makes thy children free
To follow truth, and thus to follow thee.

O clothe us with thy heavenly armour, Lord,
Thy trusty shield, thy sword of love divine;
Our inspiration be thy constant word;
We ask no victories that are not thine:
Give or withold, let pain or pleasure be;
Enough to know that we are serving thee.

J.W. Chadwick

Volvenda qui canora sidera
aeternus aeterno cursu regis
et qui de nocte profundissima
in lucem claram populos trahis,
regens et nostra corda robores
ducensque dempto fine subleves.

Ex te sumus, amore de tuo,
carique fratres Filii tui;
intres in corda turturis modo,
Paraclite, iungamur ut tibi,
tibi, qui meta nostra semper es,
illi, quod est et Frater et Comes.

Iunctis sit omne pravum odio,
iunctis, quod pulchrum, omne placeat,
iunctoque gaudeamus cantico,
iunctorum luctus in precem tremat;
iunctaque vi possimus liberi,
ut veritatem, ita te sequi.

Amoris ense, scuto solido,
praecinge nos tua panoplia;
sit constans verbum inspiratio;
victoria neu sit nisi tua;
da, sume; gaudium dolorve sit:
tibi paremus, idque sufficit.

MM 11—17.11.00

Everliving Lord,
A thousand years in your sight
Are but as yesterday;
And in your wondeful light
Time's prison fades away.

Everloving Lord,
Your first millennium passed
A thousand years ago.
The second goes by at last;
We hail the third to show.

Ever-risen Lord,
The third millennium breaks;
The dawn of your third day.
Arising, each of us takes
Your resurrection way.

Everliving,
Ever loving,
Ever-risen Lord.

N. Mortemore

Vivens usque Rex,
abit die brevius
tibi millennium,
aevi, tam es nitidus,
vanescit vinculum.

Fovens usque Rex,
secutum anterius
millennium alterum ★
valere iusserimus;
salveto tertium.

Surgens usque Rex,
millennium en! oritur, ★
Dies ut Tertius,
et nos, qui te sequimur,
tecum resurgimus,

Vivens usque,
fovens usque,
surgens usque Rex.

MM 1—6 Dec 00

★ *"millennyum" –*
a trisyllable

Fair waved the golden corn
in Canaan's pleasant land,
When full of joy, some shining morn,
Went forth the reaper-band.

To God so good and great
Their cheerful thanks they pour;
Then carry to his Temple-gate
The choicest of their store.

Like Israel, Lord, we give
Our earliest fruits to thee,
And pray that, long as we shall live,
We may thy children be.

Thine is our youthful prime,
And life and all its powers:
Be with us in our morning time,
And bless our evening hours.

In wisdom let us grow,
As years and strength are given,
That we may serve thy Church below,
And join thy saints in heaven.

J.H. Gurney

En! seges aurea
Canani finibus
messorum et laetissima
mane exiens manus!

Hi Deo gratias
magno bonoque agunt,
aristas et lectissimas
ad templum conferunt.

Ut Israel, damus
primitias tibi,
perpetuo viventibus
futuro (sis) Patri.

Floremus iuvenes
et vivimus tibi;
tu nobis prima luce ades
beaque vesperi.

Sit sapientia,
sit nobis aucta vis,
ut post terrena munera
iungamur angelis.

MM 6—11.7.99

Faithful Shepherd, feed me	*Pastor me fidelis*
In the pastures green;	*ale pascuis,*
Faithful Shepherd, lead me	*ducere et me velis*
Where thy steps are seen.	*in vestigiis.*

Faithful Shepherd, feed me
In the pastures green;
Faithful Shepherd, lead me
Where thy steps are seen.

Pastor me fidelis
ale pascuis,
ducere et me velis
in vestigiis.

Hold me fast, and guide me
In the narrow way;
So, with thee beside me,
I shall never stray.

Tene me: sectabor
stricta per viae,
neque divagabor
comitante te.

Daily bring me nearer
To thy heavenly shore;
Make my faith grow clearer,
May I love thee more.

Trahe propiorem
tuo litori;
augeasque amorem,
ut fidem, tui.

Hallow every pleasure,
Every gift and pain;
Be thyself my treasure,
Though none else I gain.

Mulcet sive mordet,
omne fac sacrum;
prae te mihi sordet
omne commodum.

Day by day prepare me
As thou seest best,
Then let angels bear me
To thy promised rest.

In dies para me
(optime vides)
angelisque da me,
sitque requies.

T.B. Pollock

MM 2—4.11.99

Father of heaven, whose love profound
A ransom for our souls hath found,
Betore thy throne we sinners bend,
To us thy pardoning love extend.

Almighty Son, incarnate Word,
Our Prophet, Priest, Redeemer, Lord,
Before thy throne we sinners bend,
To us thy saving grace extend.

Eternal Spirit, by whose breath
The soul is raised from sin and death,
Before thy throne we sinners bend,
To us thy quickening power extend.

Thrice Holy! Father, Spirit, Son;
Mysterious Godhead, Three in One,
Before thy throne we sinners bend,
Grace, pardon, life to us extend.

E. Roper

Is est amor, Pater, tuus,
a quo redempti vivimus:
ad te flectentes genua,
da veniam, precamur, da.

In carne Verbum Genite,
Salvator, Vates, Domine,
ad te flectentes genua,
da gratiam, precamur, da.

Paraclite, spirante quo
salvamur nos a tartaro,
ad te flectentes genua
per flatum nos vivifica.

In una tres essentias
ter sancta iungens Trinitas,
orantibus cum gratia
da veniam vitamque da.

MM   30—31.5.99

Father of mercies, in thy word	Verbi, Pater clemens tui,
What endless glory shines!	qui fulgor et decus!
For ever be thy name adored	Pro his sit gloria tibi
For these celestial lines.	supernis versibus.

Father of mercies, in thy word
What endless glory shines!
For ever be thy name adored
For these celestial lines.

Verbi, Pater clemens tui,
qui fulgor et decus!
Pro his sit gloria tibi
supernis versibus.

Here may the blind and hungry come,
And light and food receive;
Here shall the lowliest guest have room,
And taste and see and live.

Hinc caecus, hinc esuriens
levamen auferat;
hic est quod hospites alens
omnes accipiat.

Here springs of consolation rise
To cheer the fainting mind,
And thirsting souls receive supplies,
And sweet refreshment find.

Sunt fontes hic solacii
lassarum mentium
et sitientis animi
perenne poculum.

Here the Redeemer's welcome voice
Spreads heavenly peace around,
And life and everlasting, joys
Attend the blissful sound.

Caeleste vox Dominica
hic spargit otium
demptoque fine gaudia
sequuntur hunc sonum.

O may these heavenly pages be
My ever dear delight,
And still new beauties may I see,
And still increasing light.

His paginis dum gaudeam
semper caelestibus,
novum decus reperiam
et lumen amplius.

Divine instructor, gracious Lord,
Be thou for ever near;
Teach me to love thy sacred word,
And view my Saviour here.

Divine Doctor, Domine,
prope adsis o! mihi;
amari verbum hic iube
Christumque conspici.

Anne Steele

MM 25.1 — 5.2.01

Father, whate'er of earthly bliss
Thy sovereign will denies,
Accepted at thy throne of grace
Let this petition rise:

Give me a calm and thankful heart,
From every murmur free;
The blessings of thy grace impart,
And let me live to thee.

Let the sweet hope that thou art mine
My path of life attend;
Thy presence through my journey shine,
And crown my journey's end.

Anne Steele

Terrestre, Pater, ut neges
mihi omne gaudium,
orationem hanc probes,
cum surgat ad thronum:

mea sit pax in anima,
neu contra te fremam,
sed gratia bees tua
ut tibi serviam.

Dulcedo mihi sit viae
te meum esse spes,
meaeque praesens semitae,
ut meta, sis comes.

MM 28—30.4.01

Fierce raged the tempest o'er the deep,
Watch did thine anxious servants keep,
But thou wast wrapped in guileless sleep,
    Calm and still.

Tempestas imminet mari,
servique invigilant tui,
cum tu, quasi inscius mali,
    dormias.

"Save, Lord, we perish," was their cry,
"0 save us in our agony!"
Thy word above the storm rose high,
    "Peace, be still."

Ut morituri confremunt
tuumque auxilium petunt;
mox te iubentem audiunt
    "Sileas!"

The wild winds hushed; the angry deep
Sank, like a little child, to sleep;
The sullen billows ceased to leap,
    At thy will.

Venti fluctusque (ut) taceant
et sicut infans dormiant,
undae salire desinant,
    imperas.

So, when our life is clouded o'er,
And storm-winds drift us from the shore,
Say, lest we sink to rise no more,
    "Peace, be still."

Sic nos cum nubes opprimat,
hiems ab ora detrahat,
dic, mare ne nos hauriat,
    "Sileas!"

G. Thring

MM 12—16.7.00

Fight the good fight with all thy might,	*Ut poteris tu miles sis;*
Christ is thy strength and Christ thy right;	*ius tibi Christus, robur is;*
Lay hold on life, and it shall be	*capesse vitam, atque ea*
Thy joy and crown eternally.	*corona erit perpetua.*

Run the straight race through God's good grace,	*Cursum ope Dei tene,*
Lift up thine eyes and seek his face:	*eiusque (ad) vultum suspice;*
Life with its way before thee lies,	*vita in viam prorsus vocat*
Christ is the path and Christ the prize.	*Christus iter munusque dat.*

Cast care aside, lean on thy guide;	*Cura abeat, Dux fulciat,*
His boundless mercy will provide;	*qui bona multa commodat;*
Trust, and thy trusting soul shall prove	*esto fides, hoc comprobans:*
Christ is its life and Christ its love.	*Christus amat vivificans.*

Faint not, nor fear, his arms are near;	*Fidas ei: subest tibi;*
He changeth not and thou art dear;	*es carus immutabili;*
Only believe, and thou shalt see	*credas, et erit agnitus*
That Christ is all in all to thee.	*Christus tibi omne in omnibus.*

J.S.B. Monsell

MM   12—16.8.00

Firmly I believe and truly
God is Three and God is One;
And I next acknowledge duly
Manhood taken by the Son.

And I trust and hope most fully
in that Manhood crucified;
And each thought and deed unruly
Do to death, as he has died.

Simply to his grace and wholly
Light and life arud strength belong,
And I love supremely, solely,
Him the Holy, him the Strong.

And I hold in veneration,
For the love of him alone,
Holy Church as his creation,
And her teachings as his own.

Adoration aye be given,
With and through the angelic host,
To the God of earth and heaven,
Father, Son, and Holy Ghost.

J.H. Newman

Trinum simul unicumque
esse Deum arbitror,
id pro certo; Filiumque
incarnatum fateor.

Huïc crucifixo fidens
atque morte simili
mente et actis omne occidens
peccaturus quod fui.

Nobis vires, vita, lumen
huius fiunt gratia;
huius robur atque numen
tota miror anima.

Venerorque, quam creavit,
propter hunc Ecclesiam,
nempe cui communicavit
ipse doctrinam suam.

Angelorum sociati
coetui, perpetuo
laudem demus Trinitati,
hic et supra Domino. ★

MM   20—24.1.98

★*hic et in caelis Deo.*

For all the saints, who from their labours rest,
who thee by faith before the world confessed,
thy name, O Jesus, be forever blessed.
Alleluia, Alleluia!

Thou wast their Rock, their Fortress and their Might;
thou, Lord, their Captain in the well fought fight;
thou, in the darkness still their one true Light.
Alleluia, Alleluia!

O may thy soldiers, faithful, true, and bold,
fight as the saints who nobly fought of old,
and win, with them the victor's crown of gold.
Alleluia, Alleluia!

O blest communion, fellowship divine!
we feebly struggle, they in glory shine;
Yet all are one in thee, for all are thine.
Alleluia, Alleluia!

And when the strife is fierce, the warfare long,
steals on the ear the distant triumph song,
and hearts are brave again, and arms are strong.
Alleluia, Alleluia!

The golden evening brightens in the west;
soon, soon to faithful warriors comes their rest;
sweet is the calm of paradise the blessed.
Alleluia, Alleluia!

But lo! there breaks a yet more glorious day;
the saints triumphant rise in bright array;
the King of glory passes on his way.
Alleluia, Alleluia!

From earth's wide bounds, from ocean's farthest coast,
through gates of pearl streams in the countless host,
singing to Father, Son and Holy Ghost:
Alleluia, Alleluia!

W.W. How

Ob sanctos, qui nacturi requiem
te per suam confessi sunt fidem,
te salutamus, Jesu, celebrem.
Alleluia, Alleluia!

Saxum fuisti, turris atque vis,
dux in pugnatis bene proeliis,
illorum una lux in tenebris.
Alleluia, Alleluia!

Constanter pugnent tui milites,
Ut pugnavere sancti veteres,
laurusque mereantur similes.
Alleluia, Alleluia!

Nos debiles at illi splendidi,
divine sed sumus compositi,
in hoc uniti, quod sumus tui.
Alleluia, Alleluia!

Belli durantibus saevitiis
distans triumphus in auriculis
est, fitque virtus nova, nova vis.
Alleluia, Alleluia!

En ubi sol rubescens occidit!
Merentibus mox otium venit,
in Paradiso quod suave fit.
Alleluia, Alleluia!

Sed en ubi est aurora pulchrior
sanctorum et surgentium nitor!
It rex, supremus cuius est honor.
Alleluia, Alleluia!

Longe remotis e litoribus
innumeratus intrat en! chorus,
a quo Triunus audit Dominus
Alleluia, Alleluia!

MM   11—21.3.01

For all thy saints, O Lord,
Who strove in thee to live,
Who followed thee, obeyed, adored,
Our grateful hymn receive.

For all thy saints, O Lord,
Who strove in thee to die,
And found in thee a full reward,
Accept our thankful cry.

Thine earthly members fit
To join thy saints above,
In one communion ever knit,
One fellowship of love.

Jesu, thy name we bless,
And humbly pray that we
May follow them in holiness,
Who lived and died for thee.

All might, all praise, be thine,
Father, co-equal Son,
And Spirit, bond of love divine,
While endless ages run.

Bp R. Mant

Pro sanctis, O Deus,
conatis vivere
in te, tui cultoribus,
has grates accipe.

Pro sanctis, Domine,
qui magno te suas
mutarunt vitas munere,
grates accipias.

Iungendos redde nos
eis qui sunt supra
unoque vinclo socios
amoris colliga.

Beatus qui clues,
oramus ut tibi
eorum simus similes
vivi seu mortui.

Ut Patri, Filio
laus et potentia
iunctore cum Paraclito
esto perpetua.

MM 10—14.1.00

"For ever with the Lord!"
Amen; so let it be:
Life from the dead is in that word,
'Tis immortality.
Here in the body pent,
Absent from him I roam,
Yet nightly pitch my moving tent
A day's march nearer home.

My Father's house on high,
Home of my soul, how near
At times to faith's foreseeing eye
Thy golden gates appear!
Ah, then my spirit faints
To reach the land I love,
The bright inheritance of saints,
Jerusalem above.

"For ever with the Lord!"
Father, if 'tis thy will,
The promise of that faithful word
Even here to me fulfil.
Be thou at my right hand,
Then can I never fail;
Uphold thou me, and I shall stand,
Fight, and I must prevail.

5o when my latest breath
Shall rend the veil in twain,
By death I shall escape from death,
And life eternal gain.
Knowing as I am known,
How shall I love that word,
And oft repeat before the throne,
"For ever with the Lord!"

J.Montgomery

"Semper cum Domino!"
Amen, hoc ita sit:
his verbis vitam vindico,
nec ulla mors erit.
Seclusus corpore
ab eo nunc vagor,
sed usque vesperi die
fit domus propior.

Paterna tu domus
excelsa, quam prope
cum fide providentibus
portae nitent tuae!
Ut cor desiderat
amatam patriam,
quae clara sanctos divitat,
Jerusalem novam!

"Semper cum Domino!"
Hoc, Pater, hic, tibi
si placet id pollicito,
perficias mihi.
Dexter mihi subes:
sic non deficiam,
hostesque te, qui sustines,
pugnante subigam.

Exspirans ultimum
cum velum ruperim
per mortem pulsa morte, tum
ut vivus usque sim,
ut scitus sic sciens,
quam laetus tunc ero,
his verbis gratias agens,
"Semper cum Domino!"

MM 29.6—9.7.99

For the beauty of the earth,
For the beauty of the skies,
For the love that from our birth
Over and about us lies,
Lord of all, to thee we raise
this our grateful hymn of praise.

Tantus est quod hic decor
terrae, nec caeli minus
quodque cingit nos amor
et tegit, dum vivimus,
Accipe, rex omnium,
hoc gratorum canticum.

For the beauty of each hour
Of the day and of the night,
Hill and vale, and tree and flower,
Sun and moon and stars of light,

Quod horarum est lepos,
die, nocte quae placet,
mons et vallis, arbor, flos,
stellae, luna, sol nitet.

For the joy of human love,
Brother, sister, parent, child,
Friends on earth and friends above,
Pleasures pure and undefiled,

Quod amor familias
gratus hominum ligat
hic et supra caritas
pura comites iuvat,

For each perfect gift of thine,
To our race so freely given,
Graces human and divine,
Flowers of earth and buds of heaven,

Quad libenter praemia
nostrae genti larga das,
hic florentes et supra
florituras gratias.

For thy Church which evermore
Lifteth holy hands above,
Offering up on every shore
Her pure sacrifice of love,
Lord of all, to thee we raise
this our grateful hymn of praise.

Tua quod Ecclesia
semper elevat manus,
cuius amor victima
est locis in omnibus,
Accipe, rex omnium,
hoc gratorum canticum.

F.S. Pierpoint

MM 18—22.5.01

Forsaken once, and thrice denied,
The risen Lord gave pardon free,
Stood once again at Peter's side,
And asked him, "Lov'st thou me?"

How many times with faithless word
Have we denied his holy name,
How oft forsaken our dear Lord,
And shrunk when trial came!

Saint Peter, when the cock crew clear,
Went out, and wept his broken faith:
Strong as a rock through strife and fear,
He served his Lord till death.

How oft his cowardice of heart
We have without his love sincere,
The sin without the sorrow's smart,
The shame without the tear!

O oft forsaken, oft denied,
Forgive our shame, wash out our sin;
Look on us from thy Father's side
And let that sweet look win.

Hear when we call thee from the deep,
Still walk beside us on the shore,
Give hands to work, and eyes to weep,
And hearts to love thee more.

Mrs C.F. Alexander

Relictus, ter male agnitus,
libenter veniam dedit
iuxtaque Petrum Daminus
"Me diligisne?" ait.

At quotiens nos perfidi
te, Jesu, non agnovimus,
heu! proditores, territi
temptationibus!

Fidem, cum gallus cecinit,
flens exiit at post Petrus
ad mortem usque serviit
per omne saxeus.

Ut Petrum, vicit nos metus,
sed eius afuit amor;
peccantes haud doluimus,
nec fletus est pudor.

A nobis saepe prodite,
culpae solutionem fer;
sedens cum Patre despice,
et efficaciter.

Audi clamantes e lacu,
in ripa neu neglexeris;
colare lacrimis, menu,
amore fac magis.

MM 15—19.601

For thy mercy and thy grace,
Faithful through another year,
Hear our song of thankfulness;
Jesu, our Redeemer, hear.

In our weakness and distress,
Rock of strength, be thou our stay;
In the pathless wilderness
Be our true and living Way.

Who of us death's awful road
In the coming year shall tread,
With thy rod and staff, O God,
Comfort thou his dying bed.

Keep us faithful, keep us pure,
Keep us evermore thine own,
Help, O help us to endure,
Fit us for the promised crown.

So within thy palace gate
We shall praise on golden strings
Thee the only potentate,
Lord of Lords and King of Kings.

H.Downton

Bis dato sex mensibus
quas de dono gratiae
gratias offerimus,
O Redemptor, accipe.

Debiles miseriis
saxi more fulcias,
quique via vera sis,
nos errantes dirigas.

Si quis ad manes iter
carpet anno proximo,
hunc solare virgifer
mortis in articulo.

Nos in integra fide
semper habeas tuos
teque durantes duce
caelo fac idoneos.

Intra sic palatium
aureis te fidibus
Dominorum Dominum,
Regum Rex, laudabimus.

MM · 30.12.99—1.1.00

Forth in thy Name, O Lord, I go,
my daily labour to pursue;
thee, only thee, resolved to know
in all I think or speak or do.

The task thy wisdom hath assigned,
O let me cheerfully fulfill;
in all my works thy presence find,
and prove thy good and perfect will.

Thee may I set at my right hand,
whose eyes mine inmost substance see,
and labour on at thy command,
and offer all my works to thee.

Give me to bear thy easy yoke,
and every moment watch and pray,
and still to things eternal look,
and hasten to thy glorious day.

For thee delightfully employ
whate'er thy bounteous grace hath given;
and run my course with even joy,
and closely walk with thee to heav'n.

C. Wesley

Sacratus exeo tibi,
diurno penso debitus
unius consciis tui,
ut mente, voce et manibus.

Contentus illud exsequar
quod assignasti sapiens
benevolumque experiar
in omni facto te videns.

Te dextrum mihi statuam,
qui penitus me perspicis
constanter tibi paream
in deditis officiis.

Leve istud da iugum feram
cum prece semper vigilans;
aeterna sola videam
ad te lucentem properans.

Fac me libenter reddere
quod tu largitus es mihi,
curramque cum laeto pede
ad caelum proximus tibi.

MM 2—5.9.98

Forty days and forty nights
Thou wast fasting in the wild;
Forty days and forty nights
Tempted and yet undefiled:

Sunbeams scorching all the day;
Chilly dew-drops nightly shed;
Prowling beasts about thy way;
Stones thy pillow, earth thy bed.

Shall not we thy sorrows share,
And from earthly joys abstain,
Fasting with unceasing prayer,
Glad with thee to suffer pain?

And if Satan, vexing sore,
Flesh or spirit should assail,
Thou, his vanquisher before,
Grant we may not faint nor fail.

So shall we have peace divine;
Holier gladness ours shall be;
Round us too shall angels shine,
Such as ministered to thee.

Keep, O keep us, Saviour dear,
Ever constant by thy side;
That with thee we may appear
At the eternal Eastertide.

G.H.Smyttan & F. Pott

From all that dwell below the skies,
let the Creator's praise arise!
Let the Redeemer's Name be sung
through every land, by every tongue!

Eternal are thy mercies, Lord,
and truth eternal is thy word:
Thy praise shall sound from shore to shore
till suns shall rise and set no more.

I Watts

Quater errabas decem
per dies esuriens
noctibusque totidem,
incorruptum te tenens.

Laesit te meridie
sol et nocte glacies;
minabantur bestiae;
dura rupe fultus es.

Nonne tecum flebimus
voluptate subdita
non diremptis precibus,
tua nacti vulnera.

Temptabit-ne Satanas?
Prisco tu certamine
victor illius eras:
nos domari prohibe.

Sic divina pax erit,
sanctiora gaudia,
qualis et tibi fuit,
nobis ops angelica.

Simus, o salutifer,
fidi tibi comites,
et caeleste iugiter
celebrandum pascha des.

MM Feb97/Apr98

Sit, quot sub axe vivitis,
audita laus Artificis;
vulgetque Redemptorium
ubique linguae titulum.

Te, semper clemens Domine,
te, semper o veridice,
te litus litori canet,
dum surget sol et occidet.

MM 29.3-1.4 .99

From Greenland's icy mountains,
From India's coral strand,
Where Afric's sunny fountains
Roll down the golden sand,
From many an ancient river,
From many a palmy plain,
They call us to deliver
Their land from error's chain.

What though the spicy breezes
Blow soft o'er Ceylon's isle,
Though every prospect pleases
And only man is vile:
In vain with lavish kindness
The gifts of God are strown;
The heathen in his blindness
Bows down to wood and stone.

Can we, whose souls are lighted
With wisdom from on high,
Can we to men benighted
The lamp of life deny?
Salvation! O Salvation!
The joyful sound proclaim,
Till each remotest nation
Has learned Messiah's name.

Waft, waft, ye winds, his story,
And you, ye waters, roll,
Till, like a sea of glory,
It spreads from pole to pole;
Till o'er our ransomed nature
The Lamb for sinners slain,
Redeemer, King, Creator,
In bliss returns to reign.

Bishop Heber

*Septentrionis montes
et litus Indicum
flavumque circa fontes
Afros effluvium
palmetaque et annosa
per orbem flumina
nos invocant perosa
erroris vincula.*

*En! Tura circumvectat
Taprobanen Notus;
omne aliud delectat,
modo est homo malus.
Frustra Divina manus
pagano dona dat,
dum numen is paganus
materiam putat.*

*Nobisne illuminatis
caelesti gratia
placebit obscuratis
negare lampada?
Salvatio clametur,
laetabilis sonus,* ★
*dum Christus agnoscetur
extremis gentibus.*

*Famam differte venti,
et unda provehat,
ut magno par torrenti
inter polos eat,
dum Agnus poenae lator,
qui nobis periit,
Redemptor, Rex, Creator,
regnare coeperit.*

MM 16—21.5.97

★ *v. 1. eatque nuntius*

Give us the wings of faith to rise
Within the veil, and see
The saints above, how great their joys,
How bright their glories be.

Once they were mourning here below,
Their couch was wet with tears;
They wrestled hard, as we do now,
With sins and doubts and fears.

We ask them whence their victory came:
They, with united breath,
Ascribe the conquest to the Lamb,
Their triumph to his Death.

They marked the footsteps that he trod,
His zeal inspired their breast,
And, following their incarnate God,
They reached the promised rest.

Our glorious Leader claims our praise
For his own pattern given;
While the great cloud of witnesses
Show the same path to heaven.

I. Watts

Tolli fide pinnante da
perspicientibus
sanctarum quanta gaudia,
quam splendidum decus.

Ut nos, hi quoque fletibus
planxere madidi
et luctabantur haud secus
malorum conscii.

Quae causa eis victoriae?
Uno sese animo
Agni vicisse aiunt ope
eiusque exitio.

Eiusdem in notis pedum
eodem et duce
post incarnatum sunt Deum
potiti requie.

Laudandus ergo Dominus
exemplum ob suum;
et caelum O! petentibus
quae turba testium!

MM 23—25.3.99

Glorious things of thee are spoken,
Zion, city of our God;
He whose word cannot be broken
Formed thee for his own abode.
On the Rock of ages founded,
What can shake thy sure repose?
With salvation's walls surrounded,
Thou may'st smile at all thy foes.

See, the streams of living waters,
Springing from eternal love,
Well supply thy sons and daughters,
And all fear of want remove.
Who can faint while such a river
Ever flows their thirst to assuage,
Grace which, like the Lord the giver,
Never fails from age to age?

Round each habitation hovering,
See the cloud and fire appear
For a glory and a covering,
Showing that the Lord is near.
Thus they march, the pillar leading,
Light by night and shade by day;
Daily on the manna feeding
Which he gives them when they pray.

Saviour, since of Zion's city
I through grace a member am,
Let the world deride or pity,
I will glory in thy name.
Fading is the worldling's pleasure,
All his boasted pomp and show;
Solid joys and lasting treasure
None but Zion's children know.

J.Newton

Fama tuam nuncupavit,
Urbs beata, gloriam,
cuius se Deus dicavit
(neque fallit) incolam.
Super saxum stabilita,
certa cui tranquillitas,
tu salute communita
hostibus inrideas.

En! tuam perenni vivus
ex amore defluens
prolem locupletat rivus
egestatem submovens.
Ecquis hoc sitire debet
irrigatus flumine?
Gratiam Deus, qui praebet,
sufficit perpetue.

Super castris impendentem
ignem nubem cernite,
tegmen et decus, monentem
esse Dominum prope.
Agmen it: pilam sequuntur,
umbrat sive luminat;.
Manna per viam vescuntur,
quod Deus suppeditat.

Urbe Sion ut includar,
Christe, nactus gratiam,
sive plorer sive ludar,
tuus esse gaudeam.
Speciosa nec mansura
sunt mundana praemia;
sola Sion duratura
dat suis nutrimina.

MM Oct 96

Glory to thee, my God, this night
For all the blessings of the light;
Keep me, O keep me, King of kings,
Beneath thine own almighty wings.

Forgive me, Lord, for thy dear Son,
The ill that I this day have done;
That with the world, myself, and thee,
I, ere I sleep, at peace may be.

Teach me to live, that I may dread
The grave as little as my bed;
Teach me to die, that so I may
Rise glorious at the awful day.

O may my soul on thee repose,
And may sweet sleep mine eyelids close,
Sleep that shall me more vigorous make
To serve my God when I awake.

If in the night I sleepless lie,
My soul with heavenly thoughts supply;
Let no ill dreams disturb my rest,
No powers of darkness me molest.

Praise God, from whom all blessings flow;
Praise him, all creatures here below;
Praise him above, ye heavenly host;
Praise Father, Son, and Holy Ghost.

T.Ken

Diurnis pro favoribus
hac nocte laudo te, Deus;
per quam sub alae tegmine
me serva, regum maxime.

Remitte suasu Filii,
si hodie quid nocui,
ut, dormiturus, sim mihi
mundoque gratus et tibi.

Cum tibi vixerim placens,
nec somnum nec mortem timens,
sic moriar docente te
ut surgam ultimo die.

In te quiescam, et meos
occludat somnus oculos,
inde experrectus augeam
vires, ut tibi serviam.

Seu forte noctu vigilem,
fac de caelestibus putem;
ne mala turbent somnia
neu tenebrarum numina.

Quot estis animalia,
laudate eum qui dat bona;
nec segnius, caelicolae,
vos Trinitatem psallite.

MM 29.10.—4.11.98

Go to dark Gethsemane,
Ye that feel the tempter's power,
Your Redeemer's conflict see,
Watch with him one bitter hour;
Turn not from his griefs away:
Learn of Jesus Christ to pray.

Hortus iste vos vocat,
Satana lacessiti,
vigiles vos teneat
luctus horam Domini;
gnari preces fundere
eius more discite.

Follow to the judgement-hall,
View the Lord of Life arraigned;
O the wormwood and the gall!
O the pangs his soul sustained!
Shun not suffering, shame, or loss:
Learn of him to bear the cross.

Ad tribunal pergite.
En! Vivificans reus!
Fel, absinthium, grave
animae nocens onus!
Crucis cum dedecore
ferre damnum discite.

Calvary's mournful mountain climb;
There, adoring at his feet,
Mark that miracle of time,
God's own Sacrifice complete;
"It is finished!" hear him cry:
Learn of Jesus Christ to die.

Maestum Montem scandite;
adorate ibi Deum
et sui mirabile
scite Sacrificium,
voce fortiter mori
"Actum est" admoniti.

J.Montgomery

MM 25.2—1.3.00

God is Love: let heav'n adore him;
God is Love: let earth rejoice;
Let creation sing before him,
And exalt him with one voice.
He who laid the earth's foundation,
He who spread the heav'ns above,
He who breathes through all creation,
He is Love, eternal Love.

God is love: and he enfoldeth
All the world in one embrace;
With unfailing grasp he holdeth
Every child of every race.
And when human hearts are breaking
Under sorrow's iron rod,
Then they find that selfsame aching
Deep within the heart of God.

God is Love: and though with blindness
Sin afflicts the souls of men,
God's eternal loving-kindness
Holds and guides them even then.
Sin and death and hell shall never
O'er us final triumph gain;
God is Love, so Love for ever
O'er the universe must reign.

T.Rees

Deus Amor: terra, gaude!
Adorate, caelites!
Una, creatura, laude,
una voce celebres.
Ille telluris fundator,
caeli supra diditor,
creatorum inspirator,
sempiternus est Amor.

Deus Amor: comprehendit
unico ligamine
mundum; fortiter defendit
natos quoquo genere.
Quotiens dolor sentitur
nostro hic in animo,
idem angor invenitur
imo Dei gremio.

Deus Amor: cum caecentur
peccabundi homines,
in via Dei tenentur
bonitate sospites.
Mors, scelus nec orcus umquam
ditione nos premet;
Deus Amor; ergo numquam
mundum non Amor reget.

MM 4—12.4.01

God moves in a mysterious way
His wonders to perform;
He plants his footsteps in the sea,
And rides upon the storm.

Deep in unfathomable mines
Of never-failing skill
He treasures up his bright designs,
And works his sovereign will.

Ye fearful saints, fresh courage take;
The clouds ye so much dread
Are big with mercy, and shall break
In blessings on your head.

Judge not the Lord by feeble sense,
But trust him for his grace;
Behind a frowning providence
He hides a smiling face.

His purposes will ripen fast,
Unfolding every hour;
The bud may have a bitter taste,
But sweet will be the flower.

Blind unbelief is sure to err,
And scan his work in vain;
God is his own interpreter,
And he will make it plain.

W. Cowper

Arcanum ad modum Deus
miranda perficit:
imponit aequori gradus
et in procellis it.

Speluncis profundissimis
se meditando dat
et claris e consiliis
quod vult id ordinat.

Sancti, tollatis animos:
terrent-ne pluviae?
eaedem molli super vos
cadent aspergine.

Homo Deum-ne iudicet?
Sit gratiae fides:
sub fronte contracta latet
benigna facies.

Cotidie divina fit
seges maturior,
licetque amara gemma sit,
in flore qui sapor!

Opus scrutantes et parum
fidentes, fallimur:
suum Deus consilium
interpretabitur.

MM   22—6.5.98

God of mercy, God of grace,
Show the brightness of thy face;
Shine upon us, Saviour, shine,
Fill thy Church with light divine;
And thy saving health extend
Unto earth's remotest end.

Let the people praise thee, Lord!
Be by all that live adored;
Let the nations shout and sing
Glory to their Saviour King;
At thy feet their tribute pay,
And thy holy will obey.

Let the people praise thee, Lord;
Earth shall then her fruits afford;
God to man his blessing give,
Man to God devoted live;
All below, and all above,
One in joy and light and love.

H.F. Lyte

Clemens gratiae Deus,
nos adspecta lucidus;
fulge, divina tuam
luce plens ecclesiam,
et salutem dissipes
usque ad terrae margines.

Te collaudet populus,
exalteris omnibus;
vocem gentes elevent,
Regem Vindicem sonent,
quod debetur tribuant,
imperanti pareant.

Te collaudet populus;
laetans terrae frugibus,
prosperanti tunc homo
consecrabitur Deo;
caelo iunget inferum
caritas, lux, gaudium.

MM 10—13.1.99

God of the morning, at whose voice
The cheerful sun makes haste to rise,
And like a giant doth rejoice
To run his journey through the skies;

O, like the sun, may I fulfil
The appointed duties of the day,
With ready hand and active will
March on, and keep my heavenly way.

Give me thy counsel for my guide,
And then receive me to thy bliss:
All my desires and hopes beside
Are faint and cold, compared with this.

I. Watts

O Deus (sol enim tuo
oriri iussu properat
gaudens gigantis et modo
viam per caelum integrat),

ut sol, quodcumque acceperim,
diurno fungar munere,
et promptus impigerque sim
caelestis et memor viae.

Consilio regar tuo,
dum dentur gaudia tua:
nam hoc prae desiderio
omnino marcent alia.

MM 30.8.—l.9.99

God, that madest earth and heaven,
Darkness and light;
Who the day for toil hast given,
For rest the night;
May thine angel-guards defend us,
Slumber sweet thy mercy send us,
Holy dreams and hopes attend us,
This livelong night.

Guard us waking, guard us sleeping,
And, when we die,
May we in thy mighty keeping
All peaceful lie:
When the last dread call shall wake us,
Do not thou our God forsake us,
But to reign in glory take us
With thee on high.

Bishops Heber & Whately

Terram cum polo fecisti,
ad res diem,
noctem, Deus, aptavisti
ad requiem.
Gens caelestis nos defendat,
somnum, dum se nox extendat,
dulcem nobis dans descendat
sanctamque spem.

Simus a te custoditi
nunc placidi
vigilantes aut sopiti;
post mortui
tuba tandem experrecti
a te simus haud reiecti
sed in regni partem vecti.
supra tui.

MM 14—17.1.98

God, whose city's sure foundation
Stands upon his holy hill,
By his mighty inspiration
Chose of old and chooseth still
Men of every race and nation
His good pleasure to fulfil.

Here in England through the ages,
While the Christian years went by,
Saints, confessors, martyrs, sages,
Strong to live and strong to die,
Wrote their names upon the pages
Of God's blessed company.

Some there were like lamps of learning
Shining in a faithless night,
Same on fire with love, and burning
With a flaming zeal for right,
Some by simple goodness turning
Souls from darkness unto light.

As we now with high thanksgiving
Their triumphant names record,
Grant that we, like them, believing
In the promise of thy word,
May, like them, in all good living
Praise and magnify the Lord.

C.A. Alington

Deus, urbem qui fundavit
colle stabilem sacro,
vehementer inspiravit
e quocumque populo
quos et legat et legavit
ex suo consilio.

Nos in Anglia priores
Christiani praeeunt:
sancti, vates, confessores,
martyres perstiterunt,
atque Dei servitores
manu sua scripti sunt.

Horum barbaras pellebat
lux doctrinae tenebras,
hos et amor incendebat
et cupita veritas,
horum nocte deducebat
mera virtus animas.

Quique eorum praedicamus
nomina cum gratiis,
pariter tuis fidamus,
Domine, pollicitis,
nec minus bene vivamus
cumque laudibus tuis.

MM 24—9.4.01

Good Christian men, rejoice and sing!	*O Christiani, canite!*
Now is the triumph of our King!	*Rex noster vicit hodie.*
To all the world glad news we bring:	*Laetare, mundi popule:*
Alleluia!	*Alleluia!*

The Lord of Life is risen for ay:	*Surrexit Vitae Dominus:*
Bring flowers of song to strew his way;	*est danda canticis salus*
Let all mankind rejoice and say	*dicendum et laetantibus*
Alleluia!	*Alleluia!*

Praise we in songs of victory	*Laudetur Victor proprie*
That Love, that Life, which cannot die,	*vivens amans perpetue,*
And sing with hearts uplifted high	*sonetque elato pectore*
Alleluia!	*Alleluia!*

Thy name we bless, O risen Lord,	*Libenter uno cantico*
And sing to-day with one accord	*cantemus orto Domino,*
The life laid down, the life restored:	*ut caeso, vitae reddito*
Alleluia!	*Alleluia!*

C.A.Alington	*MM 7—10.3.99*

Good King Wenceslas looked out on the Feast of Stephen,
when the snow lay round about, deep and crisp and even.
Brightly shone the moon that night, though the frost was cruel,
when a poor man came in sight, gathering winter fuel.

"Hither, page, and stand by me, if you know it, telling,
yonder peasant, who is he? Where and what his dwelling?"
"Sire, he lives a good league hence, underneath the mountain,
right against the forest fence, by Saint Agnes' fountain."

"Bring me food and bring me wine, bring me pine logs hither,
thou and I will see him dine, when we bear them thither."
Page and monarch, forth they went, forth they went together,
through the cold wind's wild lament and the bitter weather.

"Sire, the night is darker now, and the wind blows stronger,
fails my heart, I know not how; I can go no longer."
"Mark my footsteps, my good page, tread now in them boldly,
thou shalt find the winter's rage freeze thy blood less coldly."

In his master's steps he trod, where the snow lay dinted;
heat was in the very sod which the saint had printed.
Therefore, Christian men, be sure, wealth or rank possessing,
ye who now will bless the poor shall yourselves find blessing.

J.M.Neale

Bonus ut Bohaemius
Rex prospiciebat,
terra sub Brumalibus
nivibus latebat.
Male luna temperat
hiemem nocentem,
pauperemque illuminat
ligna colligentem.

"Huc, puer, et ille quis
rusticus sit homo
dic et, id si forte scis,
qua tegatur domo."
"Distat eius hinc casa
subiacetque monti,
silvae saepi proxima
Virginisque fonti."

"Taedas cumque poculis
carnem conferamus,
quis cenare traditis
illum videamus!"
Prorsus rex et servulus
una sunt profecti,
raucis tempestatibus
hiemique obiecti.

"Fit caligo nigrior;
ventus ecce crescens!
Longius prodire cor
prohibet languescens."
"Quas premo premens nives
pone si sequere,
frigus illud senties
lenius nocere."

Regis in vestigiis
ponit ille pedes:
fit vaporis in notis
aestuosa sedes.
Ergo bene locuples
hoc considerabit:
ADIUVANTEM PAUPERES
DEUS ADIUVABIT.

MM 11—15.12.96

Gracious Spirit, Holy Ghost,
taught by thee we covet most,
of thy gifts at Pentecost,
holy, heavenly love.

Love is kind and suffers long,
love is meek and thinks no wrong,
love than death itself more strong;
therefore, give us love.

Prophecy will fade away,
melting in the light of day;
love will ever with us stay;
therefore, give us love.

Faith will vanish into sight;
hope be emptied in delight;
love in heaven will shine more bight;
therefore give us love.

Faith and hope and love we see,
joining hand in hand agree,
but the greatest of the three,
and the best, is love.

From the overshadowing
of thy gold and silver wing
shed on us, who to thee sing,
holy, heavenly love.

Bp C. Wordsworth

Pentecostes Spiritus,
e tuis muneribus
est quam prime cupimus
sancta caritas.

Hanc benignam nil gravat;
nulli malum imputat;
mortem ipsam superat:
detur caritas.

Num, qui vera praecinit,
post eventum profuit?
Usque caritas erit;
detur caritas.

Spectans fide non eget,
neque spe, qui rem tenet;
detur, quae supra nitet
usque, caritas.

Spes, fides et caritas
iungunt ecce! dexteras;
quarum superat duas
una caritas.

Alis tuis caelitus
aureis umbrantibus,
nobis nunc, qui canimus,
esto caritas.

MM 21—8.5.99

Great Shepherd of thy people, hear,
Thy presence now display;
As thou hast given a place for prayer,
So give us hearts to pray.

Within these walls let holy peace
And love and concord dwell;
Here give the troubled conscience ease,
The wounded spirit heal.

May we in faith receive thy word,
In faith present our prayers,
And in the presence of our Lord
Unbosom all our cares.

The hearing ear, the seeing eye,
The contrite heart, bestow;
And shine upon us from on high,
That we in grace may grow.

J. Newton

O magne Pastor. ovium,
exaudiens ades!
Dedisti precibus locum:
elicias preces.

Hic sancta sit tranquillitas,
amor, cancordia;
absolve mentes noxias,
fac sana vulnera.

Et auditores in fide
et supplices tui
communicemus coram te
cur simus anxii.

Oboedientes facias
et visionem da,
humilibusque luceas
alente gratia.

MM 15—17.3.98

Guide me, O thou great Jehovah,
Pilgrim through this barren land;
I am weak, but thou art mighty;
Hold me with thy powerful hand:
Bread of heaven,
Feed me now and evermore.

Open now the crystal fountain
Whence the healing stream doth flow
Let the fiery cloudy pillar
Lead me all my journey through:
Strong deliverer,
Be thou still my strength and shield.

When I tread the verge of Jordan,
Bid my anxious fears subside;
Death of death, and hell's destruction,
Land me safe on Canaan's side:
Songs and praises
I will ever give to thee.

W. Williams

Hoc in tractu sitienti
me, Jehovah, dirigas
debilemque praevalenti
dextera sustineas;
Vive Panis,
nunc et usque nutrias.

Caesa rupes flumen edat
salutare laticis;
nubes ignis antecedat
per quod est itineris;
magne Vindex,
robur et tutela sis.

Ad Jordanem cum viator
ibo, fac ne timeam;
tutum me, necis necator,
ripam fer ad alteram;
tibi laudis
usque carmina canam.

MM 15—21.1.02

Hail the day that sees him rise
To his throne above the skies;
Christ, awhile to mortals given,
Re-ascends his native heaven.

There the glorious triumph waits;
Lift your heads, eternal gates,
Wide unfold the radiant scene,
Take the King of glory in.

Lo! the heaven its Lord receives;
Yet he loves the earth he leaves;
Though returning to his throne,
Still he calls mankind his own.

See! he lifts his hands above;
See! he shows the prints of love;
Hark! his gracious lips bestow
Blessings on his Church below.

Still for us he intercedes;
His prevailing death he pleads;
Near himself prepares our place,
Firstfruits of the human race.

Lord, though parted from our sight,
High above yon azure height,
Grant our hearts may thither rise,
Following thee beyond the skies.

C. Wesley

*Christus hodie suum
superum petens thronum,
hic parumper cognitus,
redditur caelestibus.*

*Triumphanti vigiles
aperimini, fores!
Loca laeta pandite;
Rex inito gloriae.*

*Quid si caelum sumitur?
Nos dilecti linquimur.
Is recepta sede nos
usque nuncupat suos.*

*Tollit en! manus supra.
Ecce amoris stigmata!
Subter et beat sitam
alma voce Ecclesiam.*

*Rem pro nobis usque agit,
quorum causa periit,
locaturus prope se;
est enim primitiae.*

*Christe, super caerula
oculis impervia
corda nostra transeant
teque ibi reperiant.*

MM 9—16.11.98

Hail to the Lord's Anointed,	Maioribus maiorem,
Great David's greater Son!	genus Davidicum,
Hail, in the time appointed,	laudamus nunc rectorem
His reign on earth begun!	telluri debitum.
He comes to break oppression,	Vim venit elisurus
To set the captive free,	captivos liberans
To take away transgression,	et iuste regnaturus
And rule in equity.	peccata dissipans.
He comes with succour speedy	Iniqua patientes
To those who suffer wrong;	velociter iuvat,
To help the poor and needy,	confirmat impotentes,
And bid the weak be strong;	egenos divitat;
To give them songs for sighing,	e gemitu translatis
Their darkness turn to light,	ad cantum nituit,
Whose souls, condemned and dying,	pro capitis damnatis
Were precious in his sight.	qui pretium dedit.
He shall come down like showers	Ut imber is fundetur;
Upon the fruitful earth,	in eius semita
And love, joy, hope, like flowers,	amor cum spe nascetur,
Spring in his path to birth:	florescent gaudia;
before him on the mountains	praenuntiamque montes
Shall peace, the herald, go;	concordiam gerent,
And righteousness in fountains	iustitiaeque fontes
From hill to valley flaw.	deorsum profluent.
Arabia's desert-ranger	Vagans Arabianus
To him shall bow the knee;	sese proiciens
The Ethiopian stranger	et Aethiops paganus
His glory come to see;	mirabitur videns.
With offerings of devotion	Ab insulis carinae
Ships from the isles shall meet,	eum convenient
To pour the wealth of ocean	et praemia rapinae
In tribute at his feet.	aequoreae vehent.
Kings shall bow down before him,	Reges genu flectentes
And gold and incense bring;	tus, aurum conferent
All nations shall adore him,	ei quem laude gentes
His praise all people sing:	et cantibus colent.
To him shall prayer unceasing	Diurna prex ascendet

And daily vows ascend;
His kingdom still increasing,
A kingdom without end.

O'er every foe victorious,
He on his throne shall rest;
From age to age more glorious,
All-blessing and all-blest:
The tide of time shall never
His covenant remove;
His name shall stand for ever,
His changeless name of Love.

?. Montgomery.

privata termino,
et usque se distendet
divina ditio.

Is in throno sedebit
victoriis ovans;
per saecula florebit
beatus et beans.
Nec aetas variabit
eius sententias,
et nomen semper stabit ★
"Aeterna Caritas".

MN 7—13.4.97

★ *nec titulus cessabit.*

Hark! hark, my soul! angelic songs are swelling
O'er earth's green fields and ocean s wave-beat shore
How sweet the truth those blessed strains are telling
Of that new life when sin shall be no more!

Angels of Jesus, angels of light,
Singing to welcome the pilgrims of the night!

Onward we go, for still we hear them singing,
'Come, weary souls, for Jesus bids you come;'
And through the dark, its echoes sweetly ringing,
The music of the Gospel leads us home.

Far, far away, like bells at evening pealing,
The voice of Jesus sounds o'er land and sea,
And laden souls, by thousands meekly stealing,
Kind Shepherd, turn their weary steps to thee.

Rest comes at length: though life be long and dreary,
The day must dawn, and darksome night be past;
Faith's journey ends in welcome to the weary,
And heaven, the heart's true home, will come at last

Angels, sing on, your faithful watches keeping,
Sing us sweet fragments of the songs above;
Till morning's joy shall end the night of weeping,
And life's long shadows break in cloudless love.

Angels of Jesus, angels of light,
Singing to welcome the pilgrims of the night!

F.W. Faber

Heus! Angelorum carmen audiatur
per terrac prata perque litora.
Quam suaviter, quam vere nuncupatur
aetas fugato crimine nova.
Canendo Iesu nos lucidi
salutant nocte euntes angeli.

Prodimus illum ad chorum sonantem,
qui fessos Christum versus attrahat,
et, per tenebras dulce reboantem,
qui Bonus Nuntius domum vocat.

En! Procul hinc, ut tubae vespertinae,
terra marique Iesu vox canit,
cohors onusta dum sine ullo fine
se fessam ad Pastorem dirigit.

Quies erit, cum diu nos gravemur,
noctisque lux tenebras abiget;
perseveremus, mox accipiemur,
sponsumque nobis caelum veniet.

Pervigilantes, angeli, canatis,
noscamus ut qui superus canor,
dum, sole noctis fletibus fugatis,
serenus iste luceat amor.
Canendo Iesu nos lucidi
salutant nocte euntes angeli.

MM   25.11—8.12.00

Hark, my soul, it is the Lord!
'Tis thy Saviour, hear his Word;
Jesus speaks, and speaks to thee,
"Say, poor sinner, lovest thou me?"

"I delivered thee when bound,
and, when bleeding, healed thy wound;
sought thee wandering, set thee right,
turned thy darkness into light.

"Can a woman's tender care
cease toward the child she bare?
Yes, she may forgetful be,
yet will I remember thee.

"Mine is an unchanging love,
higher than the heights above,
deeper than the depths beneath,
free and faithful, strong as death.

"Thou shalt see my glory soon,
when the work of grace is done;
partner of my throne shalt be:
say, poor sinner, lovest thou me?"

Lord, it is my chief complaint
that my love is weak and faint;
yet I love thee, and adore:
O for grace to love thee more!

W. Cowper

Salvatoris, o mea,
sis auditrix, anima.
Jesus en! appellat te:
"Dic, miselle, amas-ne me?

"Tibi solvi vinculum,
te sanavi saucium,
reddidi vagum viae,
nocti lucem dans tuae.

"Femina num neglegit
filium quem peperit?
Nempe negleget prius
quam Redemptor te tuus.

"Meus altitudinis
vastae, non mutabilis,
fidus, liber est amor,
morte non infirmior.

"Gratiae post munera
cum nitebit gloria,
sedis o consors meae,
dic, miselle, amas-ne me?"

Id praecipue pudet
meus amor quod tepet:
obsecro te, Domine,
illum fac ardescere.

MM 24—26.5.97

Hark! the herald-angels sing	*Laudes cantant angeli*
Glory to the new-born King.	*Regis nuper geniti.*
Peace on earth, and mercy mild,	*Pacem terrae dat Deus*
God and sinners reconciled.	*veniamque sontibus.*
Joyful, all ye nations, rise,	*Gentes quot sunt inferae,*
Join the triumph of the skies;	*cum supernis psallite*
With the angelic host proclaim,	*nati nunc Davidica*
"Christ is born in Bethlehem."	*urbe iuncta encomia!*
Hark! the herald-angels sing	*Laudes cantant angeli*
Glory to the new-born King.	*Regis nuper geniti.*
Christ, by highest heaven adored,	*Christus, caelum quem colit,*
Christ, the everlasting Lord,	*semper dominus, venit*
Late in time behold him come,	*serus tempore suo*
Offspring of a Virgin's womb.	*virginis ex utero.*
Veiled in flesh the Godhead see!	*Ecce! tegmine Deus*
Hail, the incarnate Deity!	*corporali praeditus,*
Pleased as Man with man to dwell,	*quem Esaias nominat,*
Jesus, our Emmanuel.	*nostrum unus habitat.*
Hark! the etc.	*Laudes cantant etc.*
Hail, the heaven-born Prince of Peace!	*Sancte Pacis Rex, ave!*
Hail, the Sun of Righteousness!	*Ave, Sol Justitiae!*
Light and life to all he brings	*Lucem omnibus ferens,*
Risen with healing in his wings.	*ortus ales et medens,*
Mild he lays his glory by,	*ponis placide decus,*
Born that man no more may die,	*ne perdamur genitus,*
Born to raise the sons of earth,	*nate elator hominum,*
Born to give them second birth.	*ut nascamur iterum.*
Hark! the etc.	*Laudes cantant etc.*

C. Wesley

MM 17—21.12.98

He is risen, he is risen!
Tell it with a joyful voice;
He has burst his three days' prison;
Let the whole wide earth rejoice.
Death is conquered, man is free,
Christ has won the victory.

Come, ye sad and fearful-hearted,
With glad smile and radiant brow;
Lent's long shadows have departed,
All his woes are over now,
And the Passion that he bore:
Sin and pain can vex no more.

Come, with high and holy hymning
Chant our Lord's triumphant lay;
Not one darksome cloud is dimming
Yonder glorious morning ray,'
Breaking o'er the purple east:
Brighter far our Easter-feast.

C.F. Alexander

Eia! mortuis elatum
laeta vox enuntiet.
Tertia die levatum
tota terra celebret.
Liber homo. mors abest
victa, victor Christus est.

Tristes vos et tremefacti,
nunc estote hilares:
angor eius et peracti
quadraginta sunt dies;
liber est doloribus
nec malis obnoxius.

Vos augete nunc canorem
quem triumphans exigit;
matutinum hunc nitorem
nulla nubes occulit,
cuï, quamvis rutilet,
Pascha nostrum praenitet.

MM   21—23.4.01

He that is down needs fear no fall,
He that is low no pride;
He that is humble ever shall
Have God to be his guide.

I am content with what I have,
Little be it or much;
And, Lord, contentment still I crave,
Because thou savest such.

Fullness to such a burden is
That go on pilgrimage;
Here little, and hereafter bliss,
Is best from age to age.

Bunyan

Deiectus casum non timet
neque superbiam,
Deusque semper diriget
  summissam animam.

Seu pauper sive locuples,
contentus ego sum
eroque; nempe, Deus, es
salvator talium.

Imponit rerum copia
viantibus moras:
viventi sit inopia
et post felicitas.

MM 30—31 Jan 97

He wants not friends that hath thy love,	*Egent-ne amico quos amas*
And may converse and walk with thee,	*dignaris et colloquio*
And with thy saints here and above,	*sanctisque et hic coire das*
With whom for ever I must be.	*et superis perpetuo?*
In the blest fellowship of saints	*Sanctorum nam concilia*
Is wisdom, safety, and delight;	*salvant, erudiunt, placent;*
And when my heart declines and faints,	*depressa corda et languida*
It's raised by their heat and light.	*eorum radiis calent.*
As for my friends, they are not lost;	*Amici nec desunt mei:*
The several vessels of thy fleet,	*classis tuae navigia,*
Though parted now, by tempests tost,	*ventorum nunc dispersa vi,*
Shall safely in the haven meet.	*in portu fient integra.*
Still are we centred all in thee,	*Te circumvolvimur; caput*
Members, though distant, of one Head;	*tu, membra nos (sed dissita)*
In the same family we be,	*familiaeque unius, ut*
By the same faith and spirit led.	*fides inspirat unica.*
Before thy throne we daily meet	*Eidem genu flectimus,*
As joint-petitioners to thee;	*clientes pariter tui,*
In spirit we each other greet,	*amplectimurque mentibus*
And shall again each other see.	*congressioni debiti.*
The heavenly hosts, world without end,	*Caelestibus perpetue*
Shall be my company above;	*supra coniunctus fuero;*
And thou, my best and surest friend,	*et quis, sodalis optime,*
Who shall divide me from thy love?	*amore dividet tuo?*

R.Baxter   *MM   24—31.1.99*

Here, O my Lord, I see thee face to face;
　　Here faith would touch and handle things unseen;
Here grasp with firmer hand the eternal grace,
　　And all my weariness upon thee lean.

Here would I feed upon the Bread of God;
　　Here drink with thee the royal Wine of heaven;
Here would I lay aside each earthly load;
　　Here taste afresh the calm of sin forgiven.

I have no help but thine; nor do I need
　　Another arm save thine to lean upon:
It is enough, my Lord, enough indeed,
　　My strength is in thy might, thy might alone.

H.Bonar

Te, Deus, hic adversum video,
　　fidensque tracto siqua caeca das;
hic gratiam tenturus occupo,
　　precans ut tu me fessum fulcias.

Hic et divino nutriar Cibo
　　et hauriam caeleste Poculum;
hic onere terrestri posito
　　absolvar, et novetur otium.

Tua solius adiuvor ope,
　　nec alieno brachiost opus;
est hoc satis, sat est, O Domine,
　　tuisque solis firmor viribus.

MM 3—5.5.01

Hills of the north, rejoice;
River and mountain-spring,
Hark to the advent voice;
Valley and lowland, sing:
'hough absent long, your Lord is nigh;
He judgement brings and victory.

Isles of the southern seas,
Deep in your coral caves
Pent be each warring breeze,
Lulled be your restless waves:
He comes to reign with boundless sway,
And makes your wastes his great highway.

Lands of the east, awake,
Soon shall your sons be free;
The sleep of ages break,
And rise to liberty.
On your far hills, long cold and grey,
Has dawned the everlasting day.

Shores of the utmost west,
Ye that have waited long,
Unvisited, unblest,
Break forth in swelling song;
High raise the note, that Jesus died,
Yet lives and reigns, the Crucified.

Sing, while you journey home;
Songs be in every mouth;
Lo, from the north we come,
From east and west and south.
City of God, the bond are free,
We come to live and reign in thee!

C.E.Oakley

Gaudete, Boreae
montes et flumina;
Advenam noscite,
valles et pascua.
Qui sero Dominus subit,
iudex et victor advenit.

Esto quies aquis
mobilibus, Note:
in specubus rubris
proelia comprime.
Ubique ut regnet, is venit,
tuumque inane via fit.

Orire, Eoa gens:
libera mox eris;
somnum abiciens
solvere vinculis!
Iam lividis in collibus
sol oritur perpetuus.

Litora occidua,
grande per saeculum
sola et incognita,
crescito canticum:
cantate "Nunc, qui periit
in Cruce, vivit et regit."

Domum euntibus
carmen in ore sit,
quos locus huc suus
quemque pepulerit:
in te vivamus liberi
et dominemur, Urbs Dei.

MM 23.10—2.11.99

Latinised Hymns

His are the thousand sparkling rills
that from a thousand fountains burst,
and fill with music all the hills;
and yet he saith, "I thirst."

All fiery pangs on battlefields;
on fever beds where sick men toss,
are in that human cry he yields
to anguish on the cross.

But more than pains that racked him then,
was the deep longing thirst divine
that thirsted for the souls of men:
dear Lord! and one was mine.

O Love most patient, give me grace;
make all my soul athirst for thee;
that parched dry lip, that anguished face,
that thirst, were all for me.

Mrs C.F.Alexander

Cui tot fluenta pertinent
collesque cantibus suis
tot orta finibus replent,
torret-ne eum sitis?

Febres homo cum homine
quid sint et vulnera sciens,
se scire monstrat in Cruce
sitire se fatens.

At eum torruit sitis
 tunc altera et divinior,
id est hurnani generis
eheu! meique amor.

Sic passe Amor, feras opem:
consumar invicem siti.
Habes-ne arentis faciem?
Per me stat id tibi.

MM 31.3 3 .4.99

Holy, Holy, Holy! Lord God Almighty!
Early in the morning our song shall rise to thee;
Holy, Holy, Holy! merciful and mighty!
God in three Persons, blessed Trinity!

Holy, Holy, Holy! all the saints adore thee,
Casting down their golden crowns around the glassy sea;
Cherubim and Seraphim falling down before thee,
Which wert and art and evermore shall be.

Holy, Holy, Holy! though the darkness hide thee,
Though the eye of sinful man thy glory may not see,
Only thou art holy, there is none beside thee
Perfect in power, in love and purity.

Holy, Holy, Holy! Lord God Almighty!
All thy works shall praise thy name in earth and sky and sea;
Holy, Holy, Holy! merciful and mighty!
· God in three Persons, blessed Trinity!

R.Heber

Sancte, Sancte, Sancte! Deus Omnipollens!
Mane nostra surgat ad aures vox tuas;
Sancte, Sancte, Sancte! clemens atque pollens!
Triplex Deus, beata Trinitas!

Sancte, Sancte, Sancte! sancti te precantur
iactis mare ad vitreum coronis aureis;
Cherubim et Seraphim ecce! venerantur:
eras et es et sine fine eris.

Sancte, Sancte, Sancte! tenebris celatus
pravis cum mortalibus tu non appareas,
solus es tu sanctus (num quis aemulatus?)
integra vis amor et puritas.

Sancte, Sancte, Sancte! Deus Omnipollens!
Omnibus, quot feceris, laudatus audias;
Sancte, Sancte, Sancte! clemens atque pollens!
Triplex Deus, beata Trinitas!

MM 14—19.6.99

Hosanna in the highest
To our exalted Saviour,
Who left behind
For all mankind
These tokens of his favour:
His bleeding love and mercy,
His all-redeeming Passion;
Who here displays,
And gives the grace
Which brings us our salvation.

Louder than gathered waters,
Or bursting peals of thunder,
We lift our voice
And speak our joys
And shout our loving wonder.
Shout, all our elder brethren,
While we record the story
Of him that came
And suffered shame,
To carry us to glory.

Angels in fixed amazement
Around our altars hover
With eager gaze
Adore the grace
Of our eternal Lover:
Himself and all his fulness
Who gives to the believer;
And by this Bread
Whoe'er are fed
Shall live with God for ever.

C. Wesley

Hosanna in excelsis
sit Vindici potenti;
haec dat suae
clementiae
humanae signa genti:
cruorem, passionem,
qua nos redempti simus,
monstratque qua
cum gratia
salvati fuerimus.

Undarum superantes
et tonitrus fragorem
clamoribus
exprimimus
amantium stuporem.
Clamate, seniores,
eumque recordemur,
quo tradito
opprobrio
nos ad decus feremur.

Immobiles ad aras
stant angeli stupentes,
et gratiam
perpetuam
Amantis intuentes:
is se dabit credenti,
cui nihil inde de(e)rit;
quicumque eum
capit cibum
cum Deo semper erit.

MM 19—31.7.01

How firm a foundation, ye saints of the Lord,
Is laid for your faith in his excellent word:
What more can he say than to you he hath said
You who unto Jesus for refuge have fled?

Fear not, he is with thee, O be not dismayed;
For he is thy God, and will still give thee aid;
He'll strengthen thee, help thee and cause thee to stand
Upheld by his righteous, omnipotent hand:

In every condition, in sickness, in health,
In poverty's vale, or abounding in wealth;
At home and abroad, on the land, on the sea,
As thy days may demand shall thy strength ever be.

When through the deep waters he calls thee to go,
The rivers of grief shall not thee overflow;
For he will be with thee in trouble to bless,
And sanctify to thee thy deepest distress.

When through fiery trials thy pathway shall lie,
His grace all-sufficient shall be thy supply;
The flame shall not hurt thee, his only design
Thy dross to consume and thy gold to refine.

The soul that on Jesus has learned to repose
He will not, he will not, desert to its foes;
That soul, though all hell should endeavour to shake,
He'll never, no never, no never forsake.

"K" (?)

Fundamen habet stabile ista fides.
cui fiditis, O Domini comites,
quos ad Dominum fuga vestra trahit;
num dicere plura Deus potuit?

Noli (comes est) fieri pavidus;
nam praestat opem Deus ille tuus;
te sistere firmiter is faciet:
quae sustineat manus omne valet.

Refert neque sanus an aeger eris
nec prosperus an sine divitiis;
hic sive foris, mare terrave sit,
par temporibus tibi robur erit.

Immiserit ille doloris aquas,
non est ibi mersus ut intereas;
nam te comitabitur ipse beans,
prementia pessima sanctificans.

Cum te media vehit igne via,
praeit tibi gratia munifica.
Non flamma nocet: fugat illa lutum
aurumque ea separat inde tuum.

Si quem recubare Deus docuit,
non hostibus obiciendus erit;
et usque tenebitur is, liceat
eum domus infera quassuriat.

MM 28.2—6.3.02

How glorious is the life above
which in this ordinance we taste,
That fulness of celestial love,
That joy which shall for ever last!

That heavenly life in Christ concealed
These earthen vessels could not bear;
The part which now we find revealed
No tongue of angels can declare.

The light of life eternal darts
Into our souls a dazzling ray;
A drop of heaven o'erflows our hearts,
And floods with joy the house of clay.

Sure pledge of ecstasies unknown
Shall this divine Communion be:
The ray shall rise into a sun,
The drop shall swell into a sea.

C. Wesley

Supernae vitae qui sapor
in ore praegustantium,
Dei qua plenitate amor,
quod gaudium perpetuum!

In Christo vitam quae latet,
hanc vas terrestre non tulit,
nec angelorum praedicet
vox id quod hic apparuit.

Aeterna vitae nitidum
fert lux iubar in animas;
caelestis gutta cordium
domos inundat luteas.

Voluptas nobis quanta erit,
qui nunc Deo sic iungimur
Ut iubar solem praevenit
sic guttam mare sequitur.

MM 8—17.7.01

How lovely are thy dwellings fair,
O Lord of Hosts, how dear
Thy pleasant tabernacles are,
Where thou dost dwell so near.

My soul doth long and almost die
Thy courts, O Lord, to see;.
My heart and flesh aloud do cry,
O living God, to thee.

Happy, who in thy house reside,
Where thee they ever praise;
Happy, whose strength in thee doth bide,
And in their hearts thy ways.

They journey on from strength to strength
With joy and gladsome cheer,
Till all before our God at length
In Zion do appear.

For God, the Lord, both sun and shield,
Gives grace and glory bright;
No good from them shall be withheld
Whose ways are just and right.

J.Milton

Dilecta templa sunt tua,
O Sabaoth Deus,
et cara tabernacula,
quis es tu proximus.

Tuorum paene tegminum
amore pereo,
quantumque cor valet meum
caroque, te voco.

Caeli beatos incolas,
qui laudant usque te
viresque habent in te suas,
te suo pectore!

In dies aucto robore
laetantes prodeunt,
Deumque ad nostrum denique
in Zion veniunt.

Est sol et scutum Deus, et
decora dona dat,
nec est quod is ei neget
qui iusta faciat.

MM   22—7.8.00

How shall I sing that majesty
Which angels do admire?
Let dust in dust and silence lie;
Sing, sing, ye heavenly choir.
Thousands of thousands stand around
Thy throne, O God most high;
Ten thousand times ten thousand sound
Thy praise; but who am I?

Thy brightness unto them appears,
Whilst I thy footsteps trace;
A sound of God comes to my ears,
But they behold thy face.
They sing because thou art their Sun;
Lord, send a beam on me;
For where heav'n is but once begun
There alleluias be.

How great a being, Lord, is thine,
Which doth all beings keep!
Thy knowledge is the only line
To sound so vast a deep.
Thou art a sea without a shore,
A sun without a sphere;
Thy time is now and evermore,
Thy place is everywhere.

J. Mason

Ego-ne cantem angelis
laudatum id decus?
Cantet (tace intra te, cinis)
supernus id chorus.
Cum adstent mille milia
tuo, Deus, throno
et turba centiens ea ★
te laudet, quis ego?

Notante me vestigium,
splendorem i vident;
distantem audio Deum,
praesentem i habent.
Fac me iubar illuminet,
qui Sol es quem canunt;
qua caelum esse incipiet,
ibi Alleluia sunt.

Quot sunt, et horum maxime
et tegmen unicum,
tuae modo scientiae
profundum pervium;
tu mare cassum litore,
sol ambitu carens;
idem locaris ubique
per saecula manens.

MM   24—28.2.99

★ *et turba myriadica*

How sweet the name of Jesus sounds	*Quam dulce nomen Domini*
In a believer's ear!	*piis in auribus!*
It soothes his sorrows, heals his wounds,	*Levantur tristes, saucii,*
And drives away his fear.	*et pellitur metus.*

It makes the wounded spirit whole,	*Hoc laesum pectus integrat*
And calms the troubled breast;	*et cor lacessitum,*
'Tis manna to the hungry soul,	*esurienti manna dat*
And to the weary rest.	*et fessis otium.*

Dear name! the rock on which I build,	*Hoc construo fundamine;*
My shield and hiding-place,	*hoc praebet latebram,*
My never-failing treasury filled	*et sempiternam gratiae*
With boundless stores of grace.	*custodit copiam.*

Jesus! my Shepherd, Brother, Friend,	*Tu, Iesu, Pastor diceris,*
My Prophet, Priest, and King,	*Sacerdos, Dominus,*
My Lord, my Life, my Way, my End,	*tu Via, te peto: meis*
Accept the praise I bring.	*iuvere laudibus.*

Weak is the effort of my heart,	*Enervet cum segnities*
And cold my warmest thought;	*parumque caleam,*
But when I see thee as thou art,	*te viso tandem qualis es*
I'll praise thee as I ought.	*te digne diligam.*

Till then I would thy love proclaim	*Nunc quotiens spiravero*
With every fleeting breath;	*grates agam tibi,*
And may the music of thy name	*et mortis in articulo*
Refresh my soul in death.	*vocaberis mihi.*

J. Newton

MM 8—12.2.97

I hunger and I thirst:
Jesu, my manna be;
Ye living waters burst
Out of the rock for me.

Thou bruised and broken Bread,
My life-long wants supply;
As living souls are fed,
O feed me, or I die.

Thou true life-giving Vine,
Let me thy sweetness prove;
Renew my life with thine,
Refresh my soul with love.

Rough paths my feet have trod
Since first their course began:
Feed me, thou Bread of God;
Help me, thou Son of Man.

For still the desert lies
My thirsting soul before:
O living waters, rise
Within me evermore.

J.S.B. Monsell

Sitis mihi et fames
te, Iesu, flagitant
ut Manna; latices
e rupe profluant!

Tu, Panis fracte, me
dum vivam nutrias;
ne moriar, ale,
qui pascis animas.

Vitis vivificans,
da dulcitudines,
amore recreans,
ut vitam renoves.

Laedunt viae truces
ab initu pedem:
Panis Divine, des,
des, Homo Facte, opem.

Per locum avium
iturus sitio;
fons intus laticum
vivat perpetuo.

MM   30.7—2.8.00

I know that my Redeemer lives!
What joy the blest assurance gives!
He lives, he lives, who once was dead;
He lives, my everlasting Head!

He lives, to bless me with his love;
He lives, to plead for me above;
He lives, my hungry soul to feed;
He lives, to help in time of need.

He lives, and grants me daily breath;
He lives, and I shall conquer death;
He lives, my mansion to prepare;
He lives, to lead me safely there.

He lives, all glory to his name;
He lives, my Saviour, still the same;
What joy the blest assurance gives!
I know that my Redeemer lives!

S.Medley

Vivit Redemptor, hoc scio,
quo gaudeam pollicito!
Is vivit olim mortuus,
aeternus ille Apex meus.

Vivit, qui me beans amet
et coram Patre vindicet,
qui me ieiunum nutriat
et indigo subsideat.

Is vivit: aera traho;
quod vivit, mortem vicero;
vivus domum parat meam,
quo vivus indicat viam.

Vivit: glorificetur is,
Salvator haud mutabilis!
Quo gaudeam pollicito,
vivit Redemptor, hoc scio!

MM   12—22.11.01

I praised the earth, in beauty seen,
With garlands gay of various green;
I praised the sea, whose ample field
Shone glorious as a silver shield
And earth and ocean seemed to say,
"Our beauties are but for a day."

I praised the sun, whose chariot rolled
On wheels of amber and of gold;
I praised the moon, whose softer eye
Gleamed sweetly through the summer sky
And moon and sun in answer said,
"Our days of light are numbered."

O God, O good beyond compare,
If thus thy meaner works are fair,
If thus thy beauties gild the span
Of ruined earth and sinful man,
How glorious must the mansion be
Where thy redeemed shall dwell with thee!

R.Heber

Probavi terrae viridem
laetamque pulchritudinem,
nec aequoris ea minus
patens argenteum decus;
sunt ambo visa dicere,
"uno nitemus hoc die."

Probavi solis aureis
currum volventibus rotis,
aestivum laudans haud secus
lunare lumen mollius;
sed lux fatetur utraque
dierum terminum fore.

Minora, Deus, haec tua
sunt pulchra tamen opera,
nec inquinat corruptio
quam attulit eis homo;
sed illa praestat omnibus
promissa salvatis domus.

MM 5.12.03

I vow to thee, my country, all earthly things above,
Entire and whole and perfect, the service of my love:
The love that asks no question, the love that stands the test,
That lays upon the altar the dearest and the best;
The love that never falters, the love that pays the price,
The love that makes undaunted the final sacrifice.

And there's another country, I've heard of long ago,
Most dear to them that love her, most great to them that know.
We may not count her armies, we may not see her King;
Her fortress is a faithful heart, her pride is suffering;
And soul by soul and silently her shining bounds increase,
And her ways are ways of gentleness and all her paths are peace.

C.Spring-Rice

O Patria, habebis amorem tu meum,
prae cunctis servientem, totum et integrum,
is parens nil requirit, temptatis haud cadit,
quod optimum ad aram carumque proicit;
nec haesitat nec umquam is pretium negat,
intrepidus mactandum se ipsum dedicat.

Est altera (sic olim audivi) patria
amantibusque cara gnarisque maxima.
Nec Regem scire quimus, nec quot sint milites,
dolere ei triumphus est, est moenia fides;
silenter accedentibus augetur animis;
et in viis est comitas et pax in semitis.

MM   10—20.9.01

If God build not the house, and lay
the groundwork sure, whoever build,
It cannot stand one stormy day;
If God be not the city's shield,
If he be not their bars and wall,
In vain the watch-tower, men and all.

Sit ventus, occidet domus,
quicumque hominum struet,
fundabit nisi Dominus;
Deus nisi oppidum teget
fietque propugnaculum,
inutile est praesidium.

Though then thou wak'st when others rest,
Though rising thou prevent'st the sun,
Though with lean care thou daily feast,
Thy labour's lost and thou undone;
But God his child will feed and keep,
And draw the curtain to his sleep.

Sopitos inter vigiles
te sole sublevans prior,
curae cotidie comes,
quo tu, quo tuus is labor?
Suum sed Deus ipse alet
et dormientem conteget.
(nec)   (deseret)

P. Fletcher

MM   5—9.11.98

I'm not ashamed to own my Lord,
Or to defend his cause,
Maintain the honour of his Word,
The glory of his Cross.

Non me pudebit Domini,
eique consulam;
fidem testabor Nuntii
Crucisque gloriam.

Jesus, my God! I know his name,
His name is all my trust;
Nor will he put my soul to shame,
Nor let my hope be lost.

Deus mi scitur Jesus, et
huic credo Nomini;
nec animam deiciet,
spem sustinens mihi.

Firm as his throne his promise stands,
And he can well secure
What I've committed to his hands,
Till the decisive hour.

Ut sedes, firma pignora;
potestque efficere
quaequae sunt ei credita
prius discrimine.

Then will he own my worthless name
Before his Father's face;
And, in the New Jerusalem,
Appoint my soul a place.

Indignum, sed apud Patrem
agnoscet me suum,
assignans in Jerusalem
Nova mihi locum.

I. Watts

MM   1—12.1.02

Immortal, invisible, God only wise,
In light inaccessible hid from our eyes,
Most blessed, most glorious, the Ancient of Days,
Almighty, victorious, thy great name we praise.

Unresting, unhasting, and silent as light,
Nor wanting, nor wasting, thou rulest in might;
Thy justice like mountains high soaring above
Thy clouds which are fountains of goodness and love.

To all life thou givest, to both great and small;
In all life thou livest, the true life of all;
We blossom and flourish as leaves on the tree,
And wither and perish; but nought changeth thee.

Great Father of glory, pure Father of light,
Thine angels adore thee, all veiling their sight;
All laud we would render: O help us to see
'Tis only the splendour of light hideth thee.

W.Chalmers Smith

Omniscium Numen, aeterne Deus,
quem abdidit lumen a luminibus,
laudamus habentem perenne decus
hostesque prementem et efferimus.

Numquam properando silens graderis,
nec plus tibi dando parumve regis.
Ius montium more tuum nebulas
transfigit, amore pluente, tuas.

Magnis tu donator et exiguis,
es vivificator inesque animis,
qui, cum vigeamus, itura seges,
et deficiamus, immobilis es.

Colit te, decore nitensque Deus,
angelicus ore velato chorus.
Hic quoque colare, modoque doce
ne conspiciare iubar facere.

MM 6—15.6.99

Lmmortal love, for ever full,
For ever flowing free,
For ever shared, for ever whole,
A never-ebbing sea!

Our outward lips confess the name
All other names above;
Love only knoweth whence it came,
And comprehendeth love.

We may not climb the heavenly steeps
To bring the Lord Christ down;
In vain we search the lowest deeps,
For him no depths can drown.

In joy of inward peace, or sense
Of sorrow over sin,
He is his own best evidence;
His witness is within.

But warm, sweet, tender, even yet
A present help is he;
And faith hath still its Olivet,
And love its Galilee..

The healing of his seamless dress
Is by our beds of pain;
We touch him in life's throng and press,
And we are whole again.

Through him the first fond prayers are said
Our lips of childhood frame;
The last low whispers of our dead
Are burdened with his name.

Alone, O Love ineffable
Thy saving name is given;
To turn aside from thee is hell,
To walk with thee is heaven.

J.G.Whittier

Amoris usque profluus
O fons perpetue!
O mare tot bibentibus
inexhauribile!

Humana lingua nomen id
fatetur optimum;
sed tibi, amor, sis ipse quid
et unde, est cognitum.

Nequiquarn usque celsius
Christum persequimur,
nec ille sub gurgitibus
profundi mergitur.

In pace mentis intimae
et paenitentia
se rnonstrat ille signaque
dat intus abdita.

Manent adhuc auxilia
et suavis is calor
fides et Olivetica
Galilausque amor.

Nec eius ista demitur
stola aegrotantibus;
in vulgo tantum tangimur
et convalescimus.

Hunc parvulorum labia
precantum invocant
et morientum murmura
eundem nuncupant.

O amor ineffabilis,
arx una qui clues,
fit orcus abs te deviis,
beantur comites.

MM 15.10—2.11.98

Latinised Hymns

In heavenly love abiding
No change my heart shall fear;
And safe is such confiding,
For nothing changes here.
The storm may roar without me,
My heart may low be laid;
But God is round about me,
And can I be dismayed?

Wherever he may guide me,
No want shall turn me back;
My Shepherd is beside me,
And nothing can I lack.
His wisdom ever waketh,
His sight is never dim;
He knows the way he taketh,
And I will walk with him.

Green pastures are before me,
Which yet I have not seen;
Bright skies will soon be o'er me,
Where the dark clouds have been.
My hope I cannot measure,
My path to life is free;
My Saviour has my treasure,
And he will walk with me.

A.L.Waring

In caritate sedens
qua terrear vice?
Num fallor esse credens
nil hic mutabile?
Extra fremat procella,
deficiatque cor;
est circum me tutela
Dei, nec opprimor.

Eo ducente quibit
nil ferre perperam;
dum Pastor comes ibit,
non est quo caream.
Is sapit nec sopitur,
nec lippus inspicit;
cui via bene scitur,
is mihi dux erit.

Quae prata mi virebunt.
nondum patuerunt,
serena mox nitebunt,
quae nube tecta sunt.
Haud apta computanti
spes vitam retegit;
thesaurus est Salvanti,
et is comes erit.

MM   27.10—1.11.01

In the Cross of Christ I glory,
Towering o'er the wrecks of time;
All the light of sacred story
Gathers round its head sublime.

Christi gloriabor Cruce
tempori superstite,
circa caput altum luce
 sacrae cincta fabulae.

When the woes of life o'ertake me,
Hopes deceive and fears annoy,
Never shall the Cross forsake me
Lo! it glows with peace and joy.

Quando dolor opprimet me,
fallet spes, querar metum,
numquam Crux decipiet me:
ibi pax et gaudiurn.

When the sun of bliss is beaming
Light and love upon my way,
From the Cross the radiance streaming,
Adds more lustre to the day.

Almi solis cum levetur
via nostra radiis,
lux diurna tunc augetur
ipsa lumine Crucis.

Bane and blessing, pain and pleasure,
By the Cross are sanctified;
Peace is there that knows no measure,
Joys that through all time abide.

Almum, acre, fausta, infausta
cuncta Crux sanctificat;
gaudia illic haud exhausta,
pax quae fine careat.

J.Bowring

MM 7—11.4.00

Latinised Hymns

Jerusalem on high
My song amd city is,
My home whene'er I die,
The centre of my bliss:
  O happy place!
  When shall I be,
  My God, with thee,
  To see thy face?

There dwells my Lord, my King,
Judged here unfit to live;
There angels to him sing,
And lowly homage give:

The patriarchs of old
There from their travels cease;
The prophets there behold
Their longed-for Prince of Peace:

The Lamb's apostles there
I might with joy behold,
The harpers I might hear
Harping on harps of gold:

The bleeding martyrs, they
Within those courts are found,
Clothed in pure array,
Their scars with glory crowned:

Ah me! ah me! that I
in Kedar's tents here stay:
No place like that on high;
Lord, thither guide my way;
  O happy, etc.

S.Crossman

Quae Sion est supra
canatur urbs mihi,
futura post mea
focusque gaudii:
  felix locus,
  si videam
  ibi tuam
  frontem, Deus!

Rex est ibi meus,
addictus hic neci,
strati quem cantibus
salutant angeli:

Non inde se movent
Moyses et Abraham;
vates ratam vident
spem messianicam.

Agni satellites
quam laetus videam!
Et aureas fides
libens ibi audiam.

Pro Deo saucii
in aulis ibi sunt
notasque splendidi
cum gloria ferunt.

Heu! me tentoria
in Kedar tendere!
 maluerim supra:
duc eo, Domine:
  felix locus, etc.

MM 20—29.11.99

Jesus, lover of my soul,
let me to thy bosom fly,
while the nearer waters roll,
while the tempest still is high.
Hide me, O my Saviour, hide,
till the storm of life is past;
safe into the haven guide;
O receive my soul at last.

Other refuge have I none,
hangs my helpless soul on thee;
leave, ah! leave me not alone,
still support and comfort me.
All my trust on thee is stayed,
all my help from thee I bring;
cover my defenseless head
with the shadow of thy wing.

Thou, O Christ, art all I want,
more than all in thee I find;
raise the fallen, cheer the faint,
heal the sick, and lead the blind.
Just and holy is thy name,
I am all unrighteousness;
false and full of sin I am;
thou art full of truth and grace.

Plenteous grace with thee is found,
grace to cover all my sin;
let the healing streams abound,
make and keep me pure within.
Thou of life the fountain art,
freely let me take of thee;
spring thou up within my heart;
rise to all eternity.

Charles Wesley

Iesu, qui me diligis,
gremio me foveas,
donec tempestatum vis
volvit circum nos aquas.
Abde, mi salvator, me,
dum procella transeat;
te ducente denique
portus me recipiat.

Dest refugium mihi,
spes est nulla sine te;
ne permitte deseri,
consolare, sustine.
Solus tu salutem das,
solus es praesidium;
me nudatum contegas
ut gallina pullulum.

Praeter te desiderem
nil: tu plus quam omnia.
Me caducum, debilem,
aegrum, caecum subleva.
Sanctus, iustus tu clues;
ego scelestissimus;
tu virtute plenus es,
plenus ego fraudibus.

Ista magna gratia
quicquid pecco dissipet;
unda salutifera
intus me purificet.
Christe, fons vitalis es:
inde potem libere.
Cor intrinsecus riges
profluens perpetue.

MM 18—20.12.96

Jesus Christ is risen today,
our triumphant holy day,
who did once upon the cross,
suffer to redeem our loss.

Hymns of praise then let us sing,
unto Christ, our heavenly King,
who endured the cross and grave,
sinners to redeem and save.

But the pains which he endured,
our salvation have procured,
now above the sky he's King,
where the angels ever sing.

Lyra Davidica

Festo Christus hoc die
resurrexit splendide,
olim qui in Cruce nos
emit ante perditos.

Rex caelestis canticis
noster est laudabilis,
mortem passus in Cruce
peccatorum nomine.

At tormentum quod tulit
nobis salutare fit;
Rex et audit is supra
angelorum carmina.

MM Easter 1999 (4-5 4.99)

Jesus lives! thy terrors now
can no longer, death, appall us;
Jesus lives! by this we know
thou, O grave, canst not enthrall us.

Jesus lives! henceforth is death
but the gate of life immortal;
this shall calm our trembling breath
when we pass its gloomy portal.

Jesus lives! for us he died;
then, alone to Jesus living,
pure in heart may we abide,
glory to our Saviour giving.

Jesus lives! our hearts know well
nought from us his love shall sever;
life, nor death, nor powers of hell
tear us from his keeping ever.

Jesus lives! to him the throne
over all the world is given:
may we go where he has gone,
rest and reign with him in heaven.

??/F.E. Cox

Vivit Iesus! fugito
letum; neque enim timemus.
Vivit! sine dubio
non barathro serviemus.

Vivit! mors ab hoc die
vitae porta erit mansurae,
nec tremescent animae
quamvis atram transiturae.

Vivit, nobis mortuus;
ei soli nos vivamus;
puris usque cordibus
Salvatorem extollamus.

Vivit! hoc cognovimus:
nil amorem dissipabit;
vita, mors, diabolus
non tutela separabit

Vivit ille! Domino
terris omnibus tributis,
supra pax et ditio
nobis sit eum secutis.

MM 10-18.4.99

Jesus, Lord of life and glory,
Bend from heaven thy gracious ear;
While our waiting souls adore thee,
Friend of helpless sinners, hear:
> **By thy mercy,**
> **O deliver us, good Lord.**

From the depths of nature's blindness,
From the hardening power of sin,
From all malice and unkindness,
From the pride that lurks within:

When temptation sorely presses,
In the day of Satan's power,
In our times of deep distresses,
In each dark and trying hour:

When the world around is smiling,
In the time of wealth and ease,
Earthly joys our hearts beguiling,
In the day of health and peace:

In the weary hours of sickness,
In the times of grief and pain,
When we feel our mortal weakness,
When all human help is vain:

In the solemn hour of dying,
In the aweful judgement day,
May our souls, on thee relying,
Find thee still our Rock and stay:
> **By thy mercy,**
> **O deliver us, good Lord.**

J. Cummin

Rex decore, quo spiramus,
nos caelestis audias;
quippe tu, qui te colamus,
peccatores nos amas:
> ***qui sis clemens,***
> ***libera nos, Domine.***

Caecitatis quod innatae
sumus atque sceleris,
moti nos crudelitate
intus et superbiis,

Cum gravissime temptemur
dominante Satana
cumque curis cruciemur
nocte sub nigerrima:

Mundi bonis otiantes
cum circumdati sumus,
sine morbis exultantes,
gaudiis fallentibus,

Medicinae nos egentes
quando dolor opprimit,
quis, ut sumus impotentes,
ops humana deficit,

Morientes, cumque damus
rationem ludici,
usque in te nos fulciamus
ut in saxo stabili:
> ***qui sis clemens,***
> ***libera nos, Domine.***

MM   26.6—8.7.00

Jesus, Lord, we look to thee;
Let us in thy name agree;
Show thyself the Prince of Peace;
Bid all strife for ever cease.

By thy reconciling love
Every stumbling-block remove;
Each to each unite, endear;
Come, and spread thy banner here.

Make us of one heart and mind,
Courteous, pitiful and kind,
Lowly, meek in thought and word,
Altogether like our Lord.

Let us each for other care,
Each his brother's burden bear,
To the world a pattern give,
Show how Christ's disciples live.

Free from anger, free from pride,
Let us thus in God abide;
All the depth of love express,
All the height of holiness.

C. Wesley

Iesu, nomine tuo
uno simus animo;
Princeps Pacis vere sis:
finem fac certaminis.

Te pellatur arbitro
omnis hinc offensio
atque nos concordiae
sub vexillo cohibe.

Consentire facias,
molliat benignitas
mente et factis humiles
simus tibi compares.

Alteri sollicitus
alter subeat onus,
documentum, quomodo
vivant sancti, populo.

Ira, fastu liberi
simus incolae Dei;
alta amoris detegas,
et quae summa sanctitas.

MM 8—13.8.00

Jesus shall reign where'er the sun
Does his successive journeys run;
His kingdom stretch from shore to shore,
Till moons shall wax and wane no more.

People and realms of every tongue
Dwell on his love with sweetest song,
And infant voices shall proclaim
Their early blessings on his name.

Blessings abound where'er he reigns:
The prisoner leaps to lose his chains;
The weary find eternal rest,
And all the sons of want are blest.

To him shall endless prayer be made,
And praises throng to crown his head;
His name like incense shall arise
With every morning sacrifice.

Let every creature rise and bring
Peculiar honours to our King;
Angels descend with songs again,
And earth repeat the loud Amen.

I. Watts

Quocumque sol se diriget
regnantem Jesum sentiet;
patebit regnum, luna dum
ad mensem aptet habitum.

Amorem illius canit
quaecumque lingua sonuit
et prima vox infantium
dicabit nomen optimum.

Abundant bona qua regit,
captivus vincla deicit;
fit longa fessis requies
et divitantur pauperes.

Preces continuabimus;
cingemus illum laudibus;
surget cum ture nomen et
ad caelum mane se feret.

Summo quot animas habent
honore regem celebrent;
superna carmen integret
cohors, et terra Amen sonet.

MM 27—30.7.97

Latinised Hymns

Jesus, these eyes have never seen	O Jesu, corporalitas
That radiant form of thins;	sese interposuit
The veil of sense hangs dark betveen	opaca, neve appareas
Thy blessed face and mine.	me teque dividit.

I see thee not, I hear thee not,	Nec cerno te nec audio,
Yet thou art oft with me;	es saepe sed comes,
And earth hath ne'er so dear a spot	carusque locus iste quo
As where I meet with thee.	tu praesto latus es.

Yet, though I have not seen, and still	Cum te parum conspiciam,
Must rest in faith alone,	qui fide fretus sum,
I love thee, dearest Lord, and will,	ut diligo sic diligam
Unseen, but not unknown.	te non incognitum.

When death these mortal eyes shall seal	Mors hos cum claudet oculos
And still this throbbing heart,	silueritque cor,
The rending veil shall thee reveal	tuum mihi patebit os
All glorious as thou art.	et verus is nitor.

R.Palmer   *MM 27—29.6.99*

Jesus, we thus obey
Thy last and kindest word;
Here in thine own appointed way
We come to meet thee, Lord.

Our hearts we open wide
To make the Saviour room;
And lo, the Lamb, the Crucified,
The sinner's friend, is come.

Thy presence makes the feast;
Now let our spirits feel
The glory not to be expressed,
The joy unspeakable.

With high and heavenly bliss
Thou dost our spirits cheer;
The house of banqueting is this
And thou hast brought us here.

Now let our souls be fed
With manna from above,
And over us thy banner spread
Of everlasting love.

C. Wesley

Paremus, Jesu, sic
benigno iussui
et ultimo, quod hic
occurrimus tibi.

Aperta pectora
Salvator occupet;
en Crucifixus Hostia
et qui reos amet!

Qui sine te cibus?
Sit iam perspicuum
id ineffabile decus,
sublime gaudium.

Summa laetitia
nos hilares facis;
hic sunt triclinia tua
quo nos adduxeris.

Iam manna nutriat
supernum animas;
vexilli more nos tegat
aeterna caritas.

MM 23—26.10.01

Latinised Hymns

Jesus, where'er thy people meet,
There they behold thy mercy-seat;
Where'er they seek thee thou art found,
And every place is hallowed ground.

For thou, within no walls confined,
Inhabitest the humble mind;
Such ever bring thee when they come,
And, going, take thee to their home.

Dear Shepherd of thy chosen few,
Thy former mercies here renew;
Here to our waiting hearts proclaim
The sweetness of thy saving name.

Here may we prove the power of prayer
To strengthen faith and sweeten care,
To teach our faint desires to rise,
And bring all heaven before our eyes.

Lord, we are few, but thou art near;
Nor short thine arm, nor deaf thine ear
O rend the heavens, come quickly down,
And make a thousand hearts thine own.

W,Cowper

Quoquo tui se congregent,
sedem clementiae vident;
reperte te petentibus,
Iesu, quis haud sacer locus?

Non clausus aedificiis,
mentes summissas incolis:
ferentes quaqua veniunt,
euntes te domum vehunt.

Qui lecta pascis pecora,
priorem gratiam nova; ★
monstretur exspectantibus
hic Salvatoris titulus.

Hic et sciatur per precem
foveri cor, ali fidem:
sic altiora cupimus,
caelum fit inspectantibus.

Pauci sumus, sed tu subes,
nec vi nec auribus cares; ★★
descende nunc per aethera, ★★★
et mille corda fac tua.

MM   6—12.5.00

★   *clementias redintegra*
★★   *tu fortis neque surdus es*
★★★   *descendens divide aethera*

Just as I am. without one plea
But that thy blood was shed for me,
And that thou bidst me come to thee,
O Lamb of God, I come.

Just as I am, though tossed about
With many a conflict, many a doubt,
Fightings and fears within, without,
O Lamb of God, I come.

Just as I am, poor, wretched, blind;
Sight, riches, healing of the mind,
Yea, all I need, in thee to find,
O Lamb of God, I come.

Just as I am, thou wilt receive,
Wilt welcome, pardon, cleanse, relieve:
Because thy promise I believe,
O Lamb of God, I come.

Just as I am (thy love unknown
Has broken every barrier down),
Now to be thine, yea, thine alone,
O Lamb of God, I come.

Just as I am, of that free love
The breadth, length, depth, and height to prove,
Here for a season, then above,
O Lamb of God, I come.

C.Elliott

Ut nudus (dest quod invocem
divinum nisi sanguinem,
et quod me poscis comitem)
sic, Agne, te peto.

Ut nudus et lacessitus,
sive extra sive intrinsecus,
tot mentem agitantibus
sic, Agne, te peto.

Ut nudus, caecus, indigens
miserque, opes, quod sana mens
et visus, omne a te trahens,
sic, Agne, te peto.

Ut nudum me suscipies,
quem lauta labe subleves;
nunc quod mihi est in te fides
sic, Agne, te peto.

Ut nudus, fractis saepibus
(tu sic amas incognitus),
nunc totus ut fiam tuus,
sic, Agne, te peto.

Ut nudus, explorans ea
sit quanta caritas tua,
parumper hic et post supra,
sic, Agne, te peto.

MM 21—24.2.99

Kindly spring again is here,
Trees and fields in bloom appear;
Hark! the birds with artless lays
warble their Creator's praise.

Where in winter all was snow,
Now the flowers in clusters grow;
And the corn, in green array,
Promises a harvest-day.

On thy garden deign to smile,
Raise the plants, enrich the soil;
Soon thy presence will restore
Life to what seemed dead before.

J.Newton

Ver benignum ut redit,
rus ubique floruit;
volucrum sonat chorus
Creatoris laudibus.

Ubi nix hiberna erat,
ecce! gemma pullulat;
en aristae virides!
Larga fuerit seges.

Horto faveas tuo,
pingue solum facito;
viva te ciente erunt
quae vixisse visa sunt.

MM 5—9.2.00

King of glory, King of peace,
I will love thee;
And, that love may never cease,
I will move thee.
Thou hast granted my request,
Thou hast heard me;
Thou didst note my working breast,
Thou hast spared me.

Wherefore with my utmost art
I will sing thee,
And the cream of all my heart
I will bring thee.
Though my sins against me cried,
Thou didst clear me,
And alone, when they replied,
Thou didst hear me.

Seven whole days, not one in seven,
I will praise thee;
In my heart, though not in heaven,
I can raise thee.
Small it is in this poor sort
To enrol thee:
E'en eternity's too short
To extol thee.

G. Herbert

Te, cum pace decoris
Rex, amabo,
utque duret amor is
incitabo.
Exaudito tu mihi
adnuisti,
et commoto pectori
pepercisti.

Arte te, quanta est mihi,
celebrabo,
cordis et primum tibi
dedicabo.
Culpae reum ut prius
me solvisti,
reum rursus unicus
exaudisti.

Totam per hebdomadem
te laudabo;
corde meo hospitem
te locabo;
vix inesse eo queas
cohibenti;
deficit aeternitas
te canenti.

MM 4—9.4.00

Land of our birth, we pledge to thee	*Nativa terra, studium*
Our love and toil in years to be,	*nostrumst tibi pollicitum,*
When we are grown and take our place	*adulti quando civibus*
As men and women with our race.	*adscripti tuis erimus.*
Father in heaven, who lovest all,	*Amatos, Pater, supplices*
O help thy children when they call,	*tuos, caelestis, adiuves,*
That they may build from age to age	*ut tradant cassum vitiis*
An undefiled heritage.	*quod accepere posteris.*
Teach us to bear the yoke in youth	*Iugo iamnunc adsuesce nos,*
With steadfastness and careful truth,	*ut veritati deditos,*
That, in our time, thy grace may give	*et veritate praediti*
The truth whereby the nations live.	*simus qua vivunt populi.*
Teach us to rule ourselves alway,	*Nos continere nos doce*
Controlled and cleanly night and day,	*puros per noctem et die,*
That we may bring, if need arise,	*ut offeramus integram,*
No maimed or worthless sacrifice.	*cum tempus poscat, hostiam,*
Teach us to look in all our ends	*id velle non quod comites*
On thee for judge, and not our friends,	*sed potius quod tu probes,*
That we, with thee, may walk uncowed	*ne vulgus nos inliciat*
By fear or favour of the crowd.	*te duce neve terreat.*
Teach us the strength that cannot seek,	*Firmari nos doce neque*
By deed or thought to hurt the weak,	*infirmiores laedere,*
That, under thee, we may possess	*ut demus homines tuum*
Man's strength to comfort man's distress.	*hominibus solatium.*
Teach us delight in simple things,	*Ingenuis laetarier,*
And mirth that has no bitter, springs,	*ridere non crudeliter*
Forgiveness free of evil done,	*nocentibusque ignoscere*
And love to all men 'neath the sun.	*cunctosque amare nos doce.*
Land of our birth, our faith, our pride,	*Nativa tellus, ut tibi*
For whose dear sake our fathers died;	*sunt patres nostri mortui,*
O Motherland, we pledge to thee	*spondernus, Mater, fore nos*
Head, heart, and hand through years to be.	*totos in tempore tuos.*
R. Kipling	*MM 28.8—10.9.00*

Lead, kindly Light, amid the encircling gloom,   *Duc, alma lux, dum noctem transeo;*
Lead thou me on;   *tu dirige.*
The night is dark, and I am far from home;   *Caligo fit proculque sum domo;*
Lead thou me on.   *tu dirige.*
Keep thou my feet; I do not ask to see   *Serva pedes; spectare longius*
The distant scene; one step enough for me.   *quare velim? Sat unus est gradus.*

I was not ever thus, nor prayed that thou   *Non semper is qui dicerem tibi*
Shouldst lead me on;   *"Tu dirige",*
I loved to choose and see my path; but now   *meum tenere cursum malui;*
Lead thou me on.   *nunc dirige.*
I loved the garish day, and, spite of fears,   *Quid si superbe tunc vagatus sum?*
Pride ruled my will: remember not past years.   *Actorum ne memento temporum.*

So long thy power hath blest me, sure it still   *Manus beans tua usque ad terminum*
Will lead me on,   *me diriget*
O'er moor and fen, o'er crag and torrent, till   *trans tesqua sicca, trans aquosa, dum*
The night is gone,   *nox fugiet*
And with the morn those angel faces smile,   *et cum die ridebunt angeli,*
Which I have loved long since, and lost a while.   *cari prius, parumper perditi.*

J.H.Newman   *MM 17-18.1.97*

Lead us, heavenly Father, lead us
O'er the world's tempestuous sea;
Guard us, guide us, keep us, feed us,
For we have no help but thee;
Yet possessing every blessing
If our God our Father be.

Saviour, breathe forgiveness o'er us,
All our weakness thou dost know;
Thou didst tread this earth before us,
Thou didst feel its keenest woe;
Lone and dreary, faint and weary,
Through the desert thou didst go.

Spirit of our God, descending,
Fill our hearts with heavenly joy;
Love with every passion blending,
Pleasure that can never cloy;
Thus provided, pardoned, guided,
Nothing can our peace destroy.

J.Edmeston

Per procellas, o caelestis
pater, nos direxeris.
Custos, dux, nutrimen, vestis,
unus es qui subvenis.
Nos beati, fortunati,
quorum tu creator sis!

Quales simus tu novisti:
parce, culpam diluens.
Homo sicut nos vixisti,
dura nostra perferens,
valde pressus, solus, fessus
trans deserta te movens.

Spiritus Dei descendens
nostra laetet pectora
voluptate comprehendens
corda multifaria,
sitque tutis, absolutis
nobis pax perpetua.

MM 7—10.1.97

Let all the multitudes of light,
Their songs in concert raising,
With earth's triumphal hymns unite,
The risen Saviour praising..
Ye heavens, his festival proclaim!
Our King returneth whence he came,
With victory amazing.

For us he bore the bitter Tree,
To death's dark realm descending;
Our foe he slew, and set us free,
Man's ancient bondage ending.
No more the tyrant's chains oppress;
O conquering Love, thy name we bless,
With thee to heaven ascending.

Jesus, to thee be endless praise,
For this thy great salvation;
O holy Father, thine always
Be thanks and adoration;
Spirit of life and light, to thee
Eternal praise and glory be:
One God of all creation!

F.B.Macnutt

Sonet clarorum legio
Salvantem extollentes,
cum triumphali cantico
terrestri concinentes;
festumque, caeli, vos diem
clamate eumque reducem,
victoriam stupentes.

Qui passus in Patibulo
in tartarum descendis,
nos solvis hoste perdito
et vincula deprendis.
Iam non tyrannus opprimit;
nomen tuum beatum sit,
qui nobis coascendis.

Laudere quot erunt dies,
qui, Jesu, nos salvaris;
tu, sancte Pater, dignus es
qui semper extollaris;
gratesque tibi, Spiritus,
tibique, Trinitas, damus,
quod cuncta tu crearis.

MM 26—31.5.01

Let saints on earth in concert sing
With those whose work is done;
For all the servants of our King
In heaven and earth are one.

One family, we dwell in him,
One Church above, beneath;
Though now divided by the stream,
The narrow stream of death.

One army of the living God,
To his command we bow: /flood,
Part of the host have crossed the
And part are crossing now.

E'en now to their eternal home
There pass some spirits blest;
While others to the margin come,
Waiting their call to rest.

Jesu, be thou our constant guide,
Then, when the word is given,
Bid Jordan's narrow stream divide,
And bring us safe to heaven.

C. Wesley

Terrestribus emeriti
sanctorum concinant;
quippe omnes Regis famuli
uniti habitant.

In eo sumus una gens
et una Ecclesia:
quos separat interfluens
angusta mors aqua.

Nos una Domini cohors
ab illo regimur;
ab his est superata mors,
pars nunc transgreditur.

Sunt quorum nunc ad requiem
vehantur animae,
quas mox (eunt ad marginem)
sequentur aliae.

Iesu, constanter dirige
nos, dein arcessitos
scisso Jordanis flumine
transfer ad angelos.

MM 19—22.1.99

Let us employ all notes of joy
And praise that never endeth
To God above, whose mighty love
Our hearts and minds defendeth.
Who by his grace, in every place,
To all who need, and duly plead,
His power and presence lendeth.

For, ere he died, the Crucified
Wrought things eternal for us
By bread and wine, which Love divine
Hath given to assure us:
O taste and see; find him to be
Our great reward, our living Lord
Most willing to restore us.

The word he spoke, the bread he broke
Shall fill our lives with glory,
If we are true and loving too
And for our sins are sorry:
O do his will, and praise him still,
And still proclaim his glorious name
And deathless Gospel story.

A, Fox

Nunc iubilo cum cantico
perenniter laudetur
Deus favens nec impotens
qui homines tuetur;
is omnibus benevolus
opem dabit praesensque erit,
modo sollicitetur.

Effecit is Mactabilis
ut semper aleret nos,
amans cibo, Deus mero,
qui nunc firmificet nos:
hunc praemium, hunc Dominum
docemini constare, i
libenter recreet nos.

Is nuntians, panem fricans,
nos gloriae replebit,
benevolos nec perfidos
peccati dum pudebit;
quod vult sit et iam laus sonet
et cognitus sit titulus
Verbumque quod manebit.

MM 26—28.6.01

Let us, with a gladsome mind,	*Laeta mens benevolum*
Praise the Lord, for he is kind:	*laudet nostra Dominum.*
For his mercies aye endure,	***Cuius est perpetua***
Ever faithful, ever sure.	***cum fide clementia.***
Let us blaze his name abroad,	*Nomen publicabimus,*
For of gods he is the God:	*quod deorum est Deus.*
He with all-commanding might	*Eius est imperio*
Filled the new-made world with light:	*orbe fusa lux novo.*
He the golden-tressed sun	*Aureo soli suam*
Caused all day his course to run:	*per diem dedit viam;*
And the horned moon by night	*neque nocturnam minus*
'Mid her spangled sisters bright:	*lunae cum sororibus.*
All things living he doth feed,	*Omne sentiens alit:*
His full hand supplies their need:	*nempe manus sufficit.*
For his mercies ...	***Cuius est perpetua ...***
J. Milton (Ps 136)	*MM 24—25.6.97*

Lift high the cross, the love of Christ proclaim *Monstretur Crux amorque Domini;*
till all the world adore his sacred Name. *nomen salutent omnes populi.*

Come, brethren, follow where our Captain trod, *Ducis sequamur in vestigiis:*
our King victorious, Christ the Son of God. *est victor Rex Deique Christus is.*

Led on their way by this triumphant sign, *Post signum hoc ovans ovantia*
the hosts of God in conquering ranks combine. *Dei consociantur agmina.*

Each newborn soldier of the Crucified *Mactati quisquis miles natus sit*
bears on his brow the seal of him who died. *sigillum fronte mortui gerit.*

This is the sign which Satan's legions fear *Hoc turmae signum Satanae tremunt*
and angels veil their faces to revere. *et os velantes angeli colunt.*

Saved by this Cross whereon their Lord was slain, *Domum, qua Cruce Dominus perit*
the sons of Adam their lost home regain. *salvata, gens humana recipit.*

From north and south, from east and west they raise *Ex partibus terrarum quattuor,*
in growing unison their songs of praise. *ut una voce, tollitur canor.*

O Lord, once lifted on the glorious tree, *Clara sublatis olim Arbore,*
as thou hast promised, draw the world to thee. *ut promisisti, trahe nos ad te.*

Let every race and every language tell *Eum ne gens neu lingua taceat,*
of him who saves our souls from death and hell. *qui morte nos orcoque liberat.*

From farthest regions let them homage bring, *Quamvis remoto spondeant loco*
and on his Cross adore their Savior King. *se Vindici pendenti Regio.*

Set up thy throne, that earth's despair may cease *Ponas thronum, nobisque redde spem*
beneath the shadow of its healing peace. *ibi et cum medicina requiem.*

For thy blest Cross which doth for all atone *Cunctos quod ista Crux redemerit,*
creation's praises rise before thy throne. *laus creaturae solium subit.*

MM 21.1–2.3.01

Lift up your heads, ye gates of brass;	Portae, cedatis, aeneae
Ye bars of iron, yield!	claustrumque ferreum,
And let the King of Glory pass:	eunti Regi Gloriae
The Cross is in the field.	cum Cruce in proelium.

That banner, brighter than the star	Vexillum stella clarius
That leads the train of night,	quae nocti praeparat
Shines on the 'march, and guides from far	eius viam militibus
His servants to the fight.	ad bellum indicat.

A holy war those servants wage:	Est bellum sacrum, mysticum:
In that mysterious strife	in illo dimicant
The powers of heaven and hell engage,	de plure Bonum et Malum
For more than death or life.	quam utri pereant.

Ye armies of the living God,	Nunc ite, exercitus Dei
Sworn warriors of Christ's host,	Christique legio,
Where hallowed footsteps never trod	quo non prius pedes sacri,
Take your appointed post.	iubente Domino.

Though few and small and weak your bands,	Dux paucos debilesque vos
Strong in your Captain's strength,	fortis fortes facit;
Go to the conquest of all lands:	quot sunt domate populos:
All must be his at length.	is horum rex erit.

The spoils at his victorious feet	Victori praeda tum data
You shall rejoice to lay,	sit ad pedes ei
And lay yourselves as trophies meet,	et vos, opima spolia,
In his great judgement day.	sedenti iudici.

Then fear not, faint not, halt not now;	Vos ergo confortamini
In Jesus' name be strong!	in Iesu nomine,
To him shall all the nations bow,	cuius triumphum populi
And sing the triumph song:	augebunt undique.

Uplifted are the gates of brass,	Iam portae cedunt aeneae
The bars of iron yield;	claustrumque ferreum;
Behold the King of Glory pass:	Rex bene gessit Gloriae
The Cross hath won the field!	cum Cruce proelium.

J.Montgomery

MM 15—27.8.00

"Lift up your hearts!" We lift them, Lord, to thee;
Here at thy feet none other may we see:
"Lift up your hearts!" E'en so, with one accord,
We lift them up, we lift them to the Lord.

Above the level of the former years,
The mire of sin, the slough of guilty fears,
The mist of doubt, the blight of love's decay,
O Lord of Light, lift all our hearts today!

Above the swamps of subterfuge and shame,
The deeds, the thoughts, that honour may not name,
The halting tongue that dares not tell the whole,
O Lord of Truth, lift every Christian soul!

Lift every gift that thou thyself hast given:
Low lies the best till lifted up to heaven;
Low lie the bounding heart, the teeming brain,
Till, sent from God, they mount to God again.

Then, as the trumpet-call in after years,
"Lift up your hearts!" rings pealing in our ears,
Still shall those hearts respond with full accord,
"We lift them up, we lift them to the Lord!"

H.Montagu Butler

"Tollantur corda!" Tibi tollimus:
prostratis num videtur alius?
"Tollantur corda!" nempe Domino
uno tibi tolluntur animo.

Supra paludem culpae veterem
et nubis instar dubiam fidem
marcentem et amorem, Domine
Lucis, cor omne tollas hodie.

Supra dolorum turpium lacus
et conticenda mentis et manus
aegreque totum confessurum os,
Veri Deus, nos tollito tuos.

Dedisti: dona tolle tu tua;
iacet quod haud sustuleris supra;
iacet cor saltabundum, feta mens,
nisi Deum, qui misit, repetens.

Sic, ut sonabit ohm lituus
nostris, "Tollantur corda!" in auribus,
toto respondeamus animo
"Tolluntur ecce corda Domino!"

MM 17-3-.10.01

Latinised Hymns

Lo, he comes with clouds descending,
Once for favoured sinners slain;
Thousand thousand saints attending
Swell the triumph of his train:
Alleluia!
Christ appears on earth to reign.

Every eye shall now behold him
Robed in dreadful majesty;
ihose who set at nought and sold him,
Pierced and nailed him to the Tree,
Deeply wailng,
Shall the true Messiah see.

Those dear tokens of his Passion
Still his dazzling body bears,
Cause of endless exultation
To his ransomed worshippers:
With what rapture
Gaze we on those glorious scars!

Yea, Amen, let all adore thee,
High on thine eternal throne;
Saviour, take the power and glory,
Claim the kingdom for thine own:
Alleluia!
Thou shalt reign, and thou alone.

Wesley/Cennick

Medio venit nimborum
nobis ohm mortuus,
mille milibus sanctorum
una triumphantibus,
Alleluia!
Christus ecce! dominus.

Dirae maiestatis erunt
eius omnes arbitri
qui contemptum vendiderunt;
quemque adfixerant Cruci,
vere Christum
noscent flendo dediti.

Passionis signa amanda
stant in corpore sita,
adorantibus miranda
emptionis pretia,
laeta visu
et decora vulnera.

Amen! omnibus colaris
altus in throno sedens
gloriamque nanciscaris
tuum tibi capiens
Alleluia!
regnum unice potens.

MM 29.11—8.12.98

Lo, round the throne, a glorious band,
The saints in countless myriads stand,
Of every tongue redeemed to God,
Arrayed in garments washed in blood.

Through tribulation great they came;
They bore the cross, despised the shame;
From all their labours now they rest,
In God's eternal glory blest.

They see their Saviour face to face,
And sing the triumphs of his grace;
Him day and night they ceaseless praise,
To him the loud thanksgiving raise:

"Worthy the Lamb, for sinners slain,
Through endless years to live and reign!
Thou hast redeemed us by thy Blood,
And made us kings and priests to God."

O may we tread the sacred road
That saints and holy martyrs trod;
Wage to the end the glorious strife,
And win, like them, a crown of life.

R.Hill

En! circa thronum splendida
sanctorum multa milia,
redempta, linguis variis,
lautis in sanguine stolis.

Passos amaritudinem,
dignatos tollere crucem,
nunc liberos laboribus
in gloria beat Deus.

Nunc Salvatorem noscitant,
victricem gratiam probant,
laudantes die sitve nox;
sonatque gratiarum vox:

"Es dignus, noster Victima,
qui longa regnes saecula;
redempti sanguine tuo
sacrati sumus Domino;"

Fac nos in via pedites,
quae tulit ante martyres,
ut, dimicati strenue,
participemur gloriae.

MM 11—29.7.99

Lord, as to thy dear Cross we flee,
And plead to be forgiven,
So let thy life our pattern be,
And form our souls for heaven.

Help us, through good report and ill,
Our daily cross to bear;
Like thee, to do our Father's will,
Our brethren's griefs to share.

Let grace our selfishness expel,
Our earthliness refine,
And kindness in our bosoms dwell
As free and true as thine.

If joy shall at thy bidding fly,
And grief's dark day come on,
We in our turn would meekly cry,
"Father, thy will be done."

Kept peaceful in the midst of strife,
Forgiving and forgiven,
O may we lead the pilgrim's life,
And follow thee to heaven.

J.H. Gurney

Fac, ut ad Crucem fugimus
petentes veniam,
nos animis caelestibus
ad speciem tuam.

Bene audiamus aut male,
dum cruces tollimus,
da Patris iussa facere,
conflere fratribus.

Nobis studere nos vetet
purgetque gratia,
nostrumque pectus occupet
benignitas tua.

Cum maesta te iubente nox
laetitiam fuget,
haec nostra sit submissa vox
"Sit ut tibi placet."

Pacati prae pugnantibus,
culpando liberi,
sequamur te superius,
hic tibi dediti.

MM 20—24.11.00

Lord, enthroned in heavenly splendour,
Fist begotten from the dead,
Thou alone, our strong defender,
Liftest up thy people's head.
Alleluia!
Jesu, true and living Bread.

Here our humblest homage pay we,
Here in loving reverence bow;
Here for faith's discernment pray we,
Lest we fail to know thee now.
Alleluia!
Thou art here, we ask not how.

Though the lowliest form doth veil thee
As of old in Bethlehem,
Here as there thine angels hail thee,
Branch and Flower of Jesse's Stem.
Alleluia!
We in worship join with them.

Pachal Lamb, thine Offering, finished
Once for all, when thou wast slain,
In its fulness undiminished
Shall for evermore remain,
Alleluia!
Cleansing souls from every stain.

Life-imparting heavenly Manna,
Stricken Rock with streaming side,
Heaven and earth with loud Hosanna
Worship thee, the Lamb who died,
Alleluia!
Risen, ascended, glorified!

G.H.Bourne

Caeles in throno resplendens,
primus Orco genite,
cum valore nos defendens
plebis elator tuae,
Alleluia!
vere Panis vivide.

Te summisse reverentes
genu tibi flectirnus,
consciam fidem petentes,
nobis ut sis agnitus.
Alleluia!
Hic es: haud refert modus.

Ima forma cum tegaris
olim ut in Bethlehem,
isdem angelis laudaris:
Jesse te propaginem
Alleluia!
nos laudamus itidem.

Quod, paschalis, obtulisti,
semel, Agne, mortuus,
id aeternum praebuisti
annis haud obnoxius,
Alleluia!
cunctis purgans sordibus.

Vitam dans, caeleste Manna,
Saxum fissum, diffluum,
sonat inde et hinc Hosanna
Agnum te laudantium,
Alleluia!
vivum caelo redditum.

MM 9—12.9.98

Lord, for the years your love has kept and guided,
urged and inspired us, cheered us in our way,
sought us and saved us, pardoned and provided:
Lord of the years, we bring our thanks today.

Lord, for that word, the word of life which fires us,
speaks to our hearts and sets our souls ablaze,
teaches and trains, rebukes us and inspires us:
Lord of the word, receive your people's praise.

Lord, for our land in this our generation,
spirits oppressed by pleasure, wealth and care:
for young and old, for commonwealth and nation,
Lord of our land, be pleased to hear our prayer.

Lord, of our world where men disown and doubt you,
loveless in strength, and comfortless in pain,
hungry and helpless, lost indeed without you;
Lord of the world, we pray that Christ may reign.

Lord, of ourselves, in living power remake us
self on the cross and Christ upon the throne,
past put behind us, for the future take us;
Lord of our lives, to live for Christ alone.

T.Dudley-Smith

Amans per annos et tegens duxisti,
propulsor et levamen tu viae,
quaerens salvasti, veniam dedisti:
grates, o Rex annorum, accipe.

Pro verbo, quod vitale nos incendit
mentesque implet calore cordaque
docensque nos impellit aut reprendit,
plebs tua te laudamus, Domine.

Pro civitate et civibus, gravatis
cura seu voluptate vel lucro,
cunctis et cuiuscumque sint aetatis,
sit nostra accepta supplicatio.

Mundum, tuum sed male te fatentem
(nil eius vim luctumve temperat),
debilem, certe sine te cadentem,
tandem precamur Christus ut regat.

Tu vividus potensque recrea nos
(in cruce nos, sit Christus in throno),
quique erimus, non fuimus, voca nos,
Christoque tum vivamus unico.

MM   26.ll.—14.l2.99

Lord, her watch thy church is keeping;
When shall earth thy rule obey?
When shall end the night of weeping?
When shall break the promised day?
See the whitening harvest languish,
Waiting still the labourers' toil;
Was it vain, thy Son's deep anguish?
Shall the strong retain the spoil?

Tidings, sent to every creature,
Millions yet have never heard;
Can they hear without a preacher?
Lord almighty, give the word:
Give the word; in every nation
Let the gospel trumpet sound,
Witnessing a world's salvation
To the earth's remotest bound.

Then the end: thy church completed,
All thy chosen gathered in,
With their King in glory seated,
Satan bound, and banished sin;
Gone for ever parting, weeping,
Hunger, sorrow, death, and pain:
Lo, her watch thy church is keeping;
Come, Lord Jesus, come to reign!

H. Downton

Tibi mundus dum parebit,
vigilat Ecclesia,
dum promissa lux lucebit,
nox recedet aspera.
Ecce candentes aristae!
Sed messoribus carent.
Te-ne tanta passo, Christe,
rapta raptores tenent?

Omnibus pronuntiandum
quot ignorant milia!
Praedicantem praedicandum
poscit. Deus, impera!
Impera! Tubam praeconem
audiatis, populi!
Orbis et salvationem
noscant eius termini.

Dein electis congregatis
colligens Ecclesiam
cumque rege te locatis,
degravabis Satanam.
Inde cuncta dissipabis
quot dolemus hic mala.
Donec regem te dicabis
vigilat Ecclesia.

MM 10—13.5.97

Lord, I would own thy tender care,
And all thy love to me;
The food I eat, the clothes I wear,
Are all bestowed by thee.

'Tis thou preservest me from death
And dangers every hour;
I cannot draw another breath
Unless thou give me power.

Kind angels guard me every night,
As round my bed they stay;
Nor am I absent from thy sight
In darkness or by day.

My health and friends and parents dear
To me by God are given;
I have not any blessing here
But what is sent from heaven.

Such goodness, Lord, and constant care
I never can repay;
But may it be my daily prayer,
To love thee and obey.

Jane Taylor

O Domine, confiteor
favere te mihi:
quo nutrior. quo vestior,
id debeo tibi.

Diurno me periculo
ne moriar tegis:
spirare plane nequeo
ni posse tu facis.

Me dormientem angeli
circum custodiunt,
nec oculi, sit nox, tui,
sit lux, me neglegunt.

Salus, amicus et parens
(nam donat hos Deus),
quocumque laetor, veniens
est omne caelitus.

Est tanta caritas tua,
non umquam redderem;
sed sit diurna prex mea
ut serviens amem.

MM 11—15.8.01

Lord, in this thy mercy's day,	*Hoc clementiae tuae,*
Ere it pass for ay away,	*dum duraverit, die*
On our knees we fall and pray.	*flectimur tibi in prece.*

Holy Jesu, grant us tears,	*Iesu, lacrimare nos*
Fill us with heart-searching fears,	*fac tu corde pavidos,*
Ere that awful doom appears.	*quippe poenae debitos.*

Lord, on us thy Spirit pour	*Flatu nos tuo bea*
Kneeling lowly at the door,	*flexos ante limina,*
Ere it close for evermore.	*dum manebunt pervia.*

By thy night of agony,	*Noctem per Gethsemanes*
By thy supplicating cry,	*quasque fudisti preces,*
By thy willingness to die;	*quod mori dignatus es;*

By thy tears of bitter woe	*recordare lacrimas*
For Jerusalem below,	*de Jerusalem tuas,*
Let us not thy love forgo.	*neve amorem auferas.*

Grant us neath thy wings a place,	*Intra diem gratiae*
Lest we lose this day of grace	*nos sub alis protege*
Ere we shall behold thy face.	*te visuros, Domine.*

I. WIlliams

MM 18—20.2.99

Lord, in thy name thy servants plead,
And thou hast sworn to hear:
Thine is the harvest, thine the seed,
The fresh and fading year.

Our hope, when autumn winds blew wild,
We trusted, Lord, in thee;
And still, now spring has on us smiled,
We wait on thy decree.

The former and the latter rain,
The summer sun and air,
The green ear, and the golden grain,
All thine, are ours by prayer.

Thine too by right, and ours by grace,
The wondrous growth unseen,
The hopes that soothe, the fears that brace,
The love that shines serene.

So grant the precious things brought forth
By sun and moon below,
That thee in thy new heaven and earth
We never may forgo.

J.Keble

Qui nobis invocatus es,
es sponsus opifer:
sunt tua semen et seges,
autumnus atque ver.

Ferox tibi fidentibus
autumnus incidit,
et nunc ad te suspicimus,
ut ver reniduit.

Tuae sunt ambae pluviae,
aestiva claritas,
spicae maturae seu novae;
precantibusque das.

Quae tua sunt, augmenta tu
interiora dans,
spe molliens, firmas metu,
sereniter amans.

Sic sol te dante lunaque
hic praebeant opes
ut mundo tu perpetue
sis in novo comes.

MM 26—29.4.99

Lord, it belongs not to my care
Whether I die or live:
To love and serve thee is my share,
And this thy grace must give.

Christ leads me through no darker rooms
Than he went through before;
He that unto God's Kingdom comes
Must enter by this door.

Come, Lord, when grace hath made me meet
Thy blessed face to see;
For if thy work on earth be sweet,
What will thy glory be!

Then shall I end my sad complaints
And weary, sinful days,
And join with the triumphant saints
That sing my Saviour's praise.

My knowledge of that life is small,
The eye of faith is dim;
But 'tis enough that Christ knows all,
And I shall be with him.

R. Baxter

Non quaero, mihi sit datum
vivamne an peream;
tibi servire sit meum
tuam per gratiam.

Opacum ducis per locum?
Ibi isti tu prius;
nec itur aliis tuum
in regnum foribus.

Appareas, si fecerit
me dignum gratia;
cum dulce opus terrestre sit,
quid gloria tua!

Tum non peccatis domitus
diutius querar,
qui tecum triumphantibus
sanctis adiciar.

Non vita qualis illa sit
(lippa est fides) scio:
sat est quod Christus omne scit
comes cui tunc ero.

MM   19—28.6.99

Lord Jesus, think on me,
And purge away my sin;
From earth-born passions set me free,
And make me pure within.

Lord Jesus, think on me
With many a care opprest;
Let me thy loving servant be,
And taste thy promised rest.

Lord Jesus, think on me,
Nor let me go astray;
Through darkness and perplexity
Point thou the heavenly way.

Lord Jesus, think on me,
That, when the flood is past,
I may the eternal brightness see,
And share thy joy at last.

W. Chatfield/Bp. Synesius

Memento tu mei,
sontemque puriga;
si quid me turbat, expedi;
sit pura mens mea.

Memento tu mei
curis vexantibus;
sim pacti compos otii
amemque te tuus.

Memento tu mei,
errore ne vager,
et nocte confuso mihi
caeleste des iter.

Memento tu mei,
traiecto flumine
aeternae lucis ut mihi
sit et laetitiae.

MM   20—23.3.99

Lord of all hopefulness, Lord of all joy,
Whose trust, ever childlike, no cares could destroy,
Be there at our waking, and give us, we pray,
Your bliss in our hearts, Lord, at the break of the day.

Lord of all eagerness Lord of all faith,
Whose strong hands were skilled at the plane and the lathe
Be there at our labours, and give us, we pray,
Your strength in our hearts, Lord, at the noon of the day.

Lord of all kindliness, Lord of all grace,
Your hands swift to welcome, your arms to embrace,
Be there at our homing, and give us, we pray,
Your love in our hearts, Lord, at the eve of the day.

Lord of all gentleness, Lord of all calm,
Whose voice is contentment, whose presence is balm,
Be there at our sleeping, and give us, we pray,
Your peace in our hearts, Lord, at the end of the day.

J.Struther

Sunt tua gaudia cunctaque spes
nec sollicitudine laesa fides:
surgentibus adsis, et, O Domine,
da gaudia spemque oriente die.

Est tua navitas estque vigor
•fabrilis et, O faber, iste labor;
laboribus adsis, et, O Domine,
nobis media vigor esto die.

Est tua semper amica manus;
es, alme, benignus ut haud alius;
domum redeuntibus, O Domine,
sit gratia se minuente die.

Est tua lenitas, est requies
nec ulla querela, serenus ut es;
cubantibus adsis et, O Domine,
fiat tua pax abeunte die.

MM 6—14.3.02

Lord of all, to whom alone	*Quorum quod carissimum*
All our hearts' desires are known,	*uni tibi cognitum,*
When we stand before thy throne,	*stantes ante solium*
.Jesu, hear and save.	*salva, Domine.*

Son of Man, before whose eyes	*Christe, perspicacem te*
Every secret open lies,	*nihil fallit: in die*
At the great and last assize,	*quaestionis ultimae*
Jesu, hear and save.	*salva, Domine.*

Son of God, whose angel host	*Quo laetantur angeli*
(Thou hast said) rejoiceth most	*teste, Filio Dei,*
O'er the sinner who was lost,	*versione perditi,*
Jesu, hear and save.	*salva, Domine.*

Saviour, who didst not condemn	*Qui tangentibus tuas*
Those who touched thy garments' hem	*vestes veniam dabas,*
Mercy show to us and them:	*nobis quoque faveas*
Jesu, hear and save.	*salva, Domine.*

Lord, the Way to sinners shown,	*Peccatorum O via*
Lord, the Truth by sinners known,	*Veritasque cognita,*
Love Incarnate on the throne,	*sede, Christe, de tua*
Jesu, hear and save.	*salva, Domine.*

C.A. Alington

MM 27.10—1.11.00

Lord of beauty, thine the splendour
Shewn in earth and sky and sea,
Burning sun and moonlight tender,
Hill and river, flower and tree:
Lest we fail our praise to render
Touch our eyes that they may see.

Lord of wisdom, whom obeying
Mighty waters ebb and flow,
While unhasting, undelaying,
Planets on their courses go:
In thy laws thyself displaying,
Teach our minds thyself to know.

Lord of life, alone sustaining
All below and all above,
Lord of love, by whose ordaining
Sun and stars sublimely move;
In our earthly spirits reigning,
Lift our hearts that we may love.

Lord of beauty, bid us own thee,
Lord of truth, our footsteps guide
Till as love our hearts enthrone thee,
And, with vision purified,
Lord of all, when all have known thee,
Thou in all art glorified.

C.A. Alington

Per tuum natura lumen
est ubique lucida.
Flos et arbor, mons et flumen,
luna, sol et sidera
sunt laudanda. Tange, Numen,
tange nostra lumina.

Quo docente regularis
tractat undas impetus,
cuius motio stellaris
conservatur legibus,
nobis esse cognoscaris
legislator optimus.

Inspirator cuncta prorsum
dirigens viventia,
quo tenent superna cursum
imperante lumina,
tolle, diligende, sursum,
tolle nostra pectora.

Fac a nobis agnoscaris
dans lucernam pedibus,
cordibusque instituaris
amor ipse cognitus
et ab omnibus sciaris
omnium tu dominus.

MM 9—12 Nov 96

Lord of our life, and God of our salvation,
Star of our night, and hope of every nation,
Hear and receive thy Church's supplication,
 Lord God Almighty.

See round thine ark the hungry billows curling;
See how thy foes their banners are unfurling;
Lord, while their darts envenomed they are hurling,
 Thou canst preserve us.

Lord, thou canst help when earthly armour faileth,
Lord, thou canst save when deadly sin assaileth;
Lord, o'er thy Church nor death nor hell prevaileth:
 Grant us thy peace, Lord.

Grant us thy help till foes are backward driven,
Grant them thy truth, that they may be forgiven,
Grant peace on earth, and, after we have striven,
 Peace in thy heaven.

P. Pusey

Te salutem nos animamque dantem,
gentium stellam tenebras levantem,
almus exaudi populum precantem,
 omnia pollens.

Ad ratem fluctus-ne tuam frementes
et vides vexilla malos moventes?
Nos venenatis iaculis petentes
 hos procul arce.

Certior quocumque juvante jutor,
Christe, letalis sceleris solutor,
morte sanctorum minitante tutor,
 da, bone, pacem.

Hostium turmae duce te fugentur;
quos doce, dum crimine liberentur;
et tuis hic otia commodentur,
 otia caelo.

MM   22—27.4.99

Lord, pour thy spirit from on high,
And thine ordained servants bless;
Graces and gifts to each.supply,
And clothe thy priests with righteousness.

Within thy temple when they stand,
To teach the truth as taught by thee,
Saviour, like stars in thy right hand
Let all thy Church's pastors be.

Wisdom and zeal and faith impart,
Firmness with meekness, from above,
To bear thy people in their heart,
And love the souls whom thou dost love;

To watch and pray and never faint,
By day and night their guard to keep,
To warn the sinner, cheer the saint,
To feed thy lambs and tend thy sheep.

So, when their work is finished here,
May they in hope their charge resign;
When the Chief Shepherd shall appear,
O God, may they and we be thine.

J.Montgomery

Parentes tibi, Domine,
tuos antistites bea,
per dona tuae gratiae
amiciens iustitia.

Aedi docentes cum tuae
stabunt quod docuisti tu,
pastores sint Ecclesiae
ut sidera tua manu.

Acres doctique cum fide,
cum firmitate humiles,
plebem tuam sub pectore
ferant, amentque quos ames.

Precentur et custodiant
noctu dieque vigiles;
firment bonos, malos regant,
agnos alant, pascant oves.

Hic spe bona cum denique
ponant onus emeriti,
Pastore coram Principe
sint, simus, O Deus, tui.

MM 15—25.4.00

Lord, speak to me, that I may speak In living echoes of thy tone; As thou hast sought, so let me seek Thy erring children lost and lone.	*Ut loquar, mihi loquere,* *tuos et imiter sonos,* *ut tu petisti, Domine,* *fac perditos petam tuos.*
O lead me, Lord, that I may lead The wandering and the wavering feet; O feed me, Lord, that I may feed The hungering ones with manna sweet.	*Fac deviorum te duce* *pedum me, Domine, ducem;* *te me pascente, Domine,* *ieiunis ego manna dem.*
O strengthen me, that, while I stand Firm on the rock, and strong in thee, I may stretch out a loving hand To wrestlers with the troubled sea.	*Da robur, ut stem firmiter* *in saxo per te validus* *et contra fluctus opifer* *dem dexteram luctantibus.*
O teach me, Lord, that I may teach The precious things thou dost impart; And wing my words, that they may reach The hidden depths of many a heart.	*Me doceas, ut doceam* *quae tu probanda impertias,* *alatis verbis fodiam* *multorum cordis latebras.*
O give thine own sweet rest to me, That I may speak with soothing power A word in season, as from thee, To weary ones in needful hour.	*Da requiem mihi tuam,* *tua sermonibus vice* *ut fatigatos mulceam* *idoneis in tempore.*
O fill me with thy fullness, Lord, Until my very heart o'erflow In kindling thought and glowing word, Thy love to tell, thy praise to show.	*Cum plenitate repleas,* *dum cor hoc meum effluat* *tuas laudando gratias* *incendat mens, vox ardeat.*
O use me, Lord, use even me, Just as thou wilt, and when, and where, Until thy blessed face I see, Thy rest, thy joy, thy glory share.	*Cum non sim dignus, utere,* *si quo modo subveniam,* *dum tecum coram, Domine,* *quiescam, ovem, gaudeam.*
F.R.Havergal	*MM 10—16.3.02*

Lord, teach us how to pray aright
With reverence and with fear;
Though dust and ashes in thy sight,
We may, we must, draw near.

We perish if we cease from prayer:
0 grant us power to pray;
And, when to meet thee we prepare,
Lord, meet us by the way.

God of all grace, we bring to thee
A broken, contrite heart;
Give what thine eye delights to see,
Truth in the inward part;

Faith in the only Sacrifice
That can for sin atone,
To cast our hopes, to fix our eyes,
On Christ, on Christ alone;

Patience to watch and wait and weep,
Though mercy long delay;
Courage our fainting souls to keep,
And trust thee though thou slay.

Give these, and then thy will be done;
Thus, strengthened with all might,
We, through thy Spirit and thy Son,
Shall pray, and pray aright.

J . Montgomery

Rite et cum reverentia
orare nos doce;
sumus tibi cinis mera,
sed ire fas prope.

Dempta prece peribimus:
potentem fac eam,
et obviam euntibus
i nobis obviam.

Contritas tibi ferimus
et fractas animas;
sit nobis, qua gaudes, Deus,
interna veritas.

Uni fidamus hostiae,
peccata qui luat,
et oculosque votaque
Christus retineat.

Feramus, at cum fletibus,
seram clementiam
et exigentem haud secus
te poenam ultimam.

Sic fiat ut placet tibi,
potentiumque ope
nos Spiritus et Filii
orabimus bene.

MM 16—25.3.00

Lord, thou hast brought us to our journey's end:
Once more to thee our evening prayers ascend;
Once more we stand to praise thee for the past;
Grant prayer and praise be honest at the last.

For all the joys which thou hast deigned to share,
For all the pains which thou hast helped to bear.
For all our friends, in life and death the same,
We thank thee, Lord, and praise thy glorious name.

If from thy paths, by chastening undismayed,
If, for thy gifts ungrateful, we have strayed,
If in thy house our prayers were faint and few,
Forgive, O Lord, and build our hearts anew.

If we have learnt to feel our neighbour's need,
To fight for truth in thought and word and deed,
If these be lessons which the years have taught,
Then stablish, Lord, what thou in us hast wrought.

So be our rest thy palaces most fair,
Not built with hands, whose stones thy praise declare:
Where war is not, and all thy sons are free,
Where thou art known, and all is known in thee.

C.A.Alington

Quo duce iter confectum est, Deus,
sub noctem tibi preces tollimus,
pro donis et laudamus, Domine:
utrumque fiat integra fide.

Dignate tot nobiscum gaudia
sentire, tot sufferre vulnera,
fidos dare usque ad mortem comites,
cum laude nostras gratias habes.

Grati parum si fuimus tibi,
si pervicaces atque devii,
si defuere coram te preces,
tu corda clemens nobis integres.

Sin accolam iuvare coepimus,
verum fovere totis viribus,
haec si per annos accessere, nos
a te confirma sic dispositos.

Te sponte nexi laudant lapides,
quo tecta muro nostra sit quies,
pax et libertas ubi maxima,
tu sciris et sciuntur omnia.

MM   16—21.8.98

Lord, thy word abideth,
And our footsteps guideth;
Who its truth believeth
Light and joy receiveth.

When our foes are near us,
Then thy word doth cheer us,
Word of consolation,
Message of salvation.

When the storms are o'er us,
And dark clouds before us,
Then its light directeth,
And our way protecteth.

Who can tell the pleasure
Who recount the treasure,
By thy word imparted
To the simple-hearted?

Word of mercy, giving
Succour to the living;
Word of life, supplying
Comfort to the dying!

O that we discerning
Its most holy learning,
Lord, may love and fear thee,
Evermore be near thee.

H.W.Baker

Tua vox aeterna,
pedibus lucerna,
vera cui probatur,
Domine, is beatur.

Hostis cui minatur,
ista consolatur,
nostra confirmatrix,
boni nuntiatrix.

Unda cum tumebit,
nubes insidebit,
ista erit protectrix
et viae directrix.

Grata quis narraret,
gazas computaret,
quas dat innocenti
vox divina menti?

Larga vitae donis
et remissionis,
adiuvat viventes,
mulcet morientes.

Semper, illam gnari
docta, sancta fari,
prope te locemur,
teque veneremur.

MM 29.4-4.5.97

Lord, to our humble prayers attend,	*Rex, conscius votorum sis,*
Let thou thy peace from heaven descend,	*descendat pax a superis,*
And to our souls salvation send:	*salus mittatur animis:*
HAVE MERCY, LORD, UPON US.	*O MISERERE NOBIS.*
Rule in our hearts, thou Prince of Peace,	*Rex Pacis, corda dirigas,*
The welfare of thy Church increase,	*Ecclesiam promoveas,*
And bid all strife and discord cease:	*omnes fugans discordias:*
To all who meet for worship here	*Hic una te colentibus*
Do thou in faithfulness draw near;	*fideliter sis proximus;*
Inspire with faith and godly fear:	*fides sit et tui metus:*
O let thy priests be clothed with might,	*Vim Sacerdotes induant,*
To rule within thy Church aright,	*Ecclesiamque dum regant,*
That they may serve as in thy sight:	*ut coram, tibi serviant:*
The sovereign ruler of our land	*Qui* iure nobis imperat,*
Protect by thine almighty hand,	*hunc* manus ista protegat*
And all around the throne who stand:	*et proximos custodiat:*
Let clouds and sunshine bless the earth,	*Ne fallant sol et pluviae,*
Give flowers and fruits a timely birth,	*sint praesto flores pomaque,*
Our harvests crown with peaceful mirth:	*et gaudeamus segete:*
Let voyagers by land and sea	*Ne terreant pericula,*
In danger's hour in safety be,	*sit terra seu mari via;*
The suffering and the captive free:	*captos dolore libera:*
Around us let thine arm be cast,	*Nos amplectare, Domine;*
Till wrath and danger be o'erpast	*sit finis iracundiae,*
And tribulation's bitter blast:	*et luctus flabra supprime:*
HAVE MERCY, LORD, UPON US.	*O MISERERE NOBIS.*
J. Brownlie (from Greek)	*MM 16-21.9.01*
	* quae? hanc?

Lord, to thy loving arms	*Hunc tibi redditum*
Our brother we restore,	*benignus accipe*
Where neither sin nor sorrow harms	*dolore et culpa liberum*
Upon the further shore.	*in isto margine.*
He dwells in peace above,	*Supra nunc habitat*
Where never care may come;	*curis impervius;*
The soul that thou didst lend in love,	*te commodante venerat,*
In love thou callest home.	*tu revocas bonus.*
Lord, when we sorrow most,	*Sit dolor maximus,*
Then most one flock are we;	*tum vere iungimur;*
We grow not fewer, though the host	*nec singulis migrantibus*
Step one by one to thee.	*cohors minuitur.*
Whate'er befall, at length	*Quodcumque eveniet,*
Thus to thy heart we come;	*tu nos suscipies;*
Ah, lead us on from strength to strength;	*fac fortiores semper et*
Then draw us gently home.	*postremo reduces.*

A.C.Benson	*MM 23—4.9.98*

Love Divine, all loves excelling,
  Joy of heaven, to earth come down,
Fix in us thy humble dwelling,
  All thy faithful mercies crown.

Jesu, thou art all compassion,
  Pure unbounded love thou art;
Visit us with thy salvation,
  Enter every trembling heart.

Come, almighty to deliver,
  Let us all thy life receive;
Suddenly return, and never,
  Never more thy temples leave.

Thee we would be always blessing,
  Serve thee as thy hosts above,
Pray, and praise thee, without ceasing,
  Glory in thy perfect love.

Finish then thy new creation,
  Pure and spotless let us be;
Let us see thy great salvation,
  Perfectly restored in thee;

Changed from glory into glory,
  Till in heaven we take our place,
Till we cast our crowns before thee,
  Lost in wonder, love, and praise!

C. Wesley

O amorum praeferende,
o caeleste gaudium,
clemens inter nos descende
confirmator munerum.

Omne scis quod patiamur;
infinitus es amor;
fac salutem nanciscamur
intra tremens omne cor.

Adsis liberos facturus
universos et bea;
templa, numquam discessurus
inde, rursus occupa.

Semper erga te geramus
angelorum operam;
sine pausa te colamus
caritatem ob tuam.

Fac novam creationem:
simus omnes integri;
iubeas salvationem
per te ratam fieri,

semper aucto dum splendore
caelo simus additi
et coronas cum stupore
demus ad pedes tibi.

MM 3—17.7.97

Love's redeeming work is done;
Fought the fight, the battle won:
Lo, our Sun's eclipse is o'er!
Lo, he sets in blood no more!

Vain the stone, the watch, the seal!
Christ has burst the gates of hell;
Death in vain forbids his rise;
Christ has opened paradise.

Lives again our glorious King;
Where, O death, is now thy sting?
Dying once, he all doth save;
Where thy victory, O grave?

Soar we now where Christ has led,
Following our exalted head;
Made like him, like him we rise;
Ours the cross, the grave, the skies.

Hail the Lord of earth and heaven!
Praise to thee by both be given:
Thee we greet triumphant now;
Hail, the Resurrection thou!

C. Wesley

Rem Redemptor optime
gessit in certamine:
noster Sol renituit
nec cruentus occidit.

Quem sepulcro clauditis,
is erupit inferis.
Mors-ne tolli prohibet?
En! Elysium patet.

Rex est vitae redditus;
(ubi, mors, aculeus?)
qui salvavit homines;
num, Gehenna, victor es?

Christo tollimur duce:
is monstrator est viae;
quocum sumus homines
omnium participes.

Terrae Rex et aetheris
haud secus laudabilis,
salve nunc ovans; et O!
salve, Resurrectio!

MM 5—8.4.99

Loving Shepherd of thy sheep,	Pastor o gregis bone,
Keep thy lamb, in safety keep;	agnum tuum protege;
Nothing can thy power withstand,	omne vincere potes;
None can pluck me from thy hand.	tutum usque me tenes.

Loving Saviour, thou didst give
Thine own life that we might live,
And the hands outstretched to bless
Bear the cruel nails' impress.

Es, Salvator o bone,
nostra mortuus vice;
quas manus tendens beas,
crucis ostendunt notas.

I would praise thee every day,
Gladly all thy will obey,
Like thy blessed ones above
Happy in thy precious love.

Laudans, quot erunt dies,
paream quod imperes,
felix, par amante te
contioni superae.

Loving Shepherd, ever near,
Teach thy lamb thy voice to hear;
Suffer not my steps to stray
From the straight and narrow way.

Bone Pastor, es prope:
agnum fac audire te;
rectam neve ego viam
pravo pede deseram.

Where thou leadest I would go,
Walking in thy steps below,
Till before my Father's throne
I shall know as I am known.

Hoc in orbe te ducem
consecutus ambulem,
donec Patris ad thronum
noscam uti notus sum.

Jane.E.Leeson

MM 20—30.8.99

Master, speak! Thy servant heareth,
Waiting for thy gracious word,
Longing for the voice that cheereth;
Master, let it now be heard.
I am listening, Lord, for thee;
What hast thou to say to me?

Speak to me by name, O Master!
Let me know it is to me;
Speak, that I may follow faster,
With a step more firm and free,
Where the Shepherd leads the flock
In the shadow of the rock.

Master, speak! Though least and lowest,
Let me not unheard depart;
Master, speak! For O thou knowest
All the yearning of my heart;
Knowest all its truest need;
Speak, and make me blest indeed.

Master, speak! And make me ready,
When thy voice is truly heard,
With obedience glad and steady
Still to follow every word,
I am listening. Lord, to thee;
Master, speak, O speak to me!

F.R.Havergal

Dic, Magister, auscultanti
et manenti. servulo;
ista vox desideranti
audiatur ilico;
audituro te mihi
ecquid est quod vis loqui.

Sim, Magister, nominatus:
me vocari sic sciam;
citius sequar vocatus
gnaviusque semitam,
oves Pastor qua regit,
saxum quibus umbra sit.

Dic, licetque sim spernendus
hinc ne spretus iverim;
es, Magister, haud docendus
quid largiri te velim;
cordis haud ignarus es:
dic, ut maxime bees.

Dic, et redde me volentem
voce vere cognita
firmiter oboedientem
iussa facere omnia;
audienti te mihi
ne nolueris loqui.

MM 22.11—5.12.01

My God. accept my heart this day,
And make it always thine,
That I from thee no more may stray,
No more from thee decline.

Before the Cross of him who died,
Behold, I prostrate fall;
Let every sin be crucified,
And Christ be all in all.

Anoint me with thy heavenly grace,
And seal me for thine own;
That I may see thy glorious face,
And worship near thy throne.

Let every thought and work and word
to thee be ever given:
Then life shall be thy service, Lord,
And death the gate of heaven.

All glory to the Father be,
All glory to the Son,
All glory, Holy Ghost, to thee,
While endless ages run.

M. Bridges

Accipias tuumque cor
fac semper hoc, Deus,
hinc usque neu vitae tenor
sit a te devius.

Ad Crucem ecce! Mortui
prostratus corruo;
ubique Christus et mali
sit crucifixio.

Ungat me tua gratia,
signesque me tuum;
noscatur facies tua
colente me thronum.

Quod dicam, cogitem, geram,
id tibi dem, Deus;
sic vivus tibi serviam
et iungar mortuus.

Deo sit summa laus Patri,
laus summa Filio,
laus summa, Spiritus. tibi
exempta termino.

MM 2—9.8.01

My God, and is thy table spread,
And doth thy cup with love o'erflow?
Thither be all thy children led,
And let them all thy sweetness know.

Hail, sacred feast which Jesus makes,
Rich banquet of his Flesh and Blood!
Thrice happy he who here partakes
That sacred stream, that heavenly food.

Why are its bounties all in vain
Before unwilling hearts displayed?
Was not for them the Victim slain?
Are they forbid the children's Bread?

O let thy table honoured be,
And furnished well with joyful guests;
And may each soul salvation see,
That here its sacred pledges tastes.

P. Doddridge

Deus, mensam-ne praeparas,
amore poculum replens?
Ut illuc omnes dirigas
sapore cunctos attrahens!

Quam bene Jesus obtulit
cum carne sanguinem suum!
Beatus ille qui capit
hanc escam, hoc effluvium.

Haec tanta quare munera
monstrantur abnuentibus?
Pro his mactatur Hostia:
cenant-ne liberi secus?

Fac mensa laudetur tua
sodalibusque plena sit,
gustantibusque pignora
salvatio provenerit.

MM   5—10.10.97

My God, my Father, while I stray,
Far from my home, on life's rough way,
O teach me from my heart to say,
"Thy will be done!"

Though dark my path, and sad my lot,
Let me be still and murmur not,
Or breathe the prayer divinely taught,
"Thy will be done!"

What though in lonely grief I sigh
For friends beloved no longer nigh,
Submissive would I still reply,
"Thy will be done!"

If thou shouldst call me to resign
What I most prize, it ne'er was mine;
I only yield thee what is thine:
Thy will be done!

Let but my fainting heart be blest
With thy sweet Spirit for its guest,
My God, to thee I leave the rest:
Thy will be done!

Renew my will from day to day,
Blend it with thine, and take away
All that now makes it hard to say,
"Thy will be done!"

Charlotte Elliott

Deus Pater, vagantem me
procul per ardua viae
ex corde dicere doce
"Ut tu voles!"

Licet tenebris opprimar,
sim constans neve conquerar;
silens docente te loquar:
"Ut tu voles!"

Cum solitudinem gemam
tot comitumque absentiam,
summisse tum respondeam:
"Ut tu voles!"

Quod habeo carissimum
si poscis, haud erat meum;
cedo tibi quod est tuum,
ut tu voles.

Beato corde languido
dulci tuo Paraclito,
quod restat tibi dedico,
ut tu voles.

Mens mane nova congruat
menti tuae: fac pereat
 quodcumque dicere vetat
"Ut tu voles!"

MM 10—18.2.00

My God, my King, thy various praise
Shall fill the remnant of my days;
Thy grace employ my humble tongue,
Till death and glory raise the song.

Per quot manent mihi dies
tu laudem, Rex Deus, feres;
movebit linguam gratia,
elatus dum canam supra.

The wings of every hour shall bear
Some thankful tribute to thine ear,
And every setting sun shall see
New works of duty done for thee.

Grates, quot horae, quas agam
ascendent aurem ad tuam;
nec sol occluserit diem
quin opus tibi dedicem.

Thy truth and justice I'll proclaim;
Thy bounty flows, an endless stream;
Thy mercy swift, thine anger slow,
But dreadful to the stubborn foe.

Te verum iustum proferam
et largitatis copiam,
qui parcis quam furis prius,
es dirus obsistentibus.

But who can speak thy wondrous deeds?
Thy greatness all our thoughts exceeds;
Vast and unsearchable thy ways,
Vast and immortal be thy praise.

Sed miris es operibus
nec menti nostrae pervius;
vasta, haud scrutanda, quae facis
perpetuo laudabilis.

I. Watts

MM 3—13.8.00

My song is love unknown,
My Saviour's love for me,
Love to the loveless shown,
That they might lovely be.
O who am I,
That for my sake
My Lord should take
Frail flesh, and die?

Amavit me Deus
(est hoc meus canor),
ut non amantibus
incresceret amor.
Heu! quis ego,
sua nece
ut salvet me
factus caro?

He came from his blest throne,
Salvation to bestow;
But men made strange, and none
The longed-for Christ would know.
But O, my Friend,
My Friend indeed,
Who at my need
His life did spend!

Thronum reliquerat
salvare nos volens,
sperátus Christus, at
recognitu carens,
comes meus,
vitae suae
egente me
improvidus.

Sometimes they strew his way,	Vestem nunc ad pedes
And his sweet praises sing;	eunti cumulant
Resounding all the day	quam longa et est dies
Hosannas to their King.	"Hosanna" consonant;
Then "Crucify"	nunc "Ad crucem"
Is all their breath,	idem fremunt
And for his death	esse et volunt
They thirst and cry.	exanimem.

Why, what hath my Lord done?	Quid ille nocuit?
What makes this rage and spite?	Unde haec malitia?
He made the lame to run,	Currendo claudus it,
He gave the blind their sight.	sunt caeco lumina;
Sweet injuries!	quae dulcia
Yet they at these	parum iuvant,
Themselves displease,	et increpant
And 'gainst him rise.	quasi mala.

They rise, and needs will have	Cum eum increpent
My dear Lord made away;	mortemque cupiant,
A murderer they save,	sicario favent,
The Prince of Life they slay.	vivificum necant.
Yet cheerful he	Ad crucem is,
To suffering goes,	ut salvi sint
That he his foes	qui oderint,
From thence might free.	it hilaris.

In life, no house, no home	Dum vivit, is domum
My Lord on earth might have;	non ullam habitat,
In death, no friendly tomb	et mortuo locum
But what a stranger gave.	ignotus homo dat;
What may I say?	illi quidem
Heaven was his home;	supra est domus,
But mine the tomb	terrae datus
Wherein he lay.	ego forem.

Here might I stay and sing.	Hic diu canerem
No story so divine;	amorem, Rex, tuum
Never was love, dear King,	incomparabilem
Never was grief like thine!	et luctum unicum.
This is my Friend,	Amicus is
In whose sweet praise	mihi et comes
I all my days	quot sunt dies
could gladly spend. S. Crossman	laudabilis. MM 26.2-6.3.00

My soul, there is a country
Far beyond the stars,
Where stands a winged sentry
All skilful in the wars:

There above noise, and danger,
Sweet peace sits crowned with smiles,
And one born in a manger
Commands the beauteous files.

He is thy gracious friend,
And – O my soul, awake!
Did in pure love descend
To die here for thy sake.

If thou canst get but thither,
There grows the flower of peace,
The Rose that cannot wither,
Thy fortress and thy ease.

Leave then thy foolish ranges,
For none can thee secure
But one who never changes,
Thy God, thy life, thy cure.

H. Vaughan

Locum superstellarem
ut anima sciat!
Ibi ales militarem
rem doctus excubat;

ibi clamore ablato
renidet pax sedens,
et est praesepe nato
cohors oboediens.

Is comes tibi gratus,
neu te fefellerit,
tibi, anima, est necatus,
cum deorsum huc iit.

Ibi, illuc si mearis,
aeterna pax viret,
quae, Rosa castellaris,
labore te levet.

Desiste nunc vagari:
unus te sospitat
qui, nescius mutari,
salute te beat.

MM 10—20.8.99

My spirit longs for thee
Within my troubled breast,
Though I unworthy be
Of so divine a guest.

Of so divine a guest
unworthy though I be,
Yet has my heart no rest
Unless it come from thee.

Unless it come from thee,
In vain I look around;
In all that I can see
No rest is to be found.

No rest is to be found
But in thy blessed love:
O let my wish be crowned,
And send it from above!

J.Byrom

Ut desiderium
me distrahit Dei,
indignus ita sum
receptor Domini.

Receptor Domini
indignus ego sum;
nec habeo nisi
quod is dat otium.

Is ni dat otium,
fraudantur oculi,
nec usquam paululum
videtur otii.

Videtur otii
fons eius esse amor,
qui dum fluat mihi,
sum laeto laetior.

MM 21—24 Dec 96

New every morning is the love
Our wakening and uprising prove;
Through sleep and darkness safely brought,
Restored to life and power and thought.

New mercies, each returning day,
Hover around us while we pray;
New perils past, new sins forgiven,
New thoughts of God, new hopes of heaven.

If on our daily course our mind
Be set to hallow all we find,
New treasures still, of countless price,
God will provide for sacrifice.

The trivial round, the common task
Will furnish all we need to ask,
Room to deny ourselves, a road
To bring us daily nearer God.

Only, O Lord, in thy dear love
Fit us for perfect rest above;
And help us this and every day,
To live more nearly as we pray.

J.Keble

Dei, cum expergiscimur,
novatus amor noscitur
traiectis tuto tenebris,
vi, vita, mente redditis.

Adest orantibus nova
quotidie clementia;
culpaeque fit remissio
cum spe caelorum denuo.

Diurnis si concursibus
sancire cuncta volumus,
dabit Deus ditissimas
sibi offerendas hostias.

Parvum domesticumque opus:
est totum quod requirimus,
ubi abstinentes atque ubi
Deo fiamus obvii.

Dignos tu, Domine, modo
caelesti nos fac otio,
cotidieque adsuesce te
factis, ut prece, colere.

MM 14—19.9.00

Latinised Hymns

Now the green blade riseth from the buried grain,
Wheat that in the dark earth many days has lain;
Love lives again, that with the dead has been:
LOVE IS COME AGAIN, LIKE WHEAT THAT SPRINGETH GREEN.

In the grave they laid him, Love whom men had slain,
Thinking that never he would wake again.
Laid in the earth like grain that sleeps unseen:
Love is come again, like wheat that springeth green,

Forth he came at Easter, like the risen grain,
He that for three days in the grave had lain.
Quick from the dead my risen Lord is seen:
Love is come again, like wheat that springeth green.

When our hearts are wintry, grieving, or in pain,
Thy touch can call us back to life again;
Fields of our hearts that dead and bare have been:
LOVE IS COME AGAIN, LIKE WHEAT THAT SPRINGETH GREEN.

J.M.C.Crum

Surgit a sepulto spica semine,
sub terra quam tegebant tenebrae;
Amor revivit mortis e loco:
AMOR EN! REDIVIT SEGETIS MODO.

Sepeliverant occisurn homine,
quem non sperabant excitum fore:
par dormienti spicae sub solo,

Pascha vidit instar spicae surgere
post sepulturarn tertio die;
ex morte Christum ortum video:

Quando hiemales lugent animae,
vivificas nos tuo pollice;
sint corda nudo paria solo,
AMOR EN! REDIVIT SEGETIS MODO.

MM 11—17.5.01

Now the labourer's task is o'er,
Now the battle day is past;
Now upon the farther shore
Lands the voyager at list:
 Father, in thy gracious keeping
 Leave we now thy servant sleeping.

There the tears of earth are dried,
There its hidden things are clear;
There the work of life is tried
By a juster Judge than here:

There the sinful souls, that turn
To the Cross their dying eyes,
All the love of Christ shall learn
At his feet in Paradise:

There no more the powers of hell
Can prevail to mar their peace;
Christ the Lord shall guard them well,
He who died for their release:

'Earth to earth, and dust to dust,'
Calmly now the words we say,
Leaving him to sleep in trust
Till the resurrection-day:
 Father, in etc.

J.Ellerton

Nunc peractus est labor
et finita proelia,
ripa nunc ulterior
est petenti praebita:
scimus, Pater, te clementem;
hunc tuere dormientem.

Ibi cedunt lacrimae,
se celata detegunt;
iustiore iudice
facta iudicanda sunt:

Qui Crucem spectaverit
mortis in articulo
amor quid divinus sit
discet in elysio:

Ibi regis inferi
pax exempta viribus;
sunt in manu Domini
quos salvavit mortuus:

"Pulvis pulverem petit"
adfirmamus placidi
"dumque resurrexerit
dormit creditus tibi":
scimus, Pater, etc.

MM 8—11.3.98

Latinised Hymns

O day of rest and gladness,	*O dies gratiosa*
O day of joy and light,	*quietem adferens,*
O balm of care and sadness,	*decora, luminosa,*
Most beautiful, most bright,	*tristitiae medens,*
On thee the high and lowly	*cum imis qua praestantes*
Before the eternal throne	*adveniunt thronum*
Sing Holy, Holy, Holy,	*Ter Sanctum praedicantes*
To the great Three in One.	*Trinum et Unicum;*
On thee, at the creation,	*qua Deus imperavit*
The light first had its birth;	*"Sit lux" et lux fuit,*
On thee for our salvation	*et is qui nos salvavit*
Christ rose from depths of earth;	*barathro rediit;*
On thee our Lord victorious	*victoris ope Christi*
The Spirit sent from heaven;	*qua venit Spiritus:*
And thus on thee most glorious	*sic tu tribus luxisti*
A triple light was given.	*praeclara lucibus.*
Today on weary nations	*is manna fatigatis*
The heavenly manna falls,	*in gentibus pluit,*
To holy convocations	*et tuba convocatis*
The silver trumpet calls,	*argentea canit,*
Where Gospel-light is glowing	*lux ubi nuntiorum*
With pure and radiant beams,	*bonorum radiat*
And living water flowing	*et amnium vivorum*
With soul-refreshing streams.	*nos unda recreat.*
New graces ever gaining	*Nunc gratiam novamus*
From this our day of rest.,	*hoc nostro sabbato*
We reach the rest remaining	*ut propius eamus*
To spirits of the blest:	*sanctorum otio.*
To Holy Ghost be praises,	*Cum Patre Patre Nati*
To Father, and to Son;	*tuique, Spiritus,*
The Church her voice upraises	*sit laus, ut Trinitati*
To thee, blest Three in One.	*hic voces tollimus.*

Bp C. Wordsworth   *MM   16—24.12.00*

O Father, by whose sovereign sway
The sun and stars in order move,
Yet who hast made us bold to say
Thy nature and thy name is love:

O royal Son, whose every deed
Showed love and love's divinity,
Yet didst not scorn the humblest need
At Cana's feast in Galilee:

O Holy Spirit, who didst speak
In saint and sage since time began,
Yet givest courage to the weak
And teachest love to selfish man:

Be present in our hearts to-day,
All powerful to bless, and give
To these thy children grace that they
May love, and through their loving live.

C.A.Alington

O Pater, imperante quo
suus stellarum est tenor,
sed idem adsensu tuo
vocaris, id quod es, Amor:

rex Filius, quicquid facis,
curam divinam exhibes,
nec Galilaeis epulis
prodesse dedignatus es:

qui tot in aevis, Spiritus,
vatum per ora loqueris,
virtutem das imbellibus,
amare et alteros facis:

beatrix tota Trinitas,
adsis cum gratia beans
horum tuorum nuptias,
amore eos vivificans.

MM 1—6.5.98

O for a closer walk with God,
A calm and heavenly frame;
A light to shine upon the road
That leads me to the Lamb!

What peaceful hours I once enjoyed!
How sweet their memory still!
But they have left an aching void
The world can never fill.

Return, O holy Dove, return,
Sweet messenger of rest:
I hate the sins that made thee mourn,
And drove thee from my breast.

The dearest idol I have known,
Whate'er that idol be,
Help me to tear it from thy throne,
And worship only thee.

So shall my walk be close with God,
Calm and serene my frame;
So purer light shall mark the road
That leads me to the Lamb.

W.Cowper

*Ut vadam Deo propius,
et sit tranquilla mens;
sit et lucerna pedibus
ad Agnum me ferens.*

*Qua quondam pace fructus sum!
Memoria ut placet!
Nunc dolet eius spatium,
nec mundus id replet.*

*Iucunda nuntians redi★
Columba requiem:
invisa scelera mihi
fecere te exulem.*

*Me falso praeter te deo
si quando credidi,
fac istum deici throno
et solum te coli.*

*Sic vadam Deo propius,
erit tranquilla mens
et lux purgata nec minus
ad Agnum me ferens.*

MM 1—3.6.99

*★Quietem nuntians redi,
redi, Columba, quem
invisa scelera mihi
fecerunt exulem.*

O for a heart to praise my God,
A heart from sin set free;
A heart that's sprinkled with the blood
So freely shed for me:

A heart resigned, submissive, meek,
My great Redeemer's throne;
Where only Christ is heard to speak,
Where Jesus reigns alone:

A humble, lowly, contrite heart,
Believing, true and clean,
Which neither life nor death can part
From him him that dwells within:

A heart in every thought renewed,
And full of love divine;
Perfect and right and pure and good –
A copy, Lord, of thine!

Thy nature, gracious Lord, impart,
Come quickly from above;
Write thy new name upon my heart,
Thy new best name of Love.

C. Wesley

Sit aptum laudibus Dei
cor, culpa liberum,
effuso largiter mihi
cruore madidum;

aequum, submissum, audiens,
cui Jesus imperet,
qua Christus unus sit potens
nec alius sonet;

contritum cor et humile et
fide quod integra
nec mors nec vita dividet
ab eius incola;

cor, quicquid cogitet, novum,
divinitus amans,
nec ulla labe collitum,
tuum, Christe, imitans.

Fac qualis es, benigne, me;
huc properans eas;
signes tuo cor nomine,
quod audit "Caritas".

MM 2—10.5.00

O for a thousand tongues to sing	*Ut mille vocibus canam*
My dear Redeemer's praise,	*laudanda Domini*
The glories of my God and King,	*pronuntiando gloriam*
The triumphs of his grace!	*et gratiam Dei!*
Jesus! the name that charms our fears,	*Jesu! cum luctibus metus*
That bids our sorrows cease;	*hoc nomen dissipat;*
'Tis music in the sinner's ears,	*est melos peccatoribus,*
'Tis life and health and peace.	*vitam cum pace dat.*
He breaks the power of cancelled sin	*Insontem reddit is reum,*
He sets the prisoner free;	*captivum soluit;*
His blood can make the foulest clean	*purgat cruor foedissimum,*
His blood availed for me.	*nec mihi deficit.*
He speaks; and, listening to his voice,	*Jesu loquentis ad sonum*
New life the dead receive,	*vivunt exanimes;*
The mournful broken hearts rejoice,	*maestorum ecce gaudium*
The humble poor believe.	*et pauperum fides!*
Hear him, ye deaf; his praise, ye dumb,	*Audite, surdi, vos Deum,*
Your loosened tongues employ;	*tu, mute, eum canas;*
Ye blind, behold your saviour come;	*videte, caeci, Dominum,*
And leap, ye lame, for joy!	*tu, claude, salias;*
My gracious Master and my God,	*Intende vocem, Deus mi*
Assist me to proclaim	*et Domine, meam,*
And spread through all the earth abroad	*ut mira nominis tui*
The honours of thy name.	*ubique differam!*
C. Wesley	*MM 30.10—6.11.97*

O God of earth and altar,
Bow down and hear our cry,
Our earthly rulers falter,
Our people drift and die;
The walls of gold entomb us,
The swords of scorn divide,
Take not thy thunder from us,
But take away our pride.

From all that terror teaches,
From lies of tongue and pen,
From all the easy speeches
That comfort cruel men,
From sale and profanation
Of honour and the sword,
From sleep and from damnation,
Deliver us, good Lord!

Tie in a living tether
The prince and priest and thrall,
Bind all our lives together,
Smite us and save us all;
In ire and exultation
Aflame with faith and free,
Lift up a living nation,
A single sword to thee.

G.K. Chesterton

Cum   terra Deus arae,
adsis precantibus:
reges timent regnare,
marcetque populus;
thesauris coercemur,
fastu dissedimus:
tuus, ne gloriemur,
maneto tonitrus.

A minis aque pravis
sermone et calamo
et si sonat qua suavis
saevis oratio,
a vendito honore
et emptis ensibus
solvamur et sopore
et tartaro, Deus.

Ducem cum plebe iunctos
et flaminem liges
consociansque cunctos
caedendo sospites;
ira fideque ardentem,
ovantem, liberam
nos unam tolle gentem
ut aciem tuam.

MM 24—7.9.98

O God of grace, thy mercy send;
Let thy protecting arm defend;
Save us and keep us to the end:
Have mercy, Lord.

And through the coming hours of night
Fill us, we pray, with holy light;
Keep us all sinless in thy sight:
GRANT THIS, O LORD.

May some bright messenger abide
For ever by thy servants' side,
A faithful guardian and our guide:

From every sin in mercy free;
Let heart and conscience stainless be,
That we may live henceforth for thee:

We would not be by care opprest,
But in thy love and wisdom rest;
Give what thou seest to be the best:

While we of every sin repent,
Let our remaining years be spent
In holiness and sweet content:

And when the end of life is near,
May we, unshamed and void of fear,
Wait for the judgement to appear:
GRANT THIS, O LORD.

J. Brownlie (from Greek)

Solvamur gratia tua,
ferat munimen dextera,
protectionem usque da
et veniam.

Per imminentes tenebras
nos sanctae lucis impleas,
insontes et custodias:
HOC DES, DEUS.

Adsistat semper angelus
nobisque, qui tui sumus,
fideliter sit praevius:

Peccatis simus liberi,
nullius culpae conscii
et posthac tibi dediti:

Ne premat nos anxietas,
es sapiens et nos amas;
fac tu quod optimum scias:

Annorum nobis quod manet,
quos omnis culpae paenitet,
pax sanctitatis occupet:

Adstantes ultimum diem
ne pudeat habere spem,
dum maneamus iudicem:
HOC DES, DEUS.

MM   6—12.10.01

O God, our help in ages past,
Our hope for years to come,
Our shelter from the stormy blast,
And our eternal home;

Beneath the shadow of thy throne
Thy saints have dwelt secure;
Sufficient is thine arm alone,
And our defence is sure.

Before the hills in order steod,
Or earth received her frame,
From everlasting thou art God,
To endless years the same.

A thousand ages in thy sight
Are like an evening gone;
Short as the watch that ends the night
Before the rising sun.

Time, like an ever-rolling stream,
Bears all its sons away;
They fly forgotten, as a dream
Dies at the opening day.

O God, our help in ages past,
Our hope for years to come,
Be thou our guard while troubles last
And our eternal home.

I. Watts (P590)

Ut proavis refugium,
spes posteris, Deus,
diffractor nobis turbinum★
aeternaque domus;

tuo tegis sub solio
tu tibi deditos
valesque brachio tuo
ut tueare nos.

Dispostis nondum collibus
telluris aut bathris
ex infinito tu Deus
nec es mutabilis.

Ut pars diei saecula
sunt mille coram te,
ut ultima vigilia
venturo iubare.

Tempusque fluminis modo
quos gignit abripit:
pares fugantur somnio
cum nocte quod perit.

Ut proavis perfugium,
spes posteris, Deus,
tutela contra sis malum
aeternaque domus.

MM 11—15.5.98

★flaminibus obstaculum

O God, unseen yet ever near,
Thy presence may we feel;
And, thus inspired with holy fear,
Before thine altar kneel.

Here may thy faithful people know
The blessings of thy love,
The streams that through the desert flow,
The manna from above.

We come, obedient to thy word,
To feast on heavenly food;
Our meat the Body of the Lord,
Our drink his precious Blood.

Thus may we all thy word obey,
For we, O God, are thine;
And go rejoicing on our way,
Renewed with strength divine.

E. Osler

Non vise sed praesens Deus,
nobis cognoscere
arae genu flectentibus
humiliter tuae.

Fideles hic tui sciant
quae dederis fovens,
fontes deserta qui rigant
et manna depluens.

Tibi parentes adsumus
caeloque vescimur:
est Domini Caro cibus,
et Sanguis bibitur.

Oboedientes sic tibi
(sumus tui, Deus)
laeti pergamus et novi
divinis viribus.

MM 5—8.7.01

O help us, Lord! each hour of need
Thy heavenly succour give;
Help us in thought and word and deed
Each hour on earth we live.

O help us, when our spirits bleed
With contrite anguish sore;
And when our hearts are cold and dead,
O help us, Lord, the more.

O help us, through the power of faith
More firmly to believe;
For still the more thy servant hath,
The more shall he receive.

If strangers to thy fold we call
Imploring at thy feet
The crumbs that from thy table fall,
'Tis all we dare entreat.

But be it, Lord of Mercy, all,
So thou wilt grant but this:
The   crumbs that from thy table fall
Are light, and life, and bliss.

O help us, Jesu, from on high;
We know no help but thee:
O help us so to live and die
As thine in heaven to be.

H.H.Milman

Succurre nostris, O Deus,
quando necesse erit,
cum mente et voce manibus,
dum nobis vita sit.

Succurre diro vulneri
contriti pectoris;
sed cordium torpedini
succurrito magis.

Ut confidatur firmius,
succurre; nam tuis
donantur plus habentibus
et plura famulis.

Te nos oramus advenae
ut mendicantibus
fragmenta des dapis tuae;
nil ultra poscimus.

Nil ultra, dum tu hoc dabis
(nam clemens cor tuum)
fragmenta sint eius dapis
lux vita gaudium.

Succurre, Jesu, subveni
(num est ops alia?);
defuncti vita sic tui
vocabimur supra.

MM   2—11.2.02

O Holy Ghost, thy people bless	O Paraclete, faveas,
Who long to feel thy might,	vigensque concute;
And fain would grow in holiness	fac augeatur sanctitas,
As children of the light.	ut ortis lumine.

To thee we bring, who art the Lord,	Offerimus nos, Domine,
Our selves to be thy throne;	ut intra sedeas
Let every thought and deed and word	et mentem dicta factaque
Thy pure dominion own.	libentium regas.

Life-givng Spirit, o'er us move,	Incumbe nobis, Spiritus,
As on the formless deep;	ut pristinis aquis;
Give life and order, light and love,	da lucem dormientibus
Where now is death or sleep.	vitamque mortuis.

Great gift of our ascended King,	Monstretur Rex, qui te dedit,
His saving truth reveal;	veri pollicitor;
Our tongues inspire his praise to sing,	fac eius laus in ore sit
Our hearts his love to feel.	tangatque nos amor.

True wind of heaven, from south or north,	Fles, aura caeles, unde vis:
For joy or chastening, blow;	fove vel puriga;
The garden-spices shall spring forth	amoena, si tu iusseris,
If thou wilt bid them flow.	manabunt balsama

O Holy Ghost, of sevenfold might,	Septemplex, omnes, Spiritus,
All graces come from thee;	effundis gratias:
Grant us to know and serve aright	da cognitus regat Deus
One God in Persons three.	nos una Trinitas.

W.Baker	MM 9—15.5.01

O Jesu, blessed Lord, to thee	Ex corde tibi, Domine,
My heartfelt thanks for ever be,	meae debentur gratiae,
Who hast so lovingly bestowed	largito, quod acciperem,
On me thy Body and thy Blood.	tua cum carne sanguinem.

Break forth, my soul, for joy, and say,	Quin gloriaris, anime:
What wealth is come to me to-day!	"Ut sum ditatus hodie!"
My Saviour dwells within me now;	Locaris intra me, Deus.
"How blest am I! How good art thou!'	"Beatus ego! Tu bonus!"
T. Kingo/AJ.Mason	MM 18.5.98

O little town of Bethlehem,
How still we see thee lie!
Above thy deep and dreamless sleep
The silent stars go by:
Yet in thy dark streets shineth
The everlasting light;
The hopes and fears of all the years
Are met in thee to-night.

For Christ is born of Mary;
And, gathered all above,
While mortals sleep, the angels keep
Their watch of wondering love.
O morning stars, together
Proclaim the holy birth,
And praises sing to God the KIng,
And peace to men on earth.

How silently, how silently,
The wondrous gift is given!
So God imparts to human hearts
The blessings of his heaven.
No ear may hear his coming;
But in this world of sin,
Where meek souls will receive him, still
The dear Christ enters in.

O holy Child of Bethlehem,
Descend to us, we pray;
Cast out our sin, and enter in:
Be born in us to-day.
We hear the Christmas angels
The great glad tidings tell:
O come to us, abide with us,
Our Lord Emmanuel.

Bp Phillips Brooks

Immota, Bethlehem, iaces,
O urbs exigua;
tu dormis, et stellas movet
tranquilla vis supra:
opaca luxit in te
perpetuus dies;
quot spes bonae sunt aut malae
hac nocte tu tenes.

Nam Christum Virgo gignit,
infraque homines
cum dormiant, invigilant
Dei satellites.
Stellarum matutinus
partum canat chorus,
ut laus Deo sit Domino
et pax terrestribus.

Praebentur o quam tacite
miranda munera!
Sic cordibus nostris Deus
superna dat bona.
In mundum hunc scelestum
clam auribus venit,
et pervias in animas
parvorum Christus it.

O sancte Bethlehem Puer,
deorsum mitte te;
intransque nos fac integros;
in nobis nascere.
Est cantus angelorum
nostris in auribus:
O! nos pete nec desere,
Nobiscum tu Deus.

MM 24.12.99—3.1.00

O Lord my God! When I in awesome wonder
Consider all the works thy hand hath made,
I see the stars, I hear the mighty thunder,
Thy power throughout the universe displayed;
THEN SINGS MY SOUL, MY SAVIOUR GOD, TO THEE,
HOW GREAT THOU ART! HOW GREAT THOU ART!

When through the woods and forest glades I wander
And hear the birds sing sweetly in the trees;
When I look down from lofty mountain grandeur,
And hear the brook, and feel the gentle breeze;

And when I think that God his Son not sparing
Sent him to die – I scarce can take it in,
That on the Cross my burden gladly bearing
He bled and died to take away my sin:

When Christ shall come with shout of acclamation
And take me home – what joy shall fill my heart!
Then shall I bow in humble adoration
And there proclaim, my God, HOW GREAT THOU ART!

S.K. Hine (from Russian)

Ut me, Deus, stupefacis mirantem
tot creavisse dexteram tuam,
cum sidera tum tonitrum sonantem,
tuamque in omnibus potentiam,
SALVATOR, CANTAT ANIMA TIBI:
TU QUANTUS ES! TU QUANTUS ES!

Nemoribus et saltibus silvanis
cum dulce cantant volucres mihi,.
despicio vel arcibus montanis,
fons murmurat foventque zephyri;

Deum sciens non Filio parcentem
misisse (vix credetur) in Crucem
ibique eum peccata suggerentem,
ut solverer, fudisse sanguinem,

Quod gaudium, cum, Christe, conclamatus
domum me vocaturus venies!
Clamabo te cum Patre veneratus
humiliter "Deus, TU QUANTUS ES!"

MM 30.10 — 2.11.01

O Lord of Life, whose power sustains
The world unseen no less than this —
One family in him who reigns,
Triumphant over death, in bliss;
To thee with thankfulness we pray
For all our valiant dead today.

As nature's healing through the years
Reclothes the stricken battlefields;
So mercy gives us joy for tears,
And grief to proud remembrance yields,
And mindful hearts are glad to keep
A tryst of love with them that sleep.

Not names engraved in marble make
The best memorials of the dead,
But burdens shouldered for their sake
And tasks completed in their stead;
A braver faith and stronger prayers,
Devouter worship, nobler cares.

O help us in the silence, Lord,
To hear the whispered call of love,
And day by day thy strength afford
Our work to do, our faith to prove.
So be thy blessing richly shed
On our communion with our dead.

J.R.Darbyshire

O Vitae Domine Deus,
nos haud visosque sustinens
quos unum reddidit genus
Rex victa morte gestiens,
oramus te cum gratiis
pro nostris bene mortuis.

Ut agrum marte perditum
resumit postea seges,
mutamus fletu gaudium
pulso dolore memores,
amatis et concurrimus
laetantes dormientibus.

Inscripto marmore minus
memoriae consulitur
quam coepta si suscipimus
officioque fungimur;
crescat fides, sit prex potens,
et curet altiora mens.

Fac audiatur, Domine,
susurrans tacitis amor,
tuaque vi cotidie
fides probetur et labor;
beetur et nutu tuo
cum mortuis communio.

MM 20—26.1.01

O Lord of heaven and earth and sea,	*Totius mundi conditor,*
To thee all praise and glory be!	*sit laus tibi tibique honor;*
How shall we show our love to thee,	*sis nos (te) amare certior,*
Who givest all?	*qui cuncta das.*
The golden sunshine, vernal air,	*Flos, fructus, sol et zephyri*
Sweet flowers and fruit, thy love declare,	*probant nos a te diligi;*
When harvests ripen, thou art there,	*per te sunt fertiles agri,*
Who givest all.	*qui cuncta das.*
For peaceful homes, and healthful days,	*Et otium et sanitas,*
For all the blessings earth displays,	*terrestria quae commodas,*
We owe thee thankfulness and praise,	*cum laude poscunt gratias:*
Who givest all.	*tu cuncta das.*
Thou didst not spare thine only Son,	*Mundo daturus perdito*
But gav'st him for a world undone,	*non pepercisti Filio,*
And freely with that blessed One	*eoque cum sanctissimo*
Thou givest all.	*tu cuncta das.*
Thou giv'st the Holy Spirit's dower,	*Qui Paracletum dederis,*
Spirit of life and love and power,	*cui vita caritas et vis,*
And dost his sevenfold graces shower	*eiusdem gratias pluis*
Upon us all.	*cunctisque das.*
For souls redeemed, for sins forgiven,	*Redemptionem, veniarn,*
For means of grace and hopes of heaven,	*cum gratia spem ultimam,*
Father, what can to thee be given,	*aeterne tibi debitam,*
Who givest all?	*ut cuncta, das.*
We lose what on ourselves we spend,	*Quod nobis damus, pessum it;*
We have as treasure without end	*durans thesaurus id erit*
Whatever, Lord, to thee we lend,	*quod tibi commodatum sit,*
Who givest all;	*qui cuncta das;*
To thee, from whom we all derive	*tibi, unde venit omnibus*
Our life, our gifts, our power to give:	*quod ipsi dare possumus,*
O may we ever with thee live,	*vivamus tecum, O Deus,*
Who givest all.	*qui cuncta das.*
Bp Chr Wordsworth	*MM 30.8—9.14.01*

O Lord, to whom the spirits live
Of all the faithful passed away,
Unto their path that brightness give
Which shineth to the perfect day:
    O Lamb of God, Redeemer blest,
    Grant them eternal light and rest.

Bless thou the dead that die in thee:
As thou hast given them release,
So quicken them thy face to see,
And give them everlasting peace:
    O Lamb ...

Direct us with thine arm of might,
And bring us, perfected wth them,
To dwell within thy city bright,
The heavenly Jerusalem:
    O Lamb ...

R.F. Littledale

Cui defunctorum animae
non pereunt fideliurn,
eorum lumen da viae,
diem quod praebet integrum
    sit, Agne, eis (Redemptor es)
    aeterna lux et requies.

In te defunctos o bea;
ut liberasti vinculis,
visuros te vivifica;
fiatque longa pax eis:
    sit, Agne, ...

Factos cum eis integros
lacerto forti dirigas
splendentique urbe fige nos
Sion caelestis incolas.
    sit, Agne, ...

MM   24—5.11.99

O praise ye the Lord!	*Sit laus Domino!*
Praise him in the height;	*Audita supra*
Rejoice in his word,	*sint verba choro*
Ye angels of light;	*cum laetitia;*
Ye heavens adore him	*fer, aether, honorem,*
By whom ye were made,	*fer opifici,*
And worship before him,	*te flecte, nitorem*
In brightness arrayed.	*indutus, ei.*
O praise ye the Lord!	*Sit laus Domino*
Praise him upon earth,	*a terricolis,*
In tuneful accord,	*concordi choro,*
Ye sons of new birth;	*bis nunc genitis;*
Praise him who hath brought you	*laudate Datorem,*
His grace from above,	*qui larga tulit,*
Praise him who hath taught you	*et eius amorem,*
To sing of his love.	*ut is docuit.*
O praise ye the Lord,	*Sit laus Domino!*
All things that give sound;	*Quod sonum habet*
Each jubilant chord	*laetante globo*
Re-echo around;	*circa reboet;*
Loud organs, his glory	*sit tuba canora*
Forth tell in deep tone,	*lyraeque modi,*
And, sweet harp, the story	*ut nota decora*
Of what he hath done.	*sint facta Dci.*
O praise ye the Lord!	*Sit laus Domino!*
Thanksgiving and song	*Cum carminibus*
To him be outpoured	*per saecla Deo*
All ages along;	*grates agimus;*
For love in creation,	*salute beanti*
For heaven restored,	*caeloque novo,*
For grace of salvation,	*amanti, creanti*
O praise ye the Lord!	*sit laus Domino!*
H.W. Baker (Psl50)	*MM 14—20.2.99*

O sorrow deep!	Quis non gemit?
Who would not weep	Cui non iit
With heartfelt pain and sighing?	e pectore singultus?
God the Father's only Son	Unus Patre Genitus
In the tomb is lying.	iacet en! sepultus.

O Jesus. blest,	Jesu, comes
My help and rest,	et requies
With tears I pray thee, hear me:	subvenias dolenti:
Now, and even unto death,	prope vivo sis mihi,
Dearest Lord, be near me.	prope morienti.

J. Rist/W. Douglas   *MM Easter Eve 1999 (3.4.99)*

O thou, from whom all goodness flows,	Fons bonitatis, petii
I lift my heart to thee;	sublato corde te;
In all my sorrows, conflicts, woes,	sollicitati tu mei
Good Lord, remember me.	memento, Domine..

When on my aching burdened heart	Cum cor gravante scelerum
My sins lie heavily,	prematur pondere,
Thy pardon grant, thy peace impart:	dare clementer otium
Good Lord, remember me.	memento, Domine.

When trials sore obstruct my way,	Cum impeditus ego sim
And ills I cannot flee,	nec possim fugere,
Then let my strength be as my day:	aeques meam diei vim:
Good Lord, remember me.	memento, Domine.

If worn with pain, disease, and grief	Dolore cum tristitia
This feeble spirit be,	aegrum terente me
Grant patience, rest, and kind relief:	fac patientem et leva:
Good Lord, remember me.	memento, Domine.

And O, when in the hour of death	Cum mortis in articulo
I bow to thy decree,	cedam iubente te,
Jesu, receive my parting breath:	suscipere me gremio
Good Lord, remember me.	memento, Domine.

T.Haweis   *MM 21—3.4.00*

O thou who camest from above
The fire celestial to impart,
Kindle a flame of sacred love
On the mean altar of my heart.

There let it for thy glory burn
With inextinguishable blaze,
And trembling to its source return
In humble prayer and fervent praise.

Jesus, confirm my heart's desire
To work and speak and think for thee;
Still let me guard the holy fire
And still stir up the gift in me.

Still let me prove thy perfect will,
My acts of faith and love repeat;
Till death thy endless mercies seal,
And make the sacrifice complete.

C. Wesley

Illuminator mentium.
tibi, caelestis ignifer,
sit ara vile cor meum,
flammaque amoris occuper.

Ibi perpetuo nitens
nec exstinguenda luceat,
versusque originem tremens
preces cum laudibus vehat.

Firmes, ut mente te libens
et voce cum factis colam,
in corde scintillam tuens,
quam dator excites datam;

Testisque gratiae tuae,
cum plura fecerim bona,
(quod ultimum clementiae)
sim morte totus hostia.

MM 27—29.5.97

O valiant hearts, who to your glory came
Through dust of conflict and through battle flame;
Tranquil you lie, your knightly virtue proved,
Your memory hallowed in the land you loved.

Proudly you gathered, rank on rank, to war,
As who had heard God's message from afar;
All you had hoped for, all you had, you gave
To save mankind - yourselves you scorned to save.

Splendid you passed, the great surrender made,
Into the light that never more shall fade;
Deep your contentment in that blest abode,
Who wait the last clear trumpet-call of God.

Long years ago, as earth lay dark and still,
Rose a loud cry upon a lonely hill,
While in the frailty of our human clay
Christ, our Redeemer, passed the self-same way.

Still stands his Cross from that dread hour to this,
Like some bright star above the dark abyss;
Still, through the veil, the Victor's pitying eyes
Look down to bless our lesser Calvaries.

These were his servants, in his steps they trod,
Following through death the martyred Son of God:
Victor he rose; victorious too shall rise
They who have drunk his cup of sacrifice.

O risen Lord, O Shepherd of our dead,
Whose Cross has bought them and whose staff has led,
In glorious hope their proud and sorrowing land
Commits her children to thy gracious hand.

J.S.Arkwright

Virtute nacti claritudinem
pugnae per ignem atque pulverem,
o patriae probati milites,
est parta vobis digna requies.

Densastis agmen, ut in proelium
vocantem audientes Dominum.
Rem spemque proiecistis, populi
salutis ante vestram cupidi.

Ergo devotis lumen nituit,
nec est quod illud obscuraverit;
quo quam contenti nunc recumbitis
postremis responsuri lituis!

Meridiana fuit olim nox,
ubi est audita in colle magna vox:
tum, corpus quale nostra corpora,
eadem Christus ibat hac via.

Nec nunc minus Crux ea firma stat
stellaeque noctem more illuminat,
unde ille Victor, ut per nebulas
videns, beat minores Golgothas.

Hunc hi secuti pone dominum
mactatum morte Dei Filium,
Ut vicit hic, victores sunt et hi,
qui gustaverunt eius poculi.

Nostrorum Christe mortuorum dux
et pastor, hos redemit tua Crux,
quos, ut dolendos grande sic decus,
cum spe tuendos tibi tradimus.

MM   2—15.6.98

O worship the King all glorious above;
O gratefully sing his power and his love;
Our Shield and Defender, the Ancient of Days,
Pavilioned in splendour and girded with praise.

O tell of his might, O sing of his grace,
Whose robe is the light, whose canopy space;
His chariots of wrath the deep thunder clouds form,
And dark is his path on the wings of the storm.

The earth with its store of wonders untold,
Almighty, thy power hath founded of old;
Hath stablished it fast by a changeless decree,
And round it hath cast, like a mantle, the sea.

Thy bountiful care what tongue can recite?
It breathes in the air, it shines in the light;
It streams from the hills, it descends to the plain,
And sweetly distils in the dew and the rain.

Frail children of dust, and feeble as frail,
In thee do we trust, nor find thee to fail;
Thy mercies how tender, how firm to the end!
Our Maker, Defender, Redeemer, and Friend.

O measureless Might, ineffable Love,
While angels delight to hymn thee above,
Thy ransomed creation, though feeble their lays,
With true adoration shall sing to thy praise.

R. Grant (Ps.104)

Superna regens, laudare, Deus,
amore potens, quem nunc canimus,
ut parmula tutus, aetate vetus,
splendorem indutus et omne decus.

Tua inclyta vis et gratia sit:
cinctum radiis te inane capit,
vehuntque tonantem, irate, rotae,
et ante volantem eunt tenebrae.

Terraeque manu, o omnipotens,
fundamina tu locasti valens,
quam lege premis stabilem stabili
circumque venis, uti veste, mari.

Tuam quis opem, quae lingua, canat?
Nitens hilarem per aera flat;
ad infima vallis e collibus it,
ut ros pluvialis in imbre cadit.

Gens cineribus nata et fragiles,
te respicimus nec debilis es;
ut bona dedisti, sic et bona das:
creasti, tulisti, defendis, amas.

O splendida vis, mirandus amor!
Tibi a superis cum detur honor,
plebs, voce beata minore licet,
a te fabricata redempta canet.

MM 19—29.8.98

O worship the Lord in the beauty of holiness!
Bow down before him, his glory proclaim;
With gold of obedience, and incense of lowliness,
Kneel and adore him: the Lord is his name.

Low at his feet lay thy burden of carefulness:
High on his heart he will bear it for thee,
Comfort thy sorrows, and answer thy prayerfulness,
Guiding thy steps as may best for thee be.

Fear not to enter his courts in the slenderness
Of the poor wealth thou wouldst reckon as thine:
Truth in its beauty, and love in its tenderness,
These are the offerings to lay on his shrine.

These, though we bring them in trembling and fearfulness,
He will accept for the name that is dear;
Mornings of joy give for evenings of tearfulness,
Trust for our trembling and hope for our fear.

J.S.B. Monsell

Sit pulchra tua erga Deum reverentia;
eius acclinis edice decus;
sint aurum obsequia, tus patientia;
flecte genu: cluet is Dominus.

Ante pedes iacias onerantia:
ille onera omnia corde feret,
audierit tua verba precantia,
leniet acre, pedesque reget.

Eius ab aede ne pellat egentia
nec quod opes tibi deficiunt:
veritas atque ibi benevolentia
alma probabile munus erunt.

Pectore quod trepidante dicabitur
nomine quo datur excipiet;
nox lacrimosa die superabitur,
spesque metum procul hinc abiget.

MM 6—10.1.99

Oft in danger, oft in woe,
onward, Christian, onward go:
bear the toil, maintain the strife,
strengthened with the Bread of Life.

Onward Christians, onward go,
join the war and face the foe;
will ye flee in danger's hour?
Know ye not your Captain's power?

Let not sorrow dim your eye,
soon shall every tear be dry;
let not fears your course impede,
great your strength, if great your need.

Let your drooping hearts be glad:
march in heavenly armor clad:
fight, nor think the battle long,
victory soon shall be your song.

Onward then in battle move,
more than conquerors ye shall prove;
though opposed by many a foe,
Christian soldiers, onward go.

D. Kirke White

Per pericula viae,
Christiani, pergite;
Vitae Panis ea vis:
proelio sufficitis.

Christiani, pergite;
sitis in certamine
contra minas strenui;
num diffiditis Duci?

Ne dolete languidi;
arma ferte Domini;
an piget certaminis?
Eia! mox ovabitis.

Luctui ne cedite:
mox tollentur lacrimae;
neu retardet vos timor:
vi-ne eges? fis fortior.

Eia! pergite; magis
quam victores eritis;
hostes sint innumeri,
perge, legio Dei!

MM 19—21.4.99

Once in royal David's city
Stood a lowly cattle shed,
Where a mother laid her baby
In a manger for his bed:
Mary was that mother mild,
Jesus Christ her little child.

He came down to earth from heaven
Who is God and Lord of all,
And his shelter was a stable,
And his cradle was a stall;
With the poor and mean and lowly
Lived on earth our Saviour holy.

And through all his wondrous childhood
He would honour and obey,
Love and watch the lowly maiden,
In whose gentle arms he lay:
Christian children all must be
Mild, obedient, good as he.

For he is our childhood's pattern,
Day by day like us he grew,
He was little, weak and helpless,
Tears and smiles like us he knew;
And he feeleth for our sadness,
And he shareth in our gladness.

And our eyes at last shall see him,
Through his own redeeming love,
For that Child so dear and gentle
Is our Lord in heaven above;
And he leads his children on
To the place where he is gone.

Not in that poor lowly stable,
With the oxen standing by,
We shall see him; but in heaven,
Set at God's right hand on high;
Where like stars his children crowned
All in white shall stand around.

C.F. Alexander

---

*Fuit urbe David olim
haud insigne stabulum;
in praesepio locavit
mater ibi filium;
mater Maria fuit,
Jesus is quem peperit.*

*Coram nobis qui descendit
Deus atque Dominus,
subter tegmine bovino
super faenum positus,
fuit noster is Salvator
inter imos habitator.*

*Virgini mirandus infans,
gremio quem sustulit,
studiose veneratus,
diligenter paruit:
pari mansuetudine.
nos decebit degere.*

*Nobis enim exemplaris
crevit nostri similis;
parvus, impotens, imbellis
risit atque flevit is;
particeps fit nostri fletus
cum laetemur ipse laetus.*

*Eum, quos amans redemit,
denique videbimus,
puer enim ille lenis
est in caelo Dominus;
qui familiam agit
ipse quo praeiverit.*

*Nec cum bubus habitantem
turpiter in stabulo
sed videbimus regentem
de superno solio,
circum quem sideribus
similes nitebimus.*

MM 10—26.12.01

Once, only once, and once for all,
His precious life he gave;
Before the Cross our spirits fall,
And own it strong to save.

One Offering, single and complete,"
With lips and heart we say;
But what he never can repeat
He shows forth day by day.

For, as the priest of Aaron's line
Within the Holiest stood,
And sprinkled all the mercy-shrine
With sacrificial blood;

So he who once atonement wrought,
Our Priest of endless power,
presents himself for those he bought
In that dark noontide hour.

His Manhood pleads where now it lives
On heaven's eternal throne,
And where in mystic rite he gives
Its Presence to his own.

And so we show thy Death, O Lord,
Till thou again appear;
And feel, when we approach thy board,
We have an altar here.

All glory to the Father be,
All glory to the Son,
All glory, Holy Ghost, to thee,
While endless ages run.

W. Bright

*Semel, semel nec saepius
vitam dedit suam;
crucem prostrati colimus
ut salutiferam.*

*"Semel se totum obtulit"
ex corde dicimus;
et iterare quod nequit
diurnum fit opus.*

*Ut pontifex Leviticus
in adyto stetit,
et victimarum haustibus
sacellum maduit,*

*sic nos aeternus antistes
piator vindicat,
quos emit cum meridies
opertus fuerat.*

*Humanus is supra sedens
ibi intercessor fit,
et hic mysterium gerens
praesentem se facit.*

*Praestamus hostiam Deum
donec revenerit,
et eius hic triclinium
altare nobis fit.*

*Sit nunc ubique Filio
cum Patre gloria,
sit gloria Paraclito
nunc et per saecula.*

MM 7—18.8.97

Onward Christian soldiers!
Marching as to war,
With the Cross of Jesus
Going on before.
Christ the royal Master
Leads against the foe;
Forward into battle,
See, his banners go!

At the sign of triumph
Satan's host doth flee;
On then, Christian soldiers,
On to victory!
Hell's foundations quiver
At the shout of praise;
Brothers, lift your voices,
Loud your anthems raise.

Like a mighty army
Moves the Church of God;
Brothers, we are treading
Where the saints have trod:
We are not divided,
All one body we,
One in hope and doctrine,
One in charity.

Crowns and thrones may perish,
Kingdoms rise and wane,
But the Church of Jesus
Constant will remain:
Gates of hell can never
'Gainst that Church prevail;
We have Christ's own promise,
And that cannot fail.

Onward, then, ye people,
Join our happy throng,
Blend with ours your voices
In the triumph song:
Glory, laud and honour
Unto Christ the King,
This through countless ages
Men and angels sing.

S. Baring-Gould

Latinised Hymns

Ite, Christiani,
ut ad proelium,
Dominum sequentes
et Patibulum.
Contra Christus hostem
arma Rex gerit,
atque pugnaturus
signa corripit.

Fugit hunc triumphum
turba Satanae.
Ite, Christiani!
Ite et vincite!
Laus sonat, et ima
Tartari timent;
voces effundantur,
hymni reboent.

Agmen ecce! magnum
it Ecclesia;
sequimur sanctorum
nos itinera.
Non dissociamur;
sumus unum vas:
una spes, doctrina,
una caritas.

Brevia regnorum
mundi tempora;
usque duratura
est Ecclesia.
Contra quam inferni
porta non valet;
sponsor ipse Christus:
haud deficiet.

Addat se cohorti
laetae populus
concinatque nobis
triumphantibus.
"Laus, decus et honor
Christo Regi sit!"
cantus angelorum
hominumque erit.

MM 5—12.6.00

201

Our blest Redeemer, ere he breathed
his tender last farewell,
a Guide, a Comforter, bequeathed
with us to dwell.

He came sweet influence to impart,
a gracious, willing Guest,
while he can find one humble heart
wherein to rest.

And his that gentle voice we hear,
soft as the breath of even,
that checks each fault, that calms each fear,
and speaks of heaven.

And every virtue we possess,
and every conquest won,
and every thought of holiness,
are his alone.

Spirit of purity and grace,
our weakness, pitying, see:
O make our hearts thy dwelling place
and worthier thee.

H. Auber

Nobis beatus antequam
Redemptor abiit
Paraclitum et accolam
imposuit.

Est hospes almus animae;
qui nobis dulce flet,
in humili dum pectore
se collocet.

Is vesperi suspirio
similiter sonat;
pulsis timore et vitio,
supra vocat.

Eius, quod sanxit animas,
et quicquid vicimus,
et mente si qua sanctitas,
sunt unius.

O castae Flatus gratiae,
ignosce imbellibus,
ut captent corda nostra te
decentius.

MM 18-23 May 99

Our day of praise is done;
The evening shadows fall;
But pass not from us with the sun,
True Light that lightenest all.

Around the throne on high,
Where night can never be,
The white-robed harpers of the sky
Bring ceaseless hymns to thee.

Too faint our anthems here;
Too soon of praise we tire:
But O the strains how full and clear
Of that eternal choir!

Yet, Lord, to thy dear will
If thou attune the heart,
We in thine angels' music still
May bear our lower part.

'Tis thine each soul to calm,
Each wayward thought reclaim,
And make our life a daily psalm
Of glory to thy name.

A little while, and then
Shall come the glorious end;
And songs of angels and of men
In perfect praise shall blend.

J. Ellerton

Sub noctis tenebras
laudem confecimus:
ne tu cum sole lateas,
qui luces omnibus.

Tenebrae non erunt
ubi altus tu sedes
et candidati te canunt
usque fidicines.

Nos aegre canimus
(laudandi mox piget),
caelestis ille sed chorus
mirandum(st) ut sonet.

Sed corda, Domine,
si modulaberis,
voces licet subiungere
nostras angelicis.

Pacatas animas
in via rexeris,
vitamque psalma facias
decusque nominis.

Condentur saecula,
citoque tempus it,
commixta cum angelica
et nostra laus erit.

MM 19—22.7.00

Our Lord, his passion ended,
hath gloriously ascended,
yet though from him divided,
he leaves us not unguided;
all his benefits to crown
he hath sent his Spirit down,
burning like a flame of fire
his disciples to inspire.

God's Spirit is directing;
no more they sit expecting;
but forth to all the nation
they go with exultation;
that which God in them hath wrought
fills their life and soul and thought;
so their witness now can do
work as great in others too.

The centuries go gliding,
but still we have abiding
with us that Spirit Holy
to make us brave and lowly –
lowly, for we feel our need:
God alone is strong indeed;
brave, for with the Spirit's aid
we can venture unafraid.

O Lord of every nation,
fill us with inspiration!
We know our own unfitness,
yet for thee would bear witness.
By thy Spirit now we raise
to the heavenly Father praise:
Holy Spirit, Father, Son,
Make us know thee, ever One.

C. Burkitt

Iam Christus ab infernis
est redditus supernis,
nec eum nos videmus,
sed duce non caremus;
quippe donum ultimum
deorsum misit Spiritum,
flammae more qui suos
ureret discipulos.

Iam non opperiuntur,
sed Spiritu reguntur;
per populum vagantes
feruntur exsultantes,
plenis eo quod Deus
fecit intra cordibus;
nec minus quam passi sunt
testes ipsi faciunt.

Habemus hunc durantem
et saecla permeantem,
ut idem summittentes
fiamus et valentes:
quippe sumus pauperes
praeque Deo humiles,
idem omne possumus,
adiuvat si Spiritus.

Qui regis omnes gentes,
nostras inspira mentes;
nos male dignos scimus,
qui testes tibi simus;
sed (nam pellit Spiritus)
Patrem nunc extollimus;
unum usque, Trinitas,
nos te scire facias.

MM 4—8.6.01

Our Lord is risen from the dead;
Our Jesus is gone up on high;
The powers of hell are captive led,
Dragged to the portals of the sky.

There his triumphant chariot waits,
And angels chant the solemn lay:
Lift up your heads, ye heavenly gates;
Ye everlasting doors, give way.

Loose all your bars of massy light,
And wide unfold the ethereal scene:
He claims these mansions as his right:
Receive the King of Glory in.

Who is this King of Glory? Who?
The Lord that all our foes o'ercame,
The world, sin, death and hell o'erthrew:
And Jesus is the Conqueror's name.

C. Wesley

Surrexit Orco Dominus;
elatus Jesus est supra;
it vinctus inferum chorus
et tractus est sub aethera.

Victrices exspectant rotae,
en! angelorum cantica:
Caelorum porta, pandere!
Aeterna cede ianua!

Ut aether hic appareat,
laxate claustra luminis,
et Rex introrsus veniat;
hic iure enim locatur is.

Scitisne Rex quis ille sit?
Nostrorum victor hostium:
is dira cuncta subdidit;
Jesumque nominant eum.

MM   10—14.6.00

Out of the deep I call
To thee, O Lord, to thee:
Before thy throne of grace I fall:
Be merciful to me.

Out of the deep I cry,
The woeful deep of sin,
Of evil done in days gone by,
Of evil now within.

Out of the deep of fear,
And dread of coming shame,
From morning watch till night is near
I plead the precious name.

Lord, there is mercy now,
As ever was, with thee;
Before thy throne of grace I bow:
Be merciful to me.

H.W. Baker (Ps 130)

Ex imo gurgite
clamo, Deus, tibi
ad gratiae thronum tuae:
misereat mei.

Accipias sonum
e gurgite mali
(ut anteactorum scelerum
ita intus nunc novi).

E gurgite (metum
pudoris sentio),
dies quam longa, titulum
Salvantis invoco.

Inest, ut antea,
clementia tibi;
subiectum me throno nota:
misereat mei.

MM 6—13.11.99

Palms of glory, raiment bright,
Crowns that never fade away,
Gird and deck the sons of light:
Priests and kings and conquerors they.

Yet the conquerors bring their palms
To the Lamb amidst the throne,
And proclaim in joyful psalms
Victory through his Cross alone.

Kings for harps their crowns resign,
Crying, as they strike the chords,
"Take the Kingdom, it is thine,
King of Kings and Lord of Lords."

Round the altar priests confess,
If their robes are white as snow,
'Twas the Saviour's righteousness,
And his Blood, that made them so.

They were mortal too like us:
0, when we like them must die,
May our souls translated thus
Triumph, reign, and shine on high.

J.Montgomery

Vestis et palmae nitent
neque marcent apices,
luminosi quos habent
victor princeps antistes.

Ad pedes Agni suam
palmam victor proicit
unicaeque debitam
gloriam Cruci canit.

Positis apicibus
tractant principes lyras:
"Dominorum Dominus,
Regum" clamant "Rex regas!"

Antistes aras prope
factam esse niveam
Salvatoris sanguine
stolam indicat suam.

Nos, ut haud eis minus
moriemur, mortui
supra triumphantibus
splendeamus additi.

MM 17—21.6.97

Peace, perfect peace, in this dark world of sin?
The blood of Jesus whispers peace within.

Peace, perfect peace, by thronging duties pressed?
To do the will of Jesus, this is rest.

Peace, perfect peace, with sorrows surging round?
In Jesus' presence nought but calm is found.

Peace, perfect peace, with loved ones far away?
In Jesus' keeping we are safe, and they.

Peace, perfect peace, our future all unknown?
Jesus we know, and he is on the throne.

Peace, perfect peace, death shadowing us and ours?
Jesus has vanquished death and all its powers.

It is enough: earth's struggles soon shall cease,
And Jesus call us to heaven's perfect peace.

E.H.Bickersteth

Quae pura pax hic ubi tenebrae?
Jesus dat intus fuso sanguine.

Quae pura pax in tot officiis?
Fac Christi iussa: sic quieveris.

Quae pura pax, cum luctu cingimur?
Pax coram Jesu numquam rumpitur.

Quae pura caris pax absentibus?
Cum Jesu tuti pariter sumus.

Quae pura pax, futurum si latet?
At supra Jesus haud latens sedet.

Quae pura pax sub mortis nubibus?
Est mors potens, sed vicit Dominus.

Sat est: mox aberunt certamina
Jesu vocante longa ad otia.

MM 26.12.01-12.1.02

Pleasant are thy courts above
in the land of light and love;
pleasant are thy courts below
in this land of sin and woe:
O my spirit longs and faints
for the converse of thy saints,
for the brightness of thy face,
for thy fullness, God of grace.

Happy birds that sing and fly
round thy altars, O Most High;
happier souls that find a rest
in a heavenly Father's breast:
like the wandering dove, that found
no repose on earth around,
they can to their ark repair,
and enjoy it ever there.

Happy souls, their praises flow
even in this vale of woe;
waters in the desert rise,
manna feeds them from the skies;
on they go from strength to strength,
till they reach thy throne at length,
at thy feet adoring fall,
who hast led them safe through all.

Lord, be mine this prize to win,
guide me through a world of sin,
keep me by thy saving grace,
give me at thy side a place;
Sun and Shield alike thou art,
guide and guard my erring heart;
grace and glory flow from thee;
shower, O shower then, Lord, on me.

H.F.Lyte

Dulcis aula quae supra
est amore lucida;
nec terrestris haec minus,
ubi maeror et scelus.
Quantum placeat mihi
sanctis cum tuis loqui,
tuam nosse faciem
atque plenitudinem.

Alites beatae sunt
aram quae tuam colunt;
laetiores animae
tuo fultae pectore;
quae, palumbi similes,
nulla cui circum quies,
arcam quotiens petunt,
ibi tutae dormiunt.

Etsi luctus hic premit,
usque earum laus fluit;
umor fit in arido,
Manna funditur cibo.
Roboratae prodeunt,
dum te coram veniunt,
quem salutant humiles,
quod tulisti sospites.

Hoc nacturus praemium
ducar orbem per malum;
gratia fove tua,
teque iuxta sedem da.
Sol salusque tu: vagum
rege, tege cor meum.
Lucis fons et gratiae,
sparge utramque super me.

MM 11—15.6.97

Praise, my soul, the King of heaven,
To his feet thy tribute bring;
Ransomed, healed, restored, forgiven,
Who like me his praise should sing?
(Alleluia!)
Praise the everlasting King.

Praise him for his grace and favour
To our fathers in distress;
Praise him still the same for ever,
Slow to chide and swift to bless:
Glorious in his faithfulness.

Father-like, he tends and spares us,
Well our feeble frame he knows;
In his hands he gently bears us,
Rescues us from all our foes:
Widely as his mercy flows.

Angels, help us to adore him;
Ye behold him face to face;
Sun and moon, bow down before him,
Dwellers all in time and space:
Praise with us the God of grace.

H.F. Lyte

Sit caelorum Rex laudatus
cor tributum afferat
lotus, emptus, recreatus,
quis ut ego hunc canat?
"Alleluia! Alleluia!"
Rex aeternus audiat.

Esto laus ei qui favit
pressis ohm patribus;
cito neminem culpavit
nobis pariter bonus:
Quantum fidei decus!

More nos paterno curat:
nempe infirmos esse scit;
nos adversus hostes durat,
portaturus nos subit:
Late lenitas fluit.

Vos nobiscum adorate,
quem videtis, angeli,
una, sol, et vos laudate,
ubicumque positi:
Deum veneramini.

MM 7—12.2.00

Praise, O praise our God and King;	*Rex laudandus est Deus;*
Hymns of adoration sing:	*adorate cantibus:*
For his mercies still endure	*bonitas perpetua*
Ever faithful, ever sure.	*eius neque dubia.*
Praise him that he made the sun	*Quo iubente sol suam*
Day by day his course to run:	*it cotidie viam:*
And the silver moon by night,	*Atque lunae mollior*
Shining with her gentle light:	*noctu cernitur nitor*
Praise him that he gave the rain	*Is laudetur quod pluit*
To mature the swelling grain:	*seges ut matura sit:*
And hath bid the fruitful field	*iussit agrum fertilem*
Crops of precious increase yield:	*dare fructum divitem:*
Praise him for our harvest-store;	*Habeamus gratias*
He hath filled the garner-floor:	*plenas propter areas:*
And for richer food than this,	*Datque maius aliquid:*
Pledge of everlasting bliss:	*Paradisi pignus id:*
Glory to our bounteous King:	*Salutemus, quot sumus,*
Glory let creation sing:	*Creatorem cantibus:*
Glory to the Father, Son,	*salutetur ille Rex*
And blest Spirit, Three in One.	*noster Unus et Triplex.*
H.W. Baker	*MM 21—24.3.01*

Praise the Lord! ye heavens adore him;
praise him, angels, in the height;
sun and moon, rejoice before him;
praise him, all ye stars of light.
Praise the Lord! for he hath spoken;
worlds his mighty voice obeyed;
laws which never shall be broken
for their guidance he hath made.

Praise the Lord! for he is glorious;
never shall his promise fail;
God hath made his saints victorious;
sin and death shall not prevail.
Praise the God of our salvation!
Hosts on high, his power proclaim;
heaven and earth, and all creation,
laud and magnify his Name.

Anon. (Ps.148)

Laudet exaltata Deum
angelorum curia,
neve taceatis eum,
luna sol et sidera.
Celebrate quem locutum
audiere saecula,
quo perenne ius statutum
diriget vestigia.

Deo fida pollicenti
laus et esto gloria,
sanctos suos promoventi
cohibenti Tartara.
Deus alte, qui servavit,
praedicetur validus,
et laudetur, quod creavit,
firmamento Dominus.

MM Oct 96

Praise to the Lord, the Almighty, the King of creation!
O my soul, praise him, for he is thy health and salvation!
All ye who hear,
now to his temple draw near;
praise him in glad adoration.

Praise to the Lord, who over all things so wondrously reigneth,
shelters thee under his wings, yea, so gently sustaineth!
Hast thou not seen
all that is needful hath been
granted in what he ordaineth?

Praise to the Lord, who doth prosper thy work and defend thee;
surely his goodness and mercy here daily attend thee.
Ponder anew
what the Almighty can do,
if with his love he befriend thee.

Praise to the Lord, O let all that is in me adore him!
All that hath life and breath, come now with praises before him.
Let the amen
sound from his people again,
gladly for aye we adore him.

Neander/Catherine Winkworth

O veneremur Artificem omnipotentem,
anima mea, salutem opemque ferentem!
Quot alloquor
(frater es, es-ne soror?),
psallite Benevolentem.

Hunc venerare, qui adiuvat atque defendit.
(Ut tibi gratia cotidiana descendit!)
Ne lateat
quanta tibi faciat,
qui cum amore prehendit.

O venerare, mea anima, Dispositorem!
Qui tegat haud habeas tibi placidiorem.
Noscito, sci,
qualiter ille tibi
ordinet ex animo rem!

Ut venerabilis est! Ego totus adorem!
Omne quod est animal suum addat honorem.
Perpetuum
cantet "Amen" Dominum
populus ad Genitorem.

MM 17-25.6.98

Praise we the Lord this day,
this day so long foretold,
whose promise shone with cheering ray
on waiting saints of old.

.The prophet gave the sign
for faithful men to read:
a virgin born of David's line
shall bear the promised seed.

Ask not how this should be,
but worship and adore,
like her whom heaven's Majesty
came down to shadow o'er.

Meekly she bowed her head
to hear the gracious word,
Mary, the pure and lowly maid,
the favoured of the Lord.

Blessed shall be her name
in all the Church on earth,
through whom that wondrous mercy came,
the incarnate Saviour's birth.

Jesus, the Virgin's Son,
we praise thee and adore,
who art with God the Father one
and Spirit evermore.

Anon

Praedicta Dominum
laudemus hac die
quae cor laetavit veterum
promisso lumine.

Clarum credentibus
propheta cecinit:
Virgo, Davidicum genus,
promissum parturit.

Ne quaere quomodo:
sat venerari sit,
decore ut illa supero
umbrata paruit.

Auditur Virgini
summisse nuntius
purae Mariae humili,
cui favit Dominus,

beato nomine
piis ab omnibus,
unde est, exemplum gratiae,
Salvator genitus.

Tibi, Orte Virgine,
deflectimus genu,
unite cum Deo Patre
Sanctoque Spiritu.

MM 14—24.1.01

Prayer is the soul's sincere desire,
Uttered or unexpressed,
The motion of a hidden fire
That trembles in the breast.

Prayer is the burden of a sigh,
The falling of a tear,
The upward glancing of an eye,
When none but God is near.

Prayer is the simplest form of speech
That infant lips can try;
Prayer the sublimest strains that reach
The Majesty on high.

Prayer is the contrite sinner's voice,
Returning from his ways,
While angels in their songs rejoice,
And cry, "Behold, he prays!"

Prayer is the Christian's vital breath,
The Christian's native air,
His watchword at the gates of death;
He enters heaven with prayer.

No prayer is made on earth alone;
The Holy Spirit pleads;
And Jesus on the eternal throne
For sinners intercedes.

O thou by whom we come to God,
The Life, the Truth, the Way,
The path of prayer thyself hast trod;
Lord, teach us how to pray!

J. Montgomery

Fit prex quod anima cupit
audita seu tacens,
clam cum se flamma moverit
in pectore tremens.

Est grave prex suspirium
madens et oculus
levatioque luminum
qua solus est Deus.

Est prex quod simplicissimum
infans balbutiat,
et est sublime canticum
quod chorus erigat.

Fit peccatoris prex ubi
redivit a viis
et "en!" laetantes angeli
clamant "precatur is!"

Prex Christiani halitus,
nativae cui preces;
hanc tesseram monstrabimus
supernas ad fores.

Preci, ne fiat hic modo,
accedit Spiritus;
et es pro nobis e throno,
Jesu, causidicus.

O ducens ad Deum Via,
O Vita (et) Veritas,
(precatus ipse es antea)
precari doceas.

MM   26.11—8.12.01

Rejoice, O land, in God thy might,
his will obey, him serve aright;
for thee the saints uplift their voice:
fear not, O land, in God rejoice.

Glad shalt thou be, with blessing crowned,
with joy and peace thou shalt abound;
yea, love with thee shall make his home
until thou see God's kingdom come.

He shall forgive thy sins untold:
remember thou his love of old;
walk in his way, his word adore,
and keep his truth for evermore.

R. Bridges

O terra, gaudeas Deo,
oboediens imperio.
Sanctorum audis nenias:
confisa Deo gaudeas!

Beata delectaberis
et pace te circumdabis;
sedebit tecum caritas
dum regnum Dei videas.

Peccanti veniam dabit:
nonne olim is amor fuit?
Fac eius iussa sint rata
et veritas perpetua.

MM 16—23.10.99

Rejoice the Lord is King!
Your Lord and King adore!
Rejoice, give thanks and sing,
and triumph evermore.
Lift up your heart, lift up your voice!
Rejoice! again I say, rejoice!

Jesus, the Saviour reigns,
the God of truth and love:
when he had purged our stains,
he took his seat above.

His kingdom cannot fail;
he rules o'er earth and heaven;
the keys of death and hell
are to our Jesus given.

He sits at God's right hand
till all his foes submit,
and bow to his command,
and fall beneath his feet:
Lift up etc.

C. Wesley

Gaudete! Dominus
est Rex! Cui plaudite.
Aeternis cantibus
agantur gratiae:
Cum voce sursum pectora:
iam duplicentur gaudia!

Qui fidus nos amat,
Redemptor is regit:
ut nos purgaverat,
se supra posuit:

Is regno stabili
hic regnat et supra;
est Jesu Tartari
commissa janua:

Ad dexteram Dei
is sedem obtinet,
subiectos dum sibi
diabolos gravet.
Cum voce *etc.*

MM 8—11.5.99

Ride on! ride on in majesty!	Vehare prorsus splendide,
Hark! all the tribes Hosanna cry!	laudante civitate te!
O Saviour meek, pursue thy road	Constratum i, Salvator, per
With palms and scattered garments strowed.	vestitu palmulisque iter.

Ride on! ride on in majesty!	Vehare prorsus splendide,
In lowly pomp ride on to die:	ovans sed morti debite!
O Christ, thy triumphs now begin	O Christe, nunc instituas
O'er captive death and conquered sin.	supra malum victorias.

Ride on! ride on in majesty!	Vehare prorsus splendide!
The winged squadrons of the sky	Coetu caelorum alite
Look down with sad and wondering eyes	piaculum stupetur et
To see the approaching sacrifice.	ploratur id quod imminet.

Ride on! ride on in majesty!	Vehare prorsus splendide!
The last and fiercest strife is nigh:	Certamen ultimum(st) prope.
The Father on his sapphire throne	Elatus et Pater suum
Awaits his own anointed Son.	exspectat unctum Filium.

Ride on! ride on in majesty!	Vehare prorsus splendide,
In lowly pomp ride on to die;	ovans sed morti debite!
Bow thy meek head to mortal pain;	Homo dolori subditus,
Then take, O God, thy power, and reign.	regnabis inde tu Deus.

H.H.Milman

MM 8—13.4.01

Rock of ages, cleft for me,
let me hide myself in thee;
let the water and the blood
from thy wounded side which flowed,
be of sin the double cure,
cleanse me from its guilt and power.

Not the labour of my hands
can fulfill thy law's demands;
could my zeal no respite know,
could my tears forever flow,
all for sin could not atone;
thou must save, and thou alone.

Nothing in my hand I bring,
simply to thy cross I cling;
naked, come to thee for dress;
helpless look to thee for grace;
foul, I to the fountain fly;
wash me, Saviour, or I die.

While I draw this fleeting breath,
when mine eyelids close in death,
when I soar through tracts unknown,
see thee on thy judgment throne,
Rock of ages, cleft for me,
let me hide myself in thee.

A.M.Toplady

Saxum vetus, propter me
caesum, condar intra te;
mixtus sanguine latex,
quem profuderas, duplex
culpae medicina sit
cuius valde puduit.

Mea quod manus gerit
legi tuae deficit;
caream si requie,
fluant usque lacnimae,
non luentur scelera:
in te salus unica.

Nihil in manu fero;
Cruci totus haereo,
nudus, ut me vestias,
impotens, ut subeas,
foedus, fontem ut petam:
o lava, ne peream!

Spiritum trahens brevem,
mors cum caecet aciem,
supra cum elatus sim,
iudicem te viderim,
saxum vetus, propter me
caesum, condar intra te.

MM 1—5.8.98

Round me falls the night;
Saviour, be my light:
Through the hours in darkness shrouded
Let me see thy face unclouded;
Let thy glory shine
In this heart of mine.

Earthly work is done,
Earthly sounds are none;
Rest in sleep and silence seeking,
Let me hear thee softly speaking;
In my spirit's ear
Whisper, "I am near."

Blessed, heavenly Light,
Shining through earth's night;
Voice, that oft of love hast told me;
Arms, so strong to clasp and hold me;
Thou thy watch wilt keep,
Saviour, o'er my sleep.

W. Romanis

Cincto tenebris
lux, Salvator, sis;
videatur nocte plena
tua facies serena;
sitque interior
tuus hic nitor.

Nullus est sonus;
actumst omne opus;
sine requiem petentem
dulce audire te loquentem:
cordi dic meo
"adsum hic ego."

Lux caelestis et
cui nox locum det,
Vox amoris praedicator,
Brachiumque sustentator,
dormientem me
vigilans tene.

MM   23.9—4.10.01

Saviour, when in dust to thee	*Cum, Salvator, humiles*
Low we bow the adoring knee;	*flexo genu supplices*
When, repentant, to the skies	*oculis manantibus*
Scarce we lift our weeping eyes;	*vix ad te suspicimus,*
O by all thy pains and woe	*quod tot aegrimoniis*
Suffered once for man below,	*hic pro nobis luxeris,*
Bending from thy throne on high,	*audiatur a throno*
Hear our solemn litany.	*nostra supplicatio.*
By thy helpless infant years,	*Primis annis impotens*
By. thy life of want and tears,	*flens eras et indigens,*
By thy days of sore distress	*quadraginta dein dies*
In the savage wilderness;	*in deserto pressus es,*
By the dread mysterious hour	*totis inde viribus*
Of the insulting tempter's power:	*Satanae lacessitus:*
Turn, O turn a favouring eye,	*oculo sit in tuo*
Hear our solemn litany.	*nostra supplicatio.*
By the sacred griefs that wept	*Tu flevisti Lazarum*
O'er the grave where Lazarus slept;	*in sepulcro conditum;*
By the boding tears that flowed	*flesti tu Jerusalem*
Over Salem's loved abode;	*praesciens perniciem;*
By the mournful word that told	*inter et tuos oves*
Treachery lurked within thy fold:	*falsa movit te fides:*
From thy seat above the sky	*audiatur haec throno*
Hear our solemn litany.	*supra supplicatio.*
By thine hour of dire despair;	*Egit angor te tuum*
By thine agony of prayer;	*deprecari poculum,*
By the Cross, the nail, the thorn,	*crucem, spinas passe tu,*
Piercing spear, and torturing scorn;	*puncte contemptus acu,*
By the gloom that veiled the skies	*mactatum meridie*
O'er the dreadful Sacrifice:	*quem texere tenebrae:*
Listen to our humble cry,	*audiatur haec bono*
Hear our solemn litany.	*corde supplicatio.*
By thy deep expiring groan;	*Gemuisti moriens;*
By the sad sepulchral stone;	*lapis inde comprimens*
By the vault whose dark abode	*in sepulcro tenuit,*
Held in vain the rising God:	*quasi Deum vicerit:*
O, from earth to heaven restored,	*rursus orte Domine*
Mighty, re-ascended Lord,	*iamque caelis reddite,*
Listen, listen to the cry	*audiatur ilico*
Of our solemn litany.	*nostra supplicatio.*

R.Grant

MM 6—15.3.01

Latinised Hymns

See the destined day arise!
See, a willing sacrifice,
Jesus, to redeem our loss,
Hangs upon the shameful Cross!

Jesu, who but thou had borne,
Lifted on that Tree of scorn,
Every pang and bitter throe,
Finishing thy life of woe?

Who but thou had dared to drain,
Steeped in gall, that cup of pain,
And with tender body bear
Thorns and nails and piercing spear?

Thence the cleansing water flowed,
Mingled from thy side with blood:
Sign to all attesting eyes
Of the finished Sacrifice.

Holy Jesu, grant us grace
In that Sacrifice to place
All our trust for life renewed,
Pardoned sin, and promised good.

Bp R. Mant

Ecce! die debita,
non invitus hostia,
Jesus nostro nomine
turpi pendet a Cruce.

Ecquis, Jesu, praeter te,
ista spretus arbore,
mortem, quae te finiit
saeva, ferre potuit,

exhaurire poculum
ausus et fel additum,
membra punctus tenera
spinis, clavis, lancea?

Cuius unda latere
fluxit mixta sanguine,
testibus indicium
quod completum est Sacrum.

Quo fidamus per tuam,
Pie Jesu, gratiam,
quīs promissa sint bona,
nova vita et venia.

MM 11—16.4.01 .

Sinful, sighing to be blest;
Bound, and longing to be free;
Weary, waiting for my rest;
God, be merciful to me.

Goodness I have none to plead,
Sinfulness in all I see,
I can only bring my need:
God, be merciful to me.

Broken heart and downcast eyes
Dare not lift themselves to thee;
Yet thou canst interpret sighs:
God, be merciful to me.

From this sinful heart of mine
To thy bosom I would flee;
I am not my own, but thine:
God, be merciful to me.

There is One beside the throne,
And my only hope and plea
Are in him, and him alone:
God, be merciful to me.

He my cause will undertake,
My interpreter will be;
He's my all; and for his sake,
God, be merciful to me.

J.S.B. Monsell

Suspirantem me bees
fracto culpae compede;
fiat fesso requies
miserere, Domine.

Mihi nulla bonitas;
culpa cingit undique;
sed egenti faveas:
miserere, Domine.

Pressa cor et lumina
metuunt adire te,
noscis sed suspiria:
miserere, Domine.

Te petam (non sum meus)
hoc scelesto pectore
liberandus, ut tuus:
miserere, Domine.

Eius nomine preces,
qui stat ad thronum prope
fundo, qui mihi una spes:
miserere, Domine.

Hic opem feret mihi,
utar hoc interprete,
quo suadente tu mihi
miserere, Domine.

MM   3—9.3.01

Sing praise to God who reigns above,
The God of all creation,
The God of power, the God of love,
The God of our salvation;
With healing balm my soul he fills,
And every faithless murmur stills:
TO GOD ALL PRAISE AND GLORY.

Deo sint laudes maximae:
is omnium Creator,
amoris et potentiae
is Deus, is Salvator,
benignus, animae medens,
querelas omnes molliens;
DEUS GLORIFICETUR!

The Lord is never far away,
But, through all grief distressing,
An ever-present help and stay,
Our peace and joy and blessing;
As with a mother's tender hand,
He leads his own, his chosen band:

Deus a suo populo
non umquam separatur:
est spes et consolatio
et is qui tueatur,
ducens suos per omnia
materna quasi dextera;

Thus all my gladsome way along
I sing aloud thy praises,
That men may hear the grateful song
My voice unwearied raises.
Be joyful in the Lord, my heart;
Both soul and body bear your part:
TO GOD ALL PRAISE AND GLORY.

Te laudans mea vox canat
hinc quoad usque vivam,
et cantum mundus audiat
vocemque laudativam;
ovet cor, animae suum
sit corporique gaudium;
DEUS GLORIFICETUR!

Schutz/Cox

MM 8—14.2.02

Sleepers, wake! the watch-cry pealeth,	*Vigil "Eia, qui dormitis,"*
While slumber deep each eyelid sealeth:	*exclamat, "experrecti sitis!"*
Awake, Jerusalem, awake!	*Urbs Zion, expergiscere!*
Midnight's solemn hour is tolling,	*Media en noctis hora!*
And seraph-notes are onward rolling;	*Cantantium resplendent ora;*
They call on us our part to take.	*prudentes nunc attendite*
Come forth, ye virgins wise:	*ancillae! Clamor it:*
The Bridegroom comes, arise!	*"Maritus advenit!"*
Alleluia!	*Alleluia!*
Each lamp be bright	*Nunc lampadas*
With ready light	*parate eas*
To grace the marriage feast to-night.	*ad nuptiales epulas.*
Zion hears the voice that singeth,	*Vigilem Zion auscultat,*
With sudden joys her glad heart springeth,	*et auscultantis cor exultat,*
At once she wakes, she stands arrayed:	*en! experrecta prosilit,*
Her Light is come, her Star ascending,	*gratia dum roboratus*
Lo, girt with truth, with mercy blending,	*de ceelo properat Amatus;*
Her Bridegroom there, so long delayed.	*se sidus fulgens erigit.*
All hail! God's glorious Son,	*Corona nunc veni*
All hail! our joy and crown,	*tu Filius Dei.*
Alleluia!	*Hosanna!*
The joyful call	*Hinc nos ages*
We answer all,	*et comites*
And follow to the bridal hall.	*et prandii participes.*
Praise to him who goes before us!	*Laus tibi cantetur usque*
Let men and angels join in chorus,	*ab angelis hominibusque*
Let harp and cymbal add their sound.	*cum cymbalis et fidibus.*
Twelve the gates, a pearl each portal	*Bis sex Urbi margaritae*
We haste to join the choir immortal	*dant portas; nos et angeli te*
Within the Holy City's bound.	*supra sedentem cingimus.*
Ear ne'er heard aught like this,	*Nil oculis subit,*
Nor heart conceived such bliss.	*nil auris audiit*
Alleluia!	*tam iucundum.*
We raise the song,	*Io! Io!*
We swell the throng,	*perpetuo*
To praise thee ages all along.	*sumus in dulci iubilo!*

P.Nicolai/F.E.Cox WACHET AUF   *MM 16—27.11.01*

(I followed the German version rather than the English)

Sometimes a light surprises
The Christian while he sings:
It is the Lord who rises
With healing in his wings;
When comforts are declining,
He grants the soul again
A season of clear shining
To cheer it after rain.

In holy contemplation
We sweetly then pursue
The theme of God's salvation,
And find it ever new:
Set free from present sorrow,
We cheerfully can say,
E'en let the unknown morrow
Bring with it what it may,

It can bring with it nothing
But he will bear us through;
Who gives the lilies clothing
Will clothe his people too:
Beneath the spreading heavens
No creature but is fed;
And he who feeds the ravens
Will give his children bread.

Though vine nor fig-tree neither
Their wonted fruit should bear,
Though all the fields should wither,
Nor flocks nor herds be there;
Yet, God the same abiding,
His praise shall tune my voice;
For, while in him confiding,
I cannot but rejoice.

W.Cowper

Quondam iubar miratur
canens homo pius,
cum Deus oriatur
alis medentibus,
qui minuit dolorem,
si crevit, animi
brevemque dat nitorem,
solamen pluvii.

Salvantem praedicare
tum nos eum iuvat,
nec invenimus quare
dicandi taedeat.
Sic hodie laborum
beate liberi
quid cras sit eventurum
loquamur inscii:

"Malorum crastinorum
effugium dabit
amictor liliorum
qui nos vestiverit.
Escarum praebitor vos,
quot estis, sustinet:
si pascit ille corvos,
num natos negleget?"

Nec ficus neque vitis
carpenda praebeat
et sit Pales immitis
pecusque supprimat:
★eundem hunc manentem
laudabit os meum,★
nec fallet me fidentem
in eo gaudium.

MM 4—11.1.98

★eundem se gerentem
laudabo Dominum,★

Soldiers of Christ, arise,
And put your armour on,
Strong in the strength which God supplies
Through his eternal Son;

Strong in the Lord of Hosts,
And in his mighty power:
Who in the strength of Jesus trusts
Is more than conqueror.

Stand then in his great might,
With all his srength endued;
And take, to arm you for the fight,
The panoply of God.

From strength to strength go on,
Wrestle and fight and pray;
Tread all the powers of darkness down
And win the well-fought day;

That, having all things done,
And all your conflicts past,
Ye may o'ercome, through Christ alone,
And stand entire at last.

C. Wesley

Heus Christi milites
et accingimini!
Deusque reddat alacres
vigore Filii.

Cohortium Ducis
vis magna vestra sit;
qui Iesu Christo fidit, is
victores vicerit.

State eius maxima
virtute praediti,
et sumitote in proelia
panhopliam Dei.

Crescunto robora:
luctando cum prece
calcate inferna numina
et pugna vincite.

Donati sic rude,
labore liberi,
Christique victores ope,
tum stetis integri.

MM 10—11.3.99

Songs of praise the angels sang,
Heaven with Alleluias rang,
When creation was begun,
When God spake and it was done.

Songs of praise awoke the morn
When the Prince of Peace was born;
Songs of praise arose when he
Captive led captivity.

Heaven and earth shall pass away;
Songs of praise shall crown that day:
God will make new heavens and earth;
Songs of praise shall hail their birth.

And will man alone be dumb
Till that glorious Kingdom come?
No, the Church delights to raise
Psalms and hymns and songs of praise.

Saints below, with heart and voice,
Still in songs of praise rejoice;
Learning here, by faith and love,
Songs of praise to sing above.

Hymns of glory, songs of praise,
Father, unto thee we raise,
Jesu, glory unto thee,
With the Spirit ever be.

J. Montgomery

Alleluia superis
est cantata ab angelis,
iussit esse cum Deus,
mundum collaudantibus.

Laus est orta cum die
Pacis orto Principe,
captaque captivitas
laudes habuit suas.

Finis mundo veniet:
is laudatus incidet;
et Deus cum laude tum
mundum faciet novum.

Qui dum venerit dies
num tacebunt homines?
Fundit en! Ecclesia
multa laudis cantica.

Gestiunt inferius
Christiani laudibus,
hic discentes carmina
quae canturi sunt supra.

Cantica cum laudibus,
Pater, tibi tollimus;
decus, Iesu, sit tibi
semper et Spiritui.

MM 20—23.1.00

Songs of thankfulness and praise,
Jesu, Lord, to thee we raise,
Manifested by the star
To the sages from afar;
Branch of royal David's stem
In thy birth at Bethlehem:
Anthems be to thee addrest,
God in Man made manifest.

Manifest at Jordan's stream,
Prophet, Priest and King supreme;
And at Cana wedding-guest –
In thy Godhead manifest,
Manifest in power divine,
Changing water into wine:
Anthems be to thee addrest,
God in Man made manifest.

Manifest in making whole
Palsied limbs and fainting soul;
Manifest in valiant fight,
Quelling all the devil's might;
Manifest in gracious will,
Ever bringing good from ill:
Anthems be to thee addrest,
God in Man made manifest.

Sun and moon shall darkened be,
Stars shall fall, the heavens shall flee;
Christ will then like lightning shine,
All will see his glorious sign;
All will then the trumpet hear,
All will see the Judge appear:
Thou by all wilt be confest,
God in Man made manifest.

Grant us grace to see thee, Lord,
Mirrored in thy holy word;
May we imitate thee now,
And be pure, as pure art thou;
That we like to thee may be
At thy great Epiphany;
And may praise thee, ever blest,
God in Man made manifest.

Bp. Chr. Wordsworth

Gratias cum laudibus
tibi, Iesu, ferimus,
fecit quem exoticis
stella cognitum Magis,
rame stirpis regiae
luci Bethlehem date,
dignus Homo cantibus,
Deus idem cognitus.

Es Jordani fluctibus
Rex Propheta cognitus
cognitusque Canicis
numinosus nuptiis,
esse lympha quem Deum
versa testis in merum,
dignus Homo cantibus,
Deus idem cognitus.

Membris atque mentibus
confortandis cognitus,
cognitusque strenue
resistendo Satanae,
comiter qui traxeris
bona semper e malis,
dignus Homo cantibus,
Deus idem cognitus.

Cum caelorum lumina
occulentur omnia,
modo, Christe, fulguris
signum gentibus dabis:
omnes audient tubam,
Iudex ut fies palam;
apparebis omnibus
Homo Deus agnitus.

In scripturis, Domine,
fac te nos discernere,
et cum puritate da
imitari te tua,
Ut, cum sis Epiphanes,
simus tui similes
sisque nostris laudibus
Homo Deus agnitus.

MM 16—23.1.00

Sound aloud Jehovah's praises,
Tell abroad his aweful Name!
Heaven the ceaseless anthem raises;
Let the earth her God proclaim,
God, the hope of every nation,
God, the source of consolation,
Holy, blessed Trinity.

Heus! Jehovae laudes date,
Nomen augustum sonet;
cantat caelum prolongate:
terra eundem celebret
gentibus Deum parantem
spem solatiumque dantem,
Trinitatem optimam.

This the Name from ancient ages
Hidden in its dazzling light;
This the name that kings and sages
Prayed and strove to know aright,
Through God's wondrous Incarnation
Now revealed the world's salvation,
Ever blessed Trinity.

Nomen prae splendore ignotum
quod fuit antiquitus,
placitum parumque notum
regibus et vatibus,
Dei Nomen Incarnati
signum populi salvati,
Trinitas perpetua.

Into this great Name and holy
We all tribes and tongues baptize;
Thus the Highest owns the lowly,
Homeward, heavenward, bids them rise,
Gathers them from every nation,
bids them join in adoration
Of the blessed Trinity.

Hoc in Nomen baptizantur
populorum omnium,
a Supremo cum vocantur
humiles in superum;
omnifarii cientur,
ut coniuncti venerentur
Trinitatem optimam.

In this Name the heart rejoices,
Pouring forth its secret prayer;
In this Name we lift our voices,
And our common faith declare,
Offering praise and supplication
And the thankful life's oblation
To the blessed Trinity.

Corde laeto clam oramus
hoc impulsi Nomine;
affirmanda conclamamus
hoc ad Nomen in fide,
laudem precibus miscentes,
vitae gratias ferentes
Trinitati optimae.

Still thy Name o'er earth and ocean
Shall be carried, "God is Love,"
Whispered by the heart's devotion,
Echoed by the choirs above,
Hallowed through all worlds for ever,
Lord, of life the only giver,
Blessed, glorious Trinity.

Nomen hoc ubique latum
erit, Amor O Deus,
pio corde susurratum
angelis augentibus,
sanctus orbium regnator,
Dominus vitaeque dator,
Trinitas sacerrima.

A.Martin

MM 10—18.2.01

Still nigh me, O my Saviour, stand,
And guard in fierce temptation's hour;
Hide in the hollow of thy hand,
Show forth in me thy saving power;
Still be thine arm my sure defence:
Nor earth nor hell shall pluck me thence.

Still let thy love point out my way:
How wondrous things thy love hath wrought!
Still lead me, lest I go astray;
Direct my work, inspire my thought;
And, if I fall, soon may I hear
Thy voice, and know that love is near.

In suffering be thy love my peace,
In weakness be thy love my power;
And when the storms of life shall cease,
Jesus, in that tremendous hour,
In death as life be thou my guide
And save me, who for me hast died.

C. Wesley

Prope, O Salvator, mihi sta
custos, cum saevit Satanas;
sub manu lateam tua;
vindex potens appareas;
lacertus iste muniat;
nec est quod inde me trahat.

Ostende amans mihi viam
(fecisti mirabilia).
perverse quominus eam,
et inspiretur anima;
et si cadam, subesse mox
amantem monstret ista vox.

Quietem laboranti da
et debili potentiam;
cum hora tremendissima
turbari vita desinam,
ne mortuum regas minus:
me salva mihi mortuus,

MM 28.2—6.3.01

Sun of my soul, thou Saviour dear,
it is not night if thou be near;
O may no earthborn cloud arise
to hide thee from thy servant's eyes.

When the soft dews of kindly sleep
my wearied eyelids gently steep,
be my last thought, how sweet to rest
forever on my Saviour's breast.

Abide with me from morn till eve,
for without thee I cannot live;
abide with me when night is nigh,
for without thee I dare not die.

If some poor wandering child of thine
has spurned today the voice divine,
now, Lord, the gracious work begin;
let him no more lie down in sin.

Watch by the sick, enrich the poor
with blessings from thy boundless store;
be every mourner's sleep tonight,
like infants' slumbers, pure and light.

Come near and bless us when we wake,
ere through the world our way we take,
till in the ocean of thy love
we lose ourselves in heaven above.

J. Keble

Tu sol, Salvator, animae,
quo dissipantur tenebrae.
Te nulla nubes a meis
terrestris abdat oculis.

Cum me mulcebit somnus et
palpebras leniter premet,
aeternam fac desiderem
cum Salvatore requiem.

Diurnus adsis, quippe te
remotus nolo vivere,
et nocte, nullo nam modo
mori te cassus audeo.

Si quis vocantem filius
tuus te spreverit vagus
hac nocte, da paeniteat
ut absolutus dormiat.

Aegros tuere, de tua
beans egenos copia,
sopitis nocte qui gemunt
quo more infantes dormiunt.

Surgentes nos iuva prius
quam mane peregrabimus,
amore tandem ut tuo
mergamur caelesti freto.

MM 3—6.6.97

Take my life, and let it be
consecrated, Lord, to thee;
take my moments and my days,
let them flow in ceaseless praise.

Take my hands, and let them move
at the impulse of thy love;
take my feet, and let them be
swift and beautiful for thee.

Take my voice, and let me sing
always, only, for my King;
take my lips, and let them be
filled with messages from thee.

Take my silver and my gold,
not a mite would I withhold;
take my intellect, and use
every power as thou shalt choose.

Take my will and make it thine;
it shall be no longer mine.
take my heart, it is thine own;
it shall be thy royal throne.

Take my love; my Lord, I pour
at thy feet its treasure-store;
take my self, and I will be
ever, only, all for thee.

R Havergal

Vitam tibi, Domine,
consecratam suscipe
ut momenta sic dies
laudibus fac uberes.

Cape tu manus meas
et amore dirigas,
tibi dum mei pedes
pulchri sint et celeres.

Cape vocem: sit meum
soli tibi canticum;
ora tu reple mea:
verba nuncupent tua.

Opum mihi minimam
partem ne retineam;
mentis huius acie
ut libebit utere.

Haec voluntas non mihi
sed oboediat tibi;
pectus hoc accipias,
rex ut ibi sedeas.

Mihi quantus est amor
totum tibi largior;
cape me, tibique ero
semper omnis unico.

MM   25—9.3.98

Teach me, my God and King,
In all things thee to see;
And what I do in anything
To do it as for thee.

A man that looks on glass,
On it may stay his eye;
Or,   if he pleaseth, through it pass,
And then the heaven espy.

All may of thee partake;
Nothing can be so mean
Which, with this tincture, FOR THY SAKE,
Will not grow bright and clean.

A servant with this clause
Makes drudgery divine;
Who sweeps a room, as for thy laws,
Makes that and the action fine.

This is the famous stone
That turneth all to gold;
For that which God doth touch and own
Cannot for less be told.

G.Herbert

Ubique ut te sciam
tu, Rex, Deus, doce,
et quidquid ego peragam,
id peragam pro te.

Is qui videt vitrum
ibi oculum premat
aut, ultra dirigens eum:
caelum conspiciat.

Omnes habent tui
partem; vilissima,
suscepta gratia Dei,
fiunt candentia.

Fit gratia Dei
labor? Divinus fit:
qui verrit serviens tibi
pulchrum pulchre facit.

Non alius lapis
in aurum verteret:
quod tractat Deus ipse, quis
minoris aestimet?

MM 26—29.11.97
Revised May 99

Tell out, my soul, the greatness of the Lord;
Unnumbered blessings give my spirit voice;
Tender to me the promise off his Word;
In God my Saviour shall my heart rejoice.

Tell out, my soul, the greatness of his Name!
Make known his might, the deeds his arm has done;
His mercy sure, from age to age the same;
His Holy Name – the Lord, the Mighty One.

Tell out, my soul, the greatness of his might!
Powers and dominions lay their glory by.
Proud hearts and stubborn wills are put to flight,
The hungry fed, the humble lifted high.

Tell out, my soul, the glories of his word!
Firm is his promise, and his mercy sure.
Tell out, my soul, the greatness of the Lord
To children's children and for evermore!

T. Dudley-Smith (Magnificat)

Dic, anima, dic quantus Dominus;
vocalem fecit is laetitiam,
quod almum est mihi pollicitus,
ut Deo Salutari gaudeam.

Quantum dic Nomen ejus, anima,
quot fecerit miranda brachium,
quam sit durabilis clementia
et quam Potentis Nomen id sacrum.

Vis, anima, dic eius quanta sit:
imperio privavit proceres,
superbos e loco deposuit,
ieiunos nutrit, tollit humiles.

Dic, anima, quad eius sit decus;
stat firma fides et clementia
Dic, anima, dic quantus Dominus.
nepotibus nec non per saecula.

MM   3—25.12.01

Latinised Hymns

The Church of God a kingdom is,
Where Christ in power doth reign;
There spirits yearn till, seen in bliss,
Their Lord shall come again.

Glad companies of saints possess
This Church below, above;
And God's perpetual calm doth bless
Their paradise of love.

An altar stands within the shrine
Whereon, once sacrificed,
Is set, immaculate, divine,
The Lamb of God, the Christ.

There rich and poor, from countless lands,
Praise Christ on mystic Rood;
There nations reach forth holy hands
To take God's holy food.

There pure lifegiving streams o'erflow
The sower's garden-ground;
And faith and hope fair blossoms show,
And fruits of love abound.

O King, O Christ, this endless grace
To us and all men bring,
To see the vision of thy face
In joy, O Christ, our King.

L.B.C.L.Muirhead

Est civitas Ecclesia,
cui Christus imperat,
desiderantque pectora
dum is reveniat.

Eam sanctorum legio
laetantum habitat,
quos otio perpetuo
Deus suo beat.

Altare fanum continet,
quo, caesus antea,
purus, divinus insidet
Agnellus hostia.

Ibi omnifarii colunt
in Cruce Dominum
manusque sanctas porrigunt
sacratum ad cibum.

Ibi hortum vivi latices
satoris irrigant,
et spe coniuncta ibi fides
amorque pullulant.

O Christe, nobis gratiam
fer hanc et omnibus,
laetique faciem tuam,
O Rex, videbimus.

MM 29.1—1.2.99

The Church's one foundation
Is Jesus Christ her Lord;
She is his new creation
By water and the word:
From heaven he came and sought her
To be his holy Bride;
With his own blood he bought her,
And for her life he died.

Elect from every nation,
Yet one o'er all the earth,
Her charter of salvation
One Lord, one faith, one birth;
One holy name she blesses,
Partakes one holy food,
And to one hope she presses
With every grace endued.

Though with a scornful wonder
Men see her sore opprest,
By schisms torn asunder,
By heresies distrest,
Yet saints their watch are keeping,
Their cry goes up, "How long?"
And soon the night of weeping
Shall be the morn of song.

Mid toil and tribulation,
And tumult of her war,
She waits the consummation
Of peace for evermore;
Till with the vision glorious
Her longing eyes are blest,
And the great Church victorious
Shall be the Church at rest.

Yet she on earth hath union
With God the Three in One,
And mystic sweet communion
With those whose rest is won:
O happy ones and holy!
Lord, give us grace that we,
Like them the meek and lowly,
On high may dwell with thee.

S.J. Stone

236

*Ecclesiae fundamen
es, Christe, singulum,
quae novum est creamen
cum Verbo laticum.
Eam tu devenisti
nuptam facturus, et
tu sanguinem fudisti
ut ea viveret.*

*E gentibus collata
fit una natio;
est uno confirmata
natu, fide, Deo;
uno cibo repletam
uni se dedicat,
et unam versus metam
beata properat.*

*Stupentibus contempta
spectatur populis,
haeresibus dirempta,
distracta iurgiis;
sed sancti vigilantes
resolvi rem volunt,
et nocte lacrimantes
canturi mane sunt.*

*Manet, quae nunc turbatur
premente proelio,
durn pax conficiatur
privata termino;
dum visio donetur
aventi splendida
et requie juvetur
victrix Ecclesia.*

*Sed est et hic ligata
cum Triplici Deo
eisque sociata
qui gaudent otio.
O humiles! O sancti!
Favore Numinis
vobiscum loca nancti
iungamur angelis.*

MM 25—30.3.97

Latinised Hymns

(Hunc intellexisse parum me suspicor hymnum)

The Church triumphant in thy love,	*Sanctorum triumphantium*
Their mighty joys we know;	*sciuntur gaudia;*
They sing the Lamb in hymns above,	*hic nostrum Agno canticum,*
And we in hymns below.	*eorum fit supra.*

Thee in thy glorious realm they praise,	*In regno resplendente te*
And bow before thy throne;	*verentur ad thronum,*
We in the kingdom of thy grace:	*et nos in regno gratiae;*
The kingdoms are but one.	*sed regnum unicum.*

The holy to the Holiest leads:	*Fert sanctum ad Sanctissimum:*
From hence our spirits rise,	*hinc surgunt animae,*
And he that in thy statutes treads	*tuaeque legi deditum*
Shall meet thee in the skies.	*cernes in aethere.*

C. Wesley	*MM 30.5—4.6.00*

The day thou gavest, Lord, is ended,	*Dies finitur quem dedisti*
the darkness falls at thy behest;	*te postulante tenebras.*
to thee our morning hymns ascended,	*Tu mane carmen accepisti;*
thy praise shall sanctify our rest.	*tu dormituros audias.*

We thank thee that thy Church, unsleeping	*Lucem sequens se terra volvit:*
while earth rolls onward into light,	*laudamus quod numquam tua*
through all the world her watch is keeping	*die seu nocte se resolvit*
and rests not now by day nor night.	*pervigilans ecclesia.*

As o'er each continent and island	*Per insulas et continentes*
the dawn leads on another day,	*aurora lumen integrat,*
the voice of prayer is never silent,	*nec dest locus qui te petentes*
nor dies the strain of praise away.	*votis et laude praebeat.*

The sun that bids us rest is waking	*Quo sole sumus dormituri*
our brethren 'neath the western sky,	*cientur hoc occidui,*
and hour by hour fresh lips are making	*nec minuuntur ascensuri*
thy wondrous doings heard on high.	*de factis tuis nuntii.*

So be it, Lord; thy throne shall never,	*Nec tuum, Deus, obsolescet*
like earth's proud empires, pass away;	*ut regna temporalium,*
thy kingdom stands, and grows for ever,	*sed stabit semper, immo crescet*
till all thy creatures own thy sway.	*cunctisque fiet agnitum.*

J. Ellerton	*MM 13-15 Nov 96*

The earth, O Lord, is one wide field
Of all thy chosen seed;
The crop prepared its fruit to yield,
The labourers few indeed.

We therefore come before thee now
With fasting and with prayer,
Beseeching of thy love that thou
Wouldst send more labourers there.

Not for our land alone we pray,
Though that above the rest;
The realms and islands far away,
O let them all be blest.

Endue the bishops of thy flock
With wisdom and with grace,
Against false doctrine like a rock
To set the heart and face.

To all thy priests thy truth reveal,
And make thy judgements clear;
Make thou thy deacons full of zeal,
And humble and sincere:

And give their flocks a lowly mind
To hear – and not in vain;
That each and all may mercy find
When thou shalt come again.

J.M.Neale

Tuo devota semini
terra omnis est, Deus,
sed parva tantae segeti
messorum est manus.

Ergo venimus ante te
ieiuni supplices,
ut incrementa, Domine,
messorum ibi des.

Non nostrae solum petimus,
etsi praecipue,
sed insulis distantibus
ut sit eis bene.

Prudentes 0! tui gregis
reddas episcopos,
perversis ut sententiis
opponant cor et os.

Verique fac antistites
jurisque conscios
diaconos et humiles,
acres et integros.

Fac et submisssum his gregem,
qui vere pareat,
regressum ut te iudicem
clementem sentiat.

MM   10—21.4.00

The God of love my Shepherd is,
And he that doth me feed;
While he is mine and I am his,
What can I want or need?

He leads me to the tender grass,
Where I both feed and rest;
Then to the streams that gently pass:
In both I have the best.

Or if I stray, he doth convert,
And bring my mind in frame,
And all this not for my desert,
But for his holy name.

Yea, in death's shady black abode
Well may I walk, not fear;
For thou art with me, and thy rod
To guide, thy staff to bear.

Surely thy sweet and wondrous love
Shall measure all my days;
And, as it never shall remove,
So neither shall my praise.

G.Herbert (Ps 23)

Amat me Deus et regit,
nec nutrit alius;
sim eius (id mi sufficit)
et ille sit meus.

Ad laeta ducit pascua,
ut vescar otians,
et ad tranquilla flumina,
utrimque bona dans.

Vertit, si forte erraverim,
mentemque revocat,
non quia dignus ego sim
sed se quod deceat.

Sic mortis in caligine
securus ivero,
virga tua ducente me,
levante baculo.

Dum vixero, duraverit
mirandus iste amor;
aeternus ille, neve sit
laus mea brevior.

MM   23—8.9.00

The head that once was crowned with thorns
is crowned with glory now;
a royal diadem adorns
the mighty Victor's brow.

The highest place that heaven affords
is his, is his by right,
the King of kings, and Lord of lords,
and heaven's eternal Light;

The joy all of all who dwell above,
the joy of all below,
to whom he manifests his love
and grants his Name to know.

To them the cross with all its shame,
with all its grace is given;
their name, an everlasting name;
their joy, the joy of heaven.

They suffer with their Lord below,
they reign with him above,
their profit and their joy to know
the mystery of his love.

The cross he bore is life and health,
though shame and death to him:
his people's hope, his people's wealth,
their everlasting theme.

T. Kelly

Coronae loco spineae,
est capiti decus
datusque apex victoriae
id ornat regius.

Supremum caeli solium
is iure vindicat,
et lumen ibi, Dux ducum,
Rex regum, usque dat.

Ut incolis caelestibus
terrestribus placet
fitque isdem amor obvius,
ut nomen haud latet.

Pudorem fert cum gratia
eis Patibulum;
fama est eis perpetua,
caeleste gaudium.

Participes hic Crucis et
in caelo solii
ut scire prodest, ut placet
amorem Domini!

O salutiferam Crucem,
ut Christo noxiam!
Nostras opes nostramque spem,
laudemus usque eam.

MM 20—25.11.98

The heaven of heavens cannot contain
The universal Lord;
Yet he in humble hearts will deign
To dwell and be adored.

Where'er ascends the sacrifice
Of fervent praise and prayer,
Or in the earth or in the skies,
The heaven of God is there.

His presence there is spread abroad
Through realms, through worlds unknown;
Who seeks the mercies of his God
Is ever near his throne.

W. Drennan

*Totius mundi Rex nequit
a caelo comprimi,
submissa corda sed sinit
colentem se coli.*

*Ex corde sacrificia,
laudes cum precibus,
qua surgant, infra seu supra,
Divina ibi est domus.*

*Praeter scientiam dedit
praesentem se Deus;
cuius qui veniam petit
est ei proximus.*

MM 15—19.5.01

The heavens declare thy glory, Lord,
in every star thy wisdom shines
but when our eyes behold thy Word,
we read thy Name in fairer lines.

The rolling Sun, the changing Light,
The Nights and Days thy Power confess:
But the blest Volume thou hast writ
Reveals thy Justice and thy Grace.

Sun, moon, and stars convey thy praise
round the whole earth, and never stand:
so when thy truth begun its race,
it touched and glanced on every land.

Nor shall thy spreading Gospel rest
till through the world thy truth has run,
till Christ has all the nations blest
that see the light or feel the sun.

Great Sun of Righteousness, arise,
bless the dark world with heavenly light;
thy Gospel makes the simple wise,
thy laws are pure, thy judgments right.

Thy noblest wonders here we view
in souls renewed and sins forgiven;
Lord, cleanse my sins, my soul renew,
and make thy word my guide to heaven.

I. Watts

O dicte maximus polo
et sapiens sideribus,
in Verbo scriptus es tuo,
id si legatur, pulchrius.

Volvendo sole nox dies
te praevalentem nuncupant
sed libri guos scriptos habes
iusturn benignumque indicant.

Laudes tuas ut ubique
sol, luna, sidera vehunt,
cum coepit Ver(b)um currere
id omnes orae senserunt.

Pandi nec ante desinet
per orbem Evangelium
fruentem sole quam beet
Salvator omnem populum.

Surgens, O Sol Iustitiae,
terrestres pelle tenebras,
qui, iuris dictor optime,
ineducatos educas.

Est mira, quam hic exhibes,
cum venia novatio:
sic me cum venia noves,
et Verbo supra duc tuo.

M 31.1—5.2.01

The King of love my Shepherd is,
Whose goodness faileth never;
I nothing lack if I am his
And he is mine for ever.

Where streams of living water flow
My ransomed soul he leadeth,
And where the verdant pastures grow
With food celestial feedeth.

Perverse and foolish oft I strayed,
But yet in love he sought me,
And on his shoulder gently laid,
And home rejoicing brought me.

In death's dark vale I'll fear no ill
With thee, dear Lord, beside me;
Thy rod and staff my comfort still,
Thy Cross before to guide me.

Thou spread'st a table in my sight;
Thy unction grace bestoweth;
And O what transport of delight
From thy pure chalice floweth!

And so through all the length of days
Thy goodness faileth never:
Good Shepherd, may I sing thy praise
Within thy house for ever.

H.W.Baker (Ps 23)

Est Deus pastor dirigens
perpetuoque bonus:
bene est dum illi sim cliens
et ille mi patronus.

Aquosa iuxta flumina
me ducit is redemptum,
cui laeta praebent pascua
caeleste nutrimentum.

Me saepe gradu devio
vagantem indagavit
suoque tulit humero
domumque me portavit.

Nil mortis valle metuam
te, Deus, comitante;
me virga fulcis, semitam
Cruce mihi monstrante.

Tu mensam mihi suggeris,
unguento tu beas me;
et o! quam voluptariis
calicibus rigas me.

Sic me beas, quot sunt dies:
est bonitas aeterna;
ut laudem, Pastor, usque des
in aede te superna.

MM 13—19 Dec 97

The Lord is King! lift up thy voice,
O earth. and all ye heavens, rejoice;
From world to world the joy shall ring,
"The Lord omnipotent is King!"

The Lord is King! who then shall dare
Resist his will, distrust his care,
Or murmur at his just decrees,
Or doubt his royal promises?

He reigns! Ye saints, exalt your strains;
Your God is King, your Father reigns;
And he is at the Father's side,
The Man of love, the Crucified.

Alike pervaded by his eye
All parts of his dominion lie:
This world of ours and worlds unseen,
And thin the boundary between.

One Lord one empire all secures;
He reigns, and life and death are yours;
Through earth and heaven one song shall ring,
"The Lord omnipotent is King!"

J.Conder

Regnare Dominum canas,
tellus, et, aether, gaudeas!
Utroque mundo sit sonus:
"Est Rex Omnipotens Deus."

Regnanti num quis obstruet?
Parum curare quis putet?
Quis audet iniustum queri
oblitum aut polliciti?

Is regnat (sancti, psallite!);
 regnatque cum Deo Patre,
sedens Parenti proximus,
amans Mactatus Filius.

Dei regnantis omnia
eidem sunt perspicua:
quod scimus regnum et latens,
nec limes amplus dividens.

Vos vitae, solus quod regit,
mortisque compotes facit;
terrae caelique erit sonus:
"Est Rex Omnipotens Deus!"

MM   26.3—4.4.00

The Lord is our refuge, the Lord is our guide,
We smile upon danger with him at our side;
The billows may roll and the tempest increase;
Though earth may be shaken, his saints shall have peace.

Be near us, Redeemer, to shield us from ill; .
Speak thou but the word, and the tempest is still;
Thy presence to cheer us, thine arm to defend,
No foe shall affright us with thee for a Friend.

'The Lord is our helper: ye scorners, be awed;
Ye earthlings, be still, and acknowledge your Lord;
The proud he will humble, the lowly defend:
O, happy the people with God for a Friend!

H.F.Lyte

Ductor Deus est; ad eum fugimus:
ridenda pericla facit Dominus;
si creverit unda procellaque, fit
sanctis requies, ubi terra tremit.

Adsiste, Redemptor; abito malum;
loquare, dabitque procella locum;
tutela tuis validusque comes,
ne terreat hostis, Amicus ades.

Agnoscite, terrigenae, Dominum:
eius male temnitur auxilium;
extollit is ima, superba premit.
Felix genus, is cui Amicus erit!

MM 20—26.9.00

The Lord is risen indeed!	*Est ortus Dominus,*
Now is his work performed;	*finita et opera,*
Now is the mighty captive freed,	*captivus extra redditus,*
And death's strong castle stormed.	*arx mortis eruta.*
The Lord is risen indeed!	*Est ortus Dominus!*
Then hell has lost its prey;	*Dest praeda tartaro.*
With him is risen the ransomed seed	*Stat emptus una populus*
To reign in endless day.	*regnans perpetuo.*
The Lord is risen indeed!	*Est ortus Dominus!*
He lives, to die no more;	*Nec cadet iterum,*
He lives, the sinner's cause to plead,	*patronus peccatoribus,*
Whose curse and shame he bore.	*qūis subiit iugum.*
The Lord is risen indeed!	*Est ortus Dominus!*
Attending angels, hear!	*Attendite, angeli!*
Up to the courts of heaven with speed	*Ascendat cito nuntius*
The joyful tidings bear.	*ad atria Dei.*
Then take your golden lyres,	*Nunc vos, fidicines,*
And strike each cheerful chord;	*delectet psallere,*
Join, all ye bright celestial choirs,	*ortumque Christum, caelites*
To sing our risen Lard.	*chori, concinite.*
T.Kelly	*MM 16—23.4.01*

The Lord my pasture shall prepare
and feed me with a shepherd's care;
his presence shall my wants supply
and guard me with a watchful eye;
my noonday walks he shall attend
and all my midnight hours defend.

When in the sultry glebe I faint
or on the thirsty mountain pant,
to fertile vales and dewy meads
my weary, wandering steps he leads,
where peaceful rivers, soft and slow,
amid the verdant landscape flow.

Though in a bare and rugged way,
through devious lonely wilds, I stray,
thy bounty shall my pains beguile;
the barren wilderness shall smile,
with sudden greens and herbage crowned,
and streams shall murmur all around.

Though in the paths of death I tread,
with gloomy horrors overspread,
my steadfast heart shall fear no ill,
for thou, O Lord, art with me still;
thy friendly crook shall give me aid
and guide me through the dreadful shade.

J. Addison (Ps 23)

Deus, qui nutrimenta det,
me pastoraliter alet,
quod opus, hoc suppeditans,
custodietque vigilans:
diurnas diriget vias,
tutabitur per tenebras.

Cum tostus aestu langueam
vel sicco monte sitiam,
me fessum ducit et vagum
in laetum rus et roscidum,
qua lenta manant flumina
per arva viridantia.

Trans nuda saxa peragrem
remotam solitudinem,
in te decipitur dolor,
fit locus ipse uberior,
frondosus et circumdatus
fluentis murmurantibus.

Cum horridum sequens iter
umbrosae mortis spatier,
non est quod timeam mali:
tu semper is comes mihi,
pedumque sustinebit et
per umbras usque diriget.

MM   11—24.5.00

The Lord will come and not be slow,
his footsteps cannot err;
before him righteousness shall go,
his royal harbinger.

Truth from the earth, like to a flower,
shall bud and blossom then;
and justice, from her heavenly bower,
look down on mortal men.

Rise, God, judge thou the earth in might,
this wicked earth redress;
for thou art he who shalt by right
the nations all possess.

The nations all whom thou hast made
shall come, and all shall frame
to bow them low before thee, Lord,
and glorify thy Name.

For great thou art, and wonders great
by thy strong hand are done:
thou in thy everlasting seat
remainest God alone.

J.Milton

Adibis certum, Domine,
accelerans gradum,
et Fas procedet ante te
Regis praenuntium.

Tum germinabit floribus
similiter Fides,
Iustitia dum caelitus
spectabit homines.

Hunc mundum, Domine, potens
scelestum corrige,
cum iure gentes possidens;
nam iure sunt tuae.

Quot tu creasti, populi
omnes convenient,
ut se proiciant tibi
et nomen celebrent.

Tu magnus es, et maxima
miracula facis,
Deusque tu perpetua
in sede linqueris.

MM   9—14.8.98

The saints of God! their conflict past,
and life's long battle won at last, _
no more they need the shield or sword,
they cast them down before their Lord:
O happy saints! forever blest,
at Jesus feet' how safe your rest!

The saints of God! their wanderings done,
no more their weary course they run,
no more they faint, no more they fall,
no foes oppress, no fears appal:
O happy saints! forever blest,
in that dear home how sweet your rest!

The saints of God! life's voyage o'er,
safe landed on that blissful shore,
no stormy tempests now they dread,
no roaring billows lift their head:
O happy saints! forever blest,
in that calm haven of your rest!

The saints of God their vigil keep,
while yet their mortal bodies sleep,
till from the dust they too shall rise
and soar triumphant to the skies:
O happy saints! rejoice and sing:
he quickly comes, your Lord and King!

O God of saints! to thee we cry;
O Saviour! plead for us on high;
O Holy Ghost! our Guide and Friend,
grant us thy grace till life shall end;
that with all saints our rest may be
in that bright paradise with thee!

W.D. Maclagan

Finitis sancti proeliis
et hostibus depositis
Deo proiciunt suam
emeriti panhopliam:
sancti, divinos ad pedes
quae vobis tuta requies!

Actis sancti meatibus,
cursores haud diutius
haud fatigantur, haud cadunt;
nil opprimit, nil metuunt;
beati sancti caelites,
quae vobis grata requies!

Finita sanctis est via;
amoena nactis litora
procellae non timori sunt
nec fluctus ardui fremunt:
in portu, sancti sospites,
est parta vobis requies.

Post mortem sancti vigilant,
carnalia cum dormiant,
dum pariter surgant ea
ad caelum triumphantia;
gaudete, sancti, cantibus
quod Christus aderit citus.

Sanctorum Deus, adiuva;
tu, Christe, subveni supra;
et, dux amice Spiritus,
da gratiam dum vivimus,
ut simus sanctis comites,
sit tecum nobis requies.

MM 16—26.2.02

The Son of God goes forth to war
A kingly crown to gain;
His blood-red banner streams afar:
Who follows in his train?
Who best can drink his cup of woe.
Triumphant over pain,
Who patient bears his cross below,
He follows in his train.

The martyr first, whose eagle eye
Could pierce beyond the grave;
Who saw his Master in the sky.
And called on him to save.
Like him, with pardon on his tongue
In midst of mortal pain.,
He prayed for them that did the wrong:
Who follows in his train?

A glorious band. the chosen few
On whom the Spirit came,
Twelve valiant saints, their hope they knew,
And mocked the cross and flame.
They met the tyrant's brandished steel,
The lion's gory mane;
They bowed their necks. the death to feel:
Who follows in their train?

A noble army, men and boys,
The matron and the maid,
Around the Saviour's throne rejoice
In robes of light arrayed.
They climbed the steep ascent of heaven
Through peril, toil, and pain:
O God, to us may grace be given
To follow in their train.

R.Heber

Ad bellum prodiens thronum
en! Christus appetit;
vexillum panditur rubrum:
quis huic satelles it?
Qui eius poculum bibens.
dolorem subicit
mundanae crucis patiens,
is huic satelles it.

En! Martys sicut aquila
ultra videns necem
discernit Dominum supra
et poscit inde opem;
nec veniam minus rogat,
cum seeva mors rapit,
eius qui sibi noceat:
quis huic satelles it?

En! Parva lectorum manus,
bis sex spe validi,
cui fecit crucem Spiritus
ignemque spretui.
Nec tyrannorum gladius
nec leo terruit,
subirent cum necantibus,
quis his satelles it?

Mas gloriosa legio
commixta feminis
cingit thronum cum iubilo
lucentibus stolis.
Via scanderunt ardua
per arduas vices
tua scandamus gratia
cum his satellites.

MM 28.7—7.8.01

The spacious firmament on high,
with all the blue ethereal sky,
and spangled heavens, a shining frame,
their great Original proclaim.
The unwearied sun from day to day
does his Creator's power display;
and publishes to every land
the work of an almighty hand.

Soon as the evening shades prevail,
the moon takes up the wondrous tale,
and nightly to the listening earth
repeats the story of her birth:
whilst all the stars that round her burn,
and all the planets in their turn,
confirm the tidings, as they roll,
and spread the truth from pole to pole.

What though in solemn silence all
move round the dark terrestrial ball?
What though no real voice nor sound
amid their radiant orbs be found?
In reason's ear they all rejoice,
and utter forth a glorious voice;
for ever singing as they shine,
"The hand that made us is divine."

J.Addison

En! Firmamenti spatia
et aetheris caerulea
caelique splendentes plagae
canunt qua sint origine;
dum sol declarat in diem
Factoris firmitudinem,
omnipotentis et manus
demonstrat in terris opus.

Ut lucem vesper opprimit,
sermonem luna suscipit
suamque, ut tellus audiat,
nativitatem praedicat;
et cuncta circum sidera,
seu fixa seu palantia,
testantur in cursu suo
sonantia ad polum polo.

At grave per silentium
volvuntur circum hunc globum
nec claris vox in orbibus
nec verus ullus est sonus:
sed audit nostra ratio
cantantia cum iubilo
divinitusque splendida
se facta confitentia.

MM   1—6.10.98

Thee, living Christ, our eyes behold
Amid thy Church appearing,
All girt about thy breast with gold
And bright apparel wearing;
Thy countenance is burning light,
A sun that shineth in his might:
Lord Christ, we see thy glory.

Thy glorious feet have sought and found
Thy sons of every nation;
Thine everlasting voice doth sound
The call of our salvation;
Thine eyes of flame do search and scan
The whole outspreading realm of man:
Lord Christ, we see thy glory.

O risen Christ, who art alive,.
Amid thy Church abiding,
Who dost thy Blood and Body give
New life and strength providing,
We join in heavenly company
To sing thy praise triumphantly:
For we have seen thy glory.

E.R. Morgan

Hic, Christe, te conspicimus
nos inter apparentem
fulgentibusque vestibus
et aureis nitentem;
lucens et ardet os tuum
ut sol potens at splendidum:
videmus te decorum.

Ubique pulchro cum pede
tu tuos indagaris,
vocatque nos perpetue
vox ista salutaris;
luminibusque flammeis
humana cuncta perspicis:
videmus te decorum.

O Christe, redivivum te
nos inter habitantem
cum Corpore tum Sanguine
vitam et vim novantem
laudantes nos coniungimus
cum angelis ovantibus,
quem vidimus decorum.

MM 26—28.7.01

There is a blessed home	Beata domus est
Beyond this land of woe,	non hoc sub aethere,
Where trials never come,	tormentum unde abest
Nor tears of sorrow flow;	absuntque lacrimae;
Where faith is lost in sight,	cedit fides rei,
And patient hope is crowned,	speratum evenit;
And everlasting light	aeterna lux ibi
Its glory throws around.	splendorem digerit.

There is a land of peace,	Tranquilla regio
Good angels know it well;	supernis cognita;
Glad songs that never cease	eo neque a loco
Within its portals swell;	recedunt cantica;
Around its glorious throne	et solio Deum
Ten thousand saints adore	laudant circumdati,
Christ, with the Father one	ut Trinum, Unicum
And Spirit, evermore.	sanctorum plurimi.

Look up, ye saints of God,	Heus! comites Dei,
Nor fear to tread below	per duram hic viam
The path your Saviour trod	audete vos sequi
Of daily toil and woe;	a Christo transitam;
Wait but a little while	manete vos modo
In uncomplaining love,	amare neu gravet:
His own most gracious smile	is vultu mox bono
Shall welcome you above.	supra suscipiet.

H.W.Baker

MM 8—16.10.00

There is a book, who runs may read,
Which heavenly truth imparts,
And all the lore its scholars need,
Pure eyes and Christian hearts.
The works of God above, below,
Within us and around,
Are pages in that book, to show
How God himself is found.

The glorious sky, embracing all,
Is like the Maker's love,
Wherewith encompassed, great and small,
In peace and order move.
The moon above, the Church below,
A wondrous race they run;
But all their radiance, all their glow,
Each borrows of its sun.

The Saviour lends the light and heat
That crown his holy hill;
The saints, like stars, around his seat
Perform their courses still.
The dew of heaven is like thy grace,
It steals in silence down;
But where it lights, the favoured place
By richest fruits is known.

One name, above all glorious names,
With its ten thousand tongues
The everlasting sea proclaims,
Echoing angelic songs.
The raging fire, the roaring wind,
Thy boundless power display;
But in the gentler breeze we find
Thy Spirit's viewless way.

Two worlds are ours: 'tis only sin
Forbids us to descry
The mystic heaven and earth within,
Plain as the sea and sky.
Thou who hast given me eyes to see
And love this sight so fair,
Give me a heart to find out thee,
And read thee everywhere.

J. Keble

254

Est codex, cursor quem legat,
ut vera noverit,
dum puriter inspiciat
et Christianus sit.
Quotquot sunt opera Dei
nos, ubicumque sunt,
ut eius paginae libri
ad ipsum dirigunt.

Caelum notetur splendidum
Factonis ut amor,
amplexu cuius omnium
tranquillus est tenor.
Ut luna, sic Ecclesia
mirandum cursum it,
suus sed, ut sit lucida,
utrique sol facit.

Lux et calor colli sacro
a Salvatore sunt,
eumque siderum modo
sancti circueunt.
Descendit gratia tua
ut ros silentio,
fit et seges notissima
quo cecidit loco.

Supremum nomen nominum
proclamat plurimis
aeternum vocibus fretum,
respondens angelis.
Tu flabris borealibus
cognosceris potens
mollique zephyro tuus
clam Spiritus agens.

Duplex est mundus: extera
videntibus patent;
internum nostra vitia
discerni prohibent.
Das, Deus, oculos mihi,
ut pulchra videam;
da mentem, instar ut libri
ubique te legam.

MM 8—17.3.00

There is a green hill far away,
Without a city wall,
Where the dear Lord was crucified,
Who died to save us all.

We may not know, we cannot tell,
What pains he had to bear,
But we believe it was for us
He hung and suffered there.

He died that we might be forgiven,
He died to make us good;
That we might go at last to heaven,
Saved by his precious blood.

There was no other good enough
To pay the price of sin;
He only could unlock the gate
Of heaven, and let us in.

O dearly, dearly has he loved,
And we must love him too,
And trust in his redeeming blood,
And try his works to do.

C.F. Alexander

Stat urbis extra moenia
collis gramineus,
pro nobis ubi Christus est
in cruce mortuus.

Nescitur quantus is dolor
ei contigerit;
sed nostra pendulum vice
fuisse constitit.

Qui nobis emit veniam,
essemus ut boni,
caelorum regno per suum
cruorem debiti.

Peccati nostri pretium
is unus praestitit
solusque caeli ianuam
nobis aperuit.

Amavit ille maxime:
amemus haud secus,
fidentes eius sanguini
secundantesque opus.

MM 27.6—7.7.98

There is a land of pure delight,
Where saints immortal reign;
Infinite day excludes the night,
And pleasures banish pain.

There everlasting spring abides,
And never-withering flowers;
Death, like a narrow sea, divides
That heavenly land from ours.

Sweet fields beyond the swelling flood
Stand dressed in living green;
So to the Jews old Canaan stood,
While Jordan rolled between.

But timorous mortals start and shrink
To cross the narrow sea,
And linger shivering on the brink,
And fear to launch away.

O could we make our doubts remove,
Those gloomy doubts that rise,
And see the Canaan that we love
With unbeclouded eyes;

Could we but climb where Moses stood,
And view the landscape o'er;
Not Jordan's stream, nor death's cold flood,
Should fright us from the shore.

I. Watts

Sanctoruin regionibus
amoenitas mera
et est dies perpetuus
  nec ulla tristia.

Ver infinitum est ibi,
floresque renovat;
angustique instar nos freti
  mors inde separat

et pratis a virentibus
sic unda dirimit
Jordane Judaeis locus
ut sponsus afuit.

Nec homines tamen volunt
abire margine
sed ibi territi tremunt
timentque solvere.

Funesta dubitatio
pellatur utinam
nudoque detur oculo
spectare patriam!

Quae nobis modo visa sit
Moysi similibus,
Jordanis sive mors erit,
in flumen ibimus.

MM   24—7.4.98

There is no sorrow, Lord, too light
To bring in prayer to thee;
There is no anxious care too slight
To wake thy sympathy.

Thou who hast trod the thorny road
Wilt share each small distress;
The love which bore the greater load
Will not refuse the less.

There is no secret sigh we breathe
But meets thine ear divine;
And every cross grows light beneath
The shadow, Lord, of thine.

Life's ills without, sin's strife within,
The heart would overflow,
But for that love which died for sin,
That love which wept for woe.

J.F.Crewdson

Tam parvus ecquis est dolor
de quo non sint preces
aut ulla cura levior
quam ut tu toleres?

Feres, viae tu, luctulum,
viator spineae;
onus tulisti maximum,
non abnues leve.

Exaudis tu suspirium,
clam etsi fuerit,
nec ullum non patibulum
prae tuo lene fit.

Ne culpa premat animas
cum aegrimoniis,
tu morte culpam dissipas
et fles cum animis.

MM 13—22.10.00

They whose course on earth is o'er,
Think they of their brethren more?
They before the throne who bow,
Feel they for their brethren now?

We by enemies distrest,
They in Paradise at rest;
We the captives, they the freed –
We and they are one indeed.

Those whom many a land divides,
Many mountains, many tides,
Have they with eachother part,
Fellowship of heart with heart?

Each to each may be unknown,
Wide apart their lots be thrown;
Differing tongues their lips may speak,
One be strong, and one be weak:

Yet in Sacrament and prayer
Each with other hath a share;
Hath a share in tear and sigh,
Watch and fast and litany.

Saints departed even thus
Hold communion with us;
Still with us, beyond the veil
Praising, pleading, without fail.

With them still our hearts we raise,
Share their work and join their praise,
Rendering worship, thanks and love
To the Trinity above.

J.M.Neale

An qui vita functi sunt
comitum meminerunt?
Estne cura comitum
stratis ante solium?

Mala nos sollicitant,
illi cum Deo cubant
liberati iam, sed i
sunt eiusdem populi.

Montibus et maribus
cum findatur populus,
inter partes varias
est tamen societas.

Nulla sit scissis loco
mutua cognitio,
utque linguae dissident
vires ita discrepent;

inter se participant
quotiens sacrificant
vigiles cum lacrimis,
precibus, ieiuniis.

At ligantur haud secus
mortui viventibus,
nec, si velum dividit,
prex eorum deficit.

Iunctis ergo laudibus
sursum corda tollimus
agimusque, Trinitas
Sancta, tibi gratias.

MM 2—12.1.00

Thine for ever! God of love,
hear us from thy throne above;
thine for ever may we be
here and in eternity.

Thine for ever! O how blest
they who find in thee their rest!
Saviour, Guardian, heavenly Friend,
O defend us to the end.

Thine for ever! Lord of life,
shield us through our earthly strife;
thou, the Life, the Truth, the Way,
guide us to the realms of day.

Thine for ever! Saviour, keep
these thy frail and trembling sheep,
safe alone beneath thy care,
let us all thy goodness share.

Thine for ever! Thou our Guide,
all our wants by thee supplied,
all our sins by thee forgiven,
lead us, Lord, from earth to heaven.

Mrs. M.F. Maude

Tui semper! Quos amas,
e throno nos audias;
nunc et tu dum es, Deus,
tui semper erimus.

Tui semper! Vivere
das: viventes protege.
Vita, Veritas, Via,
ad diei duc loca.

Tui semper! Est bonum.
quod tu porgis, otium.
Vindex, custos et comes,
nos fac usque sospites.

Tui semper! Pastor es:
pasce tremulas ovcs;
tutos coram te tua
bonitate nos bea.

Tui semper! Te duce,
dante possidenda te,
sint soluta crimina;
nos et ad caelum voca.

MM 9—16.11.00

This is the day of light:
Let there be light today;
O Dayspring, rise upon our night,
And chase its gloom away.

This is our day of rest:
Our failing strength renew;
On weary brain and troubled breast
Shed thou thy freshening dew.

This is the day of peace:
Thy peace our spirits fill;
Bid thou the blasts of discord cease,
The waves of strife be still.

This is the day of prayers
Let earth to heaven draw near;
Lift up our hearts to seek thee there,
Come down to meet us here.

This is the first of days:
Send forth thy quickening breath,
And wake dead souls to love and praise,
O vanquisher of death,

J. Ellerton

Haec dies luminis
sit lumen hodie;
quin noctem tu, sol, inruis
pulsa caligine?

Haec dies otii:
minutam vim nova
et roris infundas tui
in fessa pectora.

Est pacis haec dies:
nos pacis impleas
discordiasque dissipes
litesque comprimas.

Haec est dies precis:
sit caelum propius;
ad nos huc tu descenderis,
quem ibi petimus.

Est primus hic dies:
adflans vivifica;
defunctos (victor mortis es)
ad laudem excita.

MM   12—15.12.00

This is the day the Lord hath made,
He calls the hours his own;
Let heaven rejoice, let earth be glad,
And praise surround his throne.

Today he rose and left the dead,
And Satan's empire fell;
Today the saints his triumphs spread,
And all his wonders tell.

Hosanna to the anointed King,
To David's holy Son!
O help us, Lord, descend and bring
Salvation from thy throne.

Blest be the Lord, who comes to men
With messages of grace;
Who comes, in God his Father's name,
To save our sinful race.

Hosanna in the highest strains
The Church on earth can raise;
The highest heavens in which he reigns
Shall give him nobler praise.

I. Watts

Hanc diem Dominus dedit,
horas sibi asserens
cum caelo laeta terra sit;
laudetur is sedens.

Surrexit hac de mortuis
vicitque Satanam;
a sanctis hac laudatur is
nactus victoriam.

"Hosanna!" Regi nunc sonet
uncto Davidico.
Auxilium o! defer et
salutem a throno.

Quam bonus praeco gratiae
huc, Domine, venis
reisque Patris nomine
peccantibus subis.

Laudabit hic te viribus
summis Ecclesia,
sed regna quanto melius
superna te tua!

MM   8—14.12.00

Thou art gone up on high,   *Elatus es supra*
To mansions in the skies;   *ad aetheris domum,*
And round thy throne unceasingly   *quo surgit laus perpetua*
The songs of praise arise: *cingitque solium.*
But we are lingering here,   *Nos infra sistimus,*
With sin and care oppressed;   *quos culpa subiugat;*
Lord, send thy promised Comforter,   *quem promisisti, Spiritus*
And lead us to thy rest.   *ad requiem ferat.*

Thou art gone up on high;   *Elatus es supra,*
But thou didst first come down,   *deisti sed prius,*
Through earth's most bitter misery   *et passus hic acerrima*
To pass unto thy crown;   *Regnator es ratus.*
And girt with griefs and fears   *Metus et lacrimae*
Our onward course must be;   *nos quoque maneant;*
But only let this path of tears   *sed fac eaedem denique*
Lead us at last to thee.   *te coram nos vehant.*

Thou art gone up on high;   *Elatus es supra;*
But thou shalt come again,   *sed et revenies,*
With all the bright ones of the sky   *cui cuncta caeli lumina*
Attendant in thy train.   *erunt satellites.*
Lord, by thy saving power   *Nos salva, Domine,*
So make us live and die,   *defunctos, atque ea*
That we may stand in that dread hour   *die tremenda nos habe*
At thy right hand on high.   *ad dexteram supra.*

Mrs E. Toke   *MM 29.5.—3.6.0l*

Thou didst leave thy throne and thy kingly crown,
When thou caiuest to earth for me;
But in Bethlehem's home was there found no room
For thy holy Nativity:
  O come to my heart, Lord Jesus;
  There is room in my heart for thee.

Heaven's arches rang when the angels sang,
proclaiming thy royal degree;
But in lowly birth didst thou come to earth,
And in great humility: O come etc

The foxes found rest, and the bird had its nest
in the shade of the cedar tree;
But thy couch was the sod, O thou Son of God,
In the desert of Galilee: O come etc

Thou camest, O Lord, with the living word
That should set thy people free;
But with mocking scorn and with crown of thorn
They bore thee to Calvary: O come etc

When the heavens shall ring, and the angels sing,
At thy coming to victory,
Let thy voice call me home, saying, "Yet there is room,
There is room at my side for thee:"
  O come to my heart, Lord Jesus;
  There is room in my heart for thee.

E.E.S. Elliott

Liquisti thronum et regium
apicem genitus mihi,
neque Bethlehem dedit habilem
locum isti natui:
    cor quaere meum, O Iesu;
    erit hic spatium tibi.

Etsi titulum sonuere tuum
celebrantes angeli;
haud genitus es procerum comes
sed ordinis infimi: *cor etc*

Sua vulpibus volucrique domus
sub termitibus cedri;
sed, Christe, mero cubuisti solo,
qui filius es Dei: *cor etc*

Tu nuntius is, Domine, tuis,
fiant ut liberi;
sed ludibrio cum spineo
impositus es Cruci: *cor etc*

Cum dent sonitum celebrentque tuum
triumphum angeli,
tua vox revocet "Spatium"-que "manet"
mihi dixerit "hic tibi:"
    cor quaere meum, O Iesu;
    erit hic spatium tibi.

MM 4—9.07.00

Thou to whom the sick and dying
Ever came, nor came in vain,
Still with healing word replying
To the wearied cry of pain,
Hear us, Jesu, as we meet
Suppliants at thy mercy-seat.

Still the weary, sick, and dying
Need a brother's, sister's, care,
On thy higher help relying
May we now their burden share,
Bringing all our offerings meet
Suppliants at thy mercy-seat.

May each child of thine be willing,
Willing both in hand and heart,
All the law of love fulfilling,
Ever comfort to impart;
Ever bringing offerings meet
Suppliant to thy mercy-seat.

So may sickness, sin, and sadness
To thy healing virtue yield,
Till the sick and sad, in gladness,
Rescued, ransomed, cleansèd, healed,
One in thee together meet,
Pardoned at thy judgement-seat.

G. Thring

Prope mortem aegrotantes
apte qui sanaveris,
adhuc fessos invocantes
alma voce suscipis:
nos exaudias tuae
indigos clementiae.

Fratres et sorores simus
fessis aegrotantibus;
ope tua gesserimus
grave quod portant onus,
offerentes hoc tuae
debitum clementiae.

Demus operam libentes
(cor libens sit et manus)
caritatis audientes
consolationibus:
offeramus hoc tuae
debitum clementiae.

Cum doloribus virtuti
culpa tuae cesserit:
omni vitio soluti,
quos aerumna deprimit,
iudicati tum tuae
coeant clementiae.

MM   26.8—14.9.01

Latinised Hymns

Thou, whose almighty word
Chaos and darkness heard,
And took their flight;
Hear us, we humbly pray,
And where the Gospel-day
Sheds not its glorious ray,
   Let there be light!

Thou, who didst come to bring
On thy redeeming wing
Healing and sight,
Health to the sick in mind,
Sight to the inly blind,
O now to all mankind
   Let there be light!

Spirit of truth and love,
Life-giving holy Dove,
Speed forth thy flight;
Move on the water's face
Bearing the lamp of grace,
And in earth's darkest place
   Let there be light!

Holy and blessed Three,
Glorious Trinity,
Wisdom, Love, Might;
Boundless as ocean's tide
Rolling in fullest pride
Through the earth far and wide –
   Let there be light!

J. Marriot

Cuius imperio
est facta cognito
noctis fuga,
quem Evangelium,
oramus, in locum
non fert iubar suum,
   illumina.

Qui caecis aciem
et valetudinem
cum gratia
insanis ut dares
venisti, nunc ades
et quot sunt homines
   illumina.

Spiritus nos amans,
Avis vivificans,
prorsus vola:
fer super aequora
gratiae lampada
terraeque aterrima
   illumina.

Trinitas sapiens
et amans et potens
et splendida,
sicut oceanum
volvens iubar tuum
utrumque iam polum
   illumina.

MM 13

Thou Wind of God, whose coming stirred
A world as yet unmade,
And things, which were not, woke and heard
And answered and obeyed;

By thee the lives that live and move
In earth and sea began,
And human thought and human love
Lit up the heart of man;

Until thou camest, Holy One,
In Jesus' heart to dwell,
That man, in him, might be a son
And please the Father well.

O thou, who from the Father art,
Upon our spirits move,
Until the children's thankful heart
Reflects the Father's love.

J.M.C.Crum

Divine Flatus, unde fit
quod est e nihilo
oboediensque apparuit
cienti Domino;

Quot terra gignit et mare
per te creata sunt,
lucere mens in homine
amorque coeperunt;

venisti mox sanctissimus
cor Jesu penetrans,
ut prolem ibi nos Deus
agnosceret probans.

In nos, O Patre defluens,
vis tua veniat,
dum filiorum grata mens
Patri respondeat.

MM 6—10.8.01

Three in One and One in Three,
Ruler of the earth and sea,
hear us while we lift to thee
holy chant and psalm.

Trine et Unice Deus,
es ubique Dominus;
audi nos, qui tollimus
tibi nenias.

Light of lights! with morning shine,
lift on us thy light divine;
and let charity benign
breathe on us her balm.

Lucum lampas optima,
mane nos illumina;
adflet et benefica
nobis caritas.

Light of lights! when falls the even,
let it sink on sin forgiven;
fold us in the peace of heaven;
shed a vesper calm.

Lucum lampas, vesperi
culpa simus vacui,
et caelestis otii
pacem depluas.

Three in One and One in Three,
darkling here we worship thee;
with the saints hereafter we
hope to bear the palm.

Trine et Unice Deus,
lippi quem hic colimus,
supra des posterius
ferre palmulas.

G. Rorison

MM 24—7.7.00

Through the day thy love has spared us;
Now we lay us down to rest;
Through the silent watches guard us,
Let no foe our peace molest:
Jesus, thou our guardian be;
Sweet it is to trust in thee.

Pepercisti tu diurnus:
idem dormientibus
custos noster sis nocturnus
motus absit hosticus;
super nobis vigiles:
suavis est in te fides.

Pilgrims here on earth and strangers,
Dwelling in the midst of foes,
Us and ours preserve from dangers;
In thine arms may we repose,
And, when life's sad day is past
Rest with thee in heaven at last.

E periclis peregrinos,
cicumsessos hostibus,
cum propinquis expedi nos:
pacem des et, quaesumus,
tecum post vitam gravem
sempiternam requiem.

T. Kelly

MM 9—10.11.97

Thy kingdom come, O God,
Thy rule, O Christ, begin;
Break with thine iron rod
The tyrannies of sin.

Where is thy reign of peace,
And purity, and love?
When shall all hatred cease,
As in the realms above?

When comes the promised time
That war shall be no more,
And lust, oppression, crime,
Shall flee thy face before?

We pray thee, Lord, arise,
And come in thy great might;
Revive our longing eyes,
Which languish for thy sight.

O'er heathen lands afar
Thick darkness broodeth yet;
Arise, o morning Star,
Arise, and never set!

L. Hensley

In terris incipe
regnum, Deus, tuum,
et ferro percute
mali dominium.

Quin otium tuum
hic purum retegis?
Omne absit odium
ut in caelicolis.

Quam es pollicitus
quando quies venit,
cum stuprum, vis, scelus
te viso fugerit?

Orire, Domine,
et huc potens veni;
desiderantes te
laetentur oculi.

Nulla est ubi fides,
disperge tenebras;
ut stella lucem des,
nec umquam occidas.

MM 5—9.10.98

Latinised Hymns

"Thy kingdom come", on bended knee
The passing ages pray:
And faithful souls have yearned to see
On earth that kingdom's day.

But the slow watches of the night
Not less to God belong:
And for the everlasting right
The silent stars are strong.

And lo, already on the hills
The flags of dawn appear:
Gird up your loins, ye prophet souls;
Proclaim the day is near:

The day in whose clear-shining light
All wrong shall stand revealed,
When justice shall be throned in might,
And every hurt be healed:

When knowledge, hand in hand with peace,
Shall walk the earth abroad –
The day of perfect righteousness,
The promised day of God.

F.L.Hosmer

Summisso saecula genu
Dei diem petunt,
hic pia corda quam diu
videre cupiunt.

Sed tardae non minus Deo
noctes appertinent,
et muta pro perpetuo
iure astra praevalent.

En! Est aurora in vertice
eoo rutila:
vatum cohors, accingere
diemque nuntia,

peccata clare quae nitens
recludet omnia
et aequum alte statuens★
mulcebit aspera;

qua iuncta pax scientiae
per terras iverit,
dies privata crimine,
quam Deus obtulit.

MM 10—14.10.98

★iustitiamque promovens

To God be the glory! Great things he hath done!
So loved he the world that he gave us his Son;
Who yielded his life an atonement for sin,
And opened the life-gate that all may go in.
PRAISE THE LORD! PRAISE THE LORD!
LET THE EARTH HEAR HIS VOICE!
PRAISE THE LORD! PRAISE THE LORD!
LET THE PEOPLE REJOICE!
O   COME TO THE FATHER, THROUGH JESUS THE SON!
AND GIVE HIM THE GLORY! GREAT THINGS HE HATH DONE!

O perfect redemption, the purchase of blood!
To every believer the promise of God;
The vilest offender who truly believes,
That moment from Jesus a pardon receives.

Great things he hath taught us, great things he hath done,
And great our rejoicing through Jesus the Son:
But purer, and higher, and greater will be
Our wonder, our rapture, when Jesus we see.

E. van Alstyne

Laudate Deum, quia magna facit,
qui Filium mundi amore dedit;
is omne luit moriens scelus, et
sic ianua vitae aperta patet.
CELEBRATE DEUM. TIBI, TERRA, SONUS
VENIAT, BIBAT AURE LIBENS POPULUS!
VIA FILIUS AD GENITOREM ERIT:
LAUDEMUS EUM QUIA MAGNA FACIT.

Nos sanguine soluit ille suo,
 quis dat sua pignora, crede modo;
qui pessimus est, modo crrediderit,
ei veniam simul ille dabit.

Nos magna docet, neque parva facit;
quae gaudia Filius ille dedit!
Quantoque maioribus laetitiis
videntium ipse videbitur is!

MM 21—26.1.02

To thee, O Lord, our hearts we raise
in hymns of adoration,
to thee bring sacrifice of praise
with shouts of exultation.
Bright robes of gold the fields adorn,
the hills with joy are ringing,
the valleys stand so thick with corn
that even they are singing.

And now, on this our festal day,
thy bounteous hand confessing,
Upon thine altar, Lord, we lay
the first fruits of thy blessing.
By thee the souls of men are fed
with gifts of grace supernal;
thou, who dost give us earthly bread,
give us the bread eternal.

We bear the burden of the day,
and often toil seems dreary;
but labour ends with sunset ray,
and rest comes for the weary.
May we, the angel reaping over,
stand at the last accepted,
Christ's golden sheaves, for evermore
to garners bright elected.

O blessèd is that land of God
where saints abide forever,
where golden fields spread fair and broad,
where flows the crystal river;
the strains of all its holy throng
with ours today are blending;
thrice blessèd is that harvest song
which never hath an ending.

W. Chatterton Dix

Tollentes corda canimus
te, Deus, adorantes
iustisque te clamoribus
laudamus exultantes:
est agro vestis aurea
laetusque in colle sonus,
dum celebrant declivia
suum spicarum onus.

Te coram hoc festo die
meminimus datorum
araeque reddimus tuae
primitias tuorum:
humana corda gratia
tu sustines superna:
terrestria ut nutrimina
sic praebeas aeterna.

Labor diurnus opprimit
pigetque nos sudandi;
cum nocte sed quies venit
modusque laborandi:
sic Christi seges angelis
metentibus ligemur
splendentibusque in horreis
perpetuo locemur.

Benedicatur patriae
sanctorum permanenti
cum latis agris aureae
et fluvio nitenti:
caeeleste carmen est dies
quo nostro misceatur;
o ter beata quae seges★
aeterna celebratur!

MM 26.2.—3.3.98

★ *o ter beati quīs seges*

To thee our God we fly
For mercy and for grace;
O hear our lowly cry,
And hide not thou thy face.
O Lord, stretch forth thy mighty hand
And guard and bless our fatherland.

Ad te, qui bonus es
clemensque, fugimus;
oramus humiles:
ne lateas, Deus.
Fortem protende dexteram
nostramque serva patriam.

Arise, O Lord of Hosts!
Be jealous for thy name,
And drive from out our coasts
The sins that put to shame.

Rex Sabaoth Deus,
surge et te vindica;
quod pudet his scelus
e finibus fuga.

Thy best gifts from on high
In rich abundance pour,
That we may magnify
And praise thee more and more.

Tu praemia bona
effunde caelitus:
tua usque encomia
sic iterabimus.

The powers ordained by thee
With heavenly wisdom bless;
May they thy servants be,
And rule in righteousness.

Da quos praefeceris
divine sapiant
et legibus tuis
regentes pareant.

The Church of thy dear Son
Inflame with love's pure fire,
Bind her once more in one,
And life and truth inspire.

Tu Filii tui
incende Ecclesiam
vetansque dividi
fac veram, vividam.

The pastors of thy fold
With grace and power endue,
That faithful, pure and bold,
They may be pastors true.

Fac gratia tua
pastores vigeant,
oves et integra
fide custodiant.

O let us love thy house,
And sanctify thy day,
Bring unto thee our vows,
And loyal homage pay.

Ne templa tua, ne
spernamus Sabbatum,
te voto supplice
fatentes Dominum.

Give peace, Lord, in our time;
O let no foe draw nigh,
Nor lawless deed of crime
Insult thy majesty.

Da nobis otium,
nec hostes prope sint,
nec crimina tuum
honorem laeserint.

Though vile and worthless, still
Thy people, Lord, are we;
And for our God we will
None other have but thee.
    O Lord, stretch forth, etc.

W.W. How

Indigna plebs licet,
sed tua plebs sumus;
Es Deus noster, et
non erit alius.
Fortem protende etc.

MM   22—30.1.00

To us a Child of royal birth,
Heir of the promises, is given;
The invisible appears on earth,
The Son of Man, the God of heaven.

A Saviour born, in love supreme,
He comes our fallen souls to raise;
He comes his people to redeem,
With all the fulness of his grace.

The Christ, by raptured seers foretold,
Filled with the eternal Spirit's power,
Prophet, and Priest, and King behold,
And Lord of all the worlds adore.

The Lord of Hosts, the God most high,
Who quits his throne on earth to live,
With joy we welcome from the sky,
With faith into our hearts receive.

C. Wesley

Regalis puer generis
promissus heres est datus;
videtur invisibilis
humanus hic, supra Deus.

Amore nati Vindicis
caducae surgunt animae;
redemptio fit hominis
cum plenitate gratiae.

Quem cecinere praescii,
inflavit Christum Spiritus;
is Praestes, Rex (veremini!),
Vates, mundorum Dominus.

Relicto natus est throno
Rector supremus Agminum,
excipimus quem e polo
dantes in animis locum.

MM 21—24.12.00

Trumpet of God, sound high,
Till the hearts of the heathen shake,
And the souls that in slumber lie
At the voice of the Lord awake.
Till the fenced cities fall
At the blast of the Gospel call,
Trumpet of God, sound high!

Hosts of the Lord, go forth:
Go, strong in the power of his rest,
Till the south be at one with the north,
And peace upon east and west;
Till the far-off lands shall thrill
With the gladness of God's good will,
Hosts of the Lord, go forth!

Come, as of old, like fire;
O force of the Lord, descend,
Till with love of the world's Desire
Earth burn to its utmost end;
Till the ransomed people sing
To the glory of Christ the King,
Come, as of old, like fire!

A.Brooks

Tuba Dei clamet
quatiatque profanum cor;
animas Deus excitet,
teneat licet has sopor.
Quoad oppida corruent,
sonitum sacra verba dent,
tuba Dei clamet!

Vade, cohors Dei,
firmante novata Deo,
coeant ut utrique poli,
Eous et Hesperio;
procul ut loca laeta sint
Deum ut bene iuverint,
vade, cohors Dei!

Igneus huc redi:
Domine, tua vis veniat,
dum terra calore Dei,
quam lata sit, ardeat,
redemptaque dum tribus
Christi celebret decus,
igneus huc redi!

MM 4—10.1.01 and 22.11.

'Twas by thy blood, immortal Lamb,
Thine armies trod the tempter down;
'Twas by thy word and powerful name
They gained the battle and renown.

Rejoice, ye heavens! let every star
Shine with new glories round the sky;
Saints, while ye sing the heavenly war,
Raise your Deliverer's name on high.

I.Watts

Tui per sanguinem tuum
presserunt, Agne, Satanam
potensque per vocabulum
sunt bello nacti gloriam.

Gaudete, caeli; sidera,
novate vos in aethere;
cantando, sancti, proelia
Salvantis nomen tollite.

MM 18—20.2.01

We hail thy Presence glorious,
O Christ our great high Priest,
O'er sin and death victorious,
At thy thanksgiving feast:
As thou art interceding
For us in heaven above,
Thy Church on earth is pleading
Thy perfect work of love.

Through thee in every nation
Thine own their hearts upraise,
Offering one pure Oblation,
One Sacrifice of praise:
With thee in blest communion
The living and the dead
Are joined in closest union,
One Body with one Head.

O living Bread from heaven,
Jesu, our Saviour good,
Who thine own self hast given
To be our souls' true food;
For us thy body broken
Hung on the Cross of shame:
This Bread its hallowed token
We break in thy dear name.

O stream of love unending,
Poured from the one true Vine,
With our weak nature blending
The strength of life divine;
Our thankful faith confessing
In thy life-blood outpoured,
We drink this Cup of blessing
And praise thy name, O Lord.

May we thy word believing
Thee through thy gifts receive,
That, thou within us living,
We all to God may live;
Draw us from earth to heaven
Till sin and sorrow cease,
Forgiving and forgiven,
In love and joy and peace.

Laudamus te praesentem,
O Christe Pontifex,
gratum gratos alentem,
quod est fugata nex.
Tu sicut intercessor
pro nobis es supra,
quid feceris, professor
est hic Ecclesia.

Cor gentium levatur,
quot sunt, ope tua,
dum pura dedicatur
laudantum hostia:
vivis per te defuncti
sunt uno Corpore
feliciter coniuncti
unoque Capite.

Qui bene salvavisti
nos, Panis vivide,
te verum tu dedisti
nutrimen animae:
ut corpus Cruce datum
tuum frangentibus
perinde fragmentatum
hunc Panem reddimus.

O Amor sine fine
vera vite effluens,
cum vi nostram divine
naturam nutriens,
tuo quod fisi simus
effuso sanguini,
hoc poclum nunc haurimus
cum laudibus tui.

Donatum te sumamus,
qui credimus tibi,
et te contineamus
satellites Dei;
culpa sine et dolore
clementes, liberos,
laetos cum pace amore
ad caelum trahe nos.

R.G.Parsons

Latinised Hymns

MM 7—20.1.01

We love the place, O God,
wherein thine honour dwells;
the joy of thine abode
all earthly joy excels.

It is the house of prayer,
wherein thy servants meet;
and thou, O Lord, art there
thy chosen flock to greet.

We love the sacred font;
for there the Holy Dove
to pour is ever wont
his blessing from above.

We love thine altar, Lord;
O what on earth so dear?
For there in faith adored,
we find thy presence near.

We love the word of life,
the word that tells of peace,
of comfort in the strife,
and joys that never cease.

We love to sing below
for mercies freely given;
but O we long to know
the triumph-song of heaven.

Lord Jesus, give us grace
on earth to love thee more,
in heaven to see thy face,
and with thy saints adore.

Bullock/Baker

Amamus ut locum
ubi est honor tuus!
Terrestre gaudium
tua anteit domus.

Hic fundimus precem
tui satellites;
et ipse tu gregem
collectum hic foves.

Lavabrum ut placet,
Columba ubi suum
defundere solet
beantem spiritum!

Quid tua Doinine,
est ara carius,
colentes ubi te
adesse fidimus?

Id Verbum ut placet,
quod monstrat otium,
pugnae solamen et
perenne iubilum!

Clementias iuvat
hic canere datas:
cantare liceat
supra victorias!

Da, Jesu, gratiam:
amemus hic magis,
et caelo te palam
colamus cum tuis.

MM 1—10.8.99

We sing the praise of him who died,
Of him who died upon the Cross:
The sinner's hope let men deride;
For this we count the world but loss.

Inscribed upon the Cross we see
In shining letters 'God is love';
He bears our sins upon the Tree;
He brings us mercy from above.

The Cross! it takes our guilt away;
It holds the fainting spirit up;
It cheers with hope the gloomy day,
And sweetens every bitter cup;

It makes the coward spirit brave,
And nerves the feeble arm for fight;
It takes all terror from the grave,
And gilds the bed of death with light;

The balm of life, the cure of woe,
The measure and the pledge of love,
The sinner's refuge here below,
The angels' theme in heaven above.

T.Kelly

Laudamus Cruce mortuum,
spem dantem peccatoribus;
sit ceteris ludibrium,
prae Cruce mundum spernimus.

Crucis nitens inscriptio
amorem Deum nominat,
qui salvat in patibulo
caeloque gratia rigat.

Crux culpam nobis abluit,
caducum fulcit animum,
caliginemque dirimit,
delenit acre poculum.

Imbellem Crux intrepidum,
fortemque timidum facit;
per eam funus liberum
terrore, mors aurata fit.

Solamen et lenitio,
ferens amoris pignora,
Crux hic effugium reo
dat angelisque cantica.

MM 4—7.3.98

We three Kings of Orient are;
Bearing gifts we traverse afar
Field and fountain, moor and mountain,
Following yonder star:

O STAR OF WONDER, STAR OF NIGHT,
STAR WITH ROYAL BEAUTY BRIGHT,
WESTWARD LEADING, STILL PROCEEDING,
GUIDE US TO THY PERFECT LIGHT.

Born a King on Bethlehem plain,
Gold I bring to crown him again
King for ever, ceasing never
Over us all to reign:

Frankincense to offer have I;
Incense owns a deity nigh:
Prayer and praising all men raising
Worship him, God most high:

Myrrh is mine: its bitter perfume
Breathes a life of gathering gloom;
Sorrowing, sighing, bleeding, dying,
Sealed in a stone cold tomb:

Glorious now behold him arise,
King and God and Sacrifice!
Heaven sings Alleluia; Alle-
-luia the earth replies.

Misit huc Magos Oriens:
stella tres nos ducit agens
rura rivos campum clivos
donaque transferens.

O SIDUS ADMIRABILE
CLARA PULCHRITUDINE
NOS PRAECEDENS, NUSQUAM SEDENS
NOS AD LUMEN DIRIGE!

Natus est ad Bethlehem Rex:
aureus confirmet apex;
totus sine cuncto fine
pareat illi grex:

Numinosum offero tus:
noscitatur ture Deus;
ornent iuncti Summum cuncti
cum prece laudibus:

Ecce! myrrha acerbum olens,
umbras imminere docens!
Cruciatum immolatum
en lapis opprimens!

Iamque vindicatus ovat,
se victorem nuntiat;
angelorum terra chorum
laude reduplicat.

MM 10—19.1.02

We turn to you, O God of every nation,	*Te petimus, O Deus populorum;*
Giver of life and origin of good;	*fons bonitatis, nos vivificas,*
Your love is at the heart of all creation,	*amans tuorum umbo creatorum,*
Your hurt is people's broken brotherhood.	*quem laesa laeserit fraternitas.*

We turn to you, that we may be forgiven
For crucifying Christ on earth again.
We know that we have never wholly striven,
Forgetting self, to love the other man.

Te petimus clementiam quaerentes
qui Christum rursus fiximus cruci
parum constituisse nos scientes
consulere prae nobis alteri.

Free every heart from pride and self-reliance,
Our ways of thought inspire with simple grace
Break down among us barriers of defiance,
Speak to the soul of all the human race.

Confisi nobis ne superbiamus,
te capiat spirantem nostra mens.
O frange claustra, neve resistamus
intus te sentiat humana gens.

On men who fight on earth for right relations
We pray the light of love from hour to hour.
Grant wisdom to the leaders of the nations,
The gift of carefulness to those in power.

Hic ut amici simus qui nitantur,
eis amoris lumen poscimus:
ut sapienter populi regantur
eorum cura sit potentibus.

Teach us, good Lord, to serve the need of others,
Help us to give and not to count the cost.
Unite us all, for we are born as brothers:
Defeat our Babel with your Pentecost.

Vicinis, serviendo dedicati,
quocumque largiamur pretio;
nativae redde nos fraternitati;
fac consonos cum Spiritu tuo.

F. Kaan

MM 22.9—8.10.01

What a wonderful change in my life has been wrought
   SINCE JESUS CAME INTO MY HEART!
I have light in my soul for which long I had sought,

    FLOODS OF JOY O'ER MY SOUL
    LIKE THE SEA BILLOWS ROLL,

I'm possessed of a hope that is steadfast and sure,
And no dark clouds of doubt now my pathway obscure,

There's a light in the valley of death now for me,
And the gates of the city beyond I can see,

I shall go there to dwell in that city, I know,
And I'm happy, so happy, as onward I go!
   SINCE JESUS CAME INTO MY HEART.

K.J.D.Matthews

Mea vita novatur ita ut stupeam,
   COR JESUS UBI INTROIIT:
mihi lux fovet illa petita animam,

    MIHI LAETITIAE
    CUMULANTUR AQUAE,

Data spes stabilis, bene fida, mihi,
nec opacat iter nigra nox dubii,

Ubi mors, ibi ave mihi vise nitor!
Procul Urbs mihi cernitur ulterior,

Erit Urbs habitanda mihi illa, scio;
ita terque quaterque beatus eo,
   COR JESUS UBI INTROIIT.

MM 7-13.12.01

When came in flesh the incarnate Word,
The heedless world slept on,
And only simple shepherds heard
That God had sent his Son.

When comes the Saviour at the last,
From east to west shall shine
The aweful pomp, and earth aghast
Shall tremble at the sign.

Lord, who could dare see thee descend
In state, unless he knew
Thou art the sorrowing sinner's friend,
The gracious and the true?

Dwell in our hearts, O Saviour blest:
So shall thine advent's dawn
'Twixt us and thee, our bosom-guest,
Be but the veil withdrawn.

J.Anstice

Mundum, cum factum est caro,
sopitum iniit
missumque rusticis modo
Verbum apparuit.

Valde tremendus iterum
Salvator veniet,
lustrata quod miraculum
tum terra metuet.

Quis te videre, Domine,
ovantem audeat,
peccantes te diligere
ex corde ni sciat?

Sis tu, Salvator, incola
nostris in cordibus,
ut revelatio mera
adventus sit tuus.

MM 4—10.12.00

When God of old came down from heaven,	*Olim descenderat Deus*
in power and wrath he came;	*et fortis et furens,*
before his feet the clouds were riven,	*miscens tenebras ignibus*
half darkness and half flame:	*nimbosque dividens.*
But when he came the second time,	*Sed iterum descendit is*
he came in power and love;	*et fortis et amans,*
softer than gale at morning prime	*aurorae vento similis*
hovered his holy Dove.	*columbamque imitans.*
The fires, that rushed on Sinai down	*Flammaeque Sinaiticae*
in sudden torrents dread,	*dira illa flumina*
now gently light, a glorious crown,	*sanctorum molli decore*
on every sainted head.	*adornant capita.*
And as on Israel's awestruck ear	*Utque Israel in auribus*
the voice exceeding loud,	*vox mira cecinit,*
the trump that angels quake to hear,	*supernos terrens lituus*
thrilled from the deep, dark cloud;	*qui nube sonuit,*
So, when the Spirit of our God	*sic, venit cum Paraclitus*
came down his flock to find,	*pecus suum petens,*
a voice from heaven was heard abroad,	*e caelo sparsus est sonus*
a rushing, mighty wind.	*ventusque violens.*
It fills the Church of God; it fills	*Hoc plena fit Dei domus*
the sinful world around;	*et quicquid exterum:*
only in stubborn hearts and wills	*solis abest a cordibus*
no place for it is found.	*is pervicacium.*
Come Lord, come Wisdom, Love and Power,	*O docte amans potensque, nos*
open our ears to hear;	*fac audiamus te:*
let us not miss the accepted hour;	*amatos sive territos*
save, Lord, by love or fear.	*salves in tempore.*
J.Keble	*MM 8—14.12.98*

When I survey the wondrous cross
on which the Prince of Glory died,
my richest gain I count but loss,
and pour contempt on all my pride.

Forbid it, Lord, that I should boast,
save in the cross of Christ, my God:
all the vain things that charm me most,
I sacrifice them to his blood.

See, from his head, his hands, his feet,
sorrow and love flow mingled down!
Did e'er such love and sorrow meet,
or thorns compose so rich a crown?

Were the whole realm of nature mine,
that were an offering far too small;
love so amazing, so divine,
demands my soul, my life, my all.

I. Watts.

In mentem mihi cum venit
Crucis Deo letiferae,
damnosum omne lucrum fit
pudetque me superbiae.

Ne causa gloriandi sit
nisi in pendente Domino.
Inane quicquid placuit
eius Cruori consecro.

Amorem luctu confluum
stillant caput, pedes, manus
Insigne quod confluvium!
Quod fronte spineum decus!

Totus-ne mundus est mihi?
Non sufficit, si offero.
Amori tam mirabili
me ipsum dare debeo.

MM 17—24.10.97

When morning gilds the skies,	*Cum mane luxerit*
My heart awaking cries,	*excitum cor canit*
MAY JESUS CHRIST BE PRAISED:	*SIT JESU CHRISTO LAUS.*
Alike at work and prayer	*Laborans, seu precor,*
To Jesus I repair; …	*ad Dominum feror,* …

Whene'er the sweet church bell	*Campana nos vocat*
Peels over hill and dell, …	*et rus circurnsonat* …
O hark to what it sings,	*num quis suavior*
As joyously it rings: …	*auditur hoc canor* …

My tongue shall never tire	*Augendi nec chorum*
Of chanting with the choir, …	*taedebit os meum* …
This song of sacred joy,	*Nec laeti carminis*
It never seems to cloy,…	*habuerim nimis* …

Does sadness fill my mind?	*Dolet-ne cor meum?*
A solace here I find …	*Hic est solatium* …
Or fades my earthly bliss?	*Fallente gaudio*
My comfort still is this: …	*levatus hoc ero* …

The night becomes as day,	*Dies fit ipsa nox,*
When from the heart we say …	*sit haec ex corde vox* …
The powers of darkness fear,	*Cedunt diaboli*
When this sweet chant they hear, …	*huic grato carmini* …

Be this, while life is mine,	*Dum vivus fuero*
My canticle divine …	*hoc utar cantico* …
Be this the eternal song	*Quod sit perpetuum*
Through ages all along,	*per omne saeculum,*
MAY JESUS CHRIST BE PRAISED.	*SIT JESU CHRISTO LAUS.*

Anon/E.Caswall   *MM   24.3—2.4.01*
(Beim frühen Morgenlicht)

When the trumpet of the Lord shall sound, and time shall be no more,
And the morning breaks, eternal, bright and fair;
When the saved of earth shall gather over on the other shore,
And the roll is called up yonder, I'll be there.

On that bright and cloudless morning when the dead in Christ shall rise,
And the glory of his resurrection share,
When his chosen ones shall gather to their home beyond the skies
And the roll is called up yonder, I'll be there.

Let us labour for the Master from the dawn till setting sun:
Let us talk of all his wond'rous love and care;
Then when all of life is over, and our work on earth is done
And the roll is called up yonder, I'll be there.

J.M.Black

Tuba finem ubi temporis edixerit Dei,
venietque lux privata termino,
steterint ubi caelestibus litoribus pii,
ego quoque numerandus adero.

Sine nube cum nitebit ea lux, dominici
orientur oriente Domino;
ut ad alta lecta turba ea levabitur, ibi
ego quoque numerandus adero.

Tenebras adusque pensa properabimus Eri,
et agemus gratias benefico;
ubi et ultimo labore soluemur famuli,
ego quoque numerandus adero.

MM 16-18.12.01

Where is this stupendous stranger?
Prophets, shepherds, kings, advise:
Lead me to my Master's manger,
Show me where my Saviour lies.

O most mighty, O most holy,
Far beyond the seraph's thought,
Art thou then so meek and lowly
As unheeded prophets taught?

O the magnitude of meekness,
Worth from worth immortal sprung,
O the strength of infant weakness,
If eternal is so young.

Good all-bounteous, all-creative,
Whom no ills from good dissuade,
Is incarnate, and a native
Of the very world he made.

C.Smart

Ille ubi advena stupendus,
vates, pastores, magi?
Ad praesepe sum ducendus
nam Salvator est ibi.

Praeter angelorum mentem
fortis et sanctissime,
humilem te nec potentem
num credidimus fore?

Quae maiestas se negantis
(optimus fit e bono)!
Quale robur est infantis,
erit si perpetuo!

Largus en! Deus Creator,
bonitati deditus,
mundi natus habitator
est, quem fecit, ipsius.

MM 24—26.10.00

While shepherds watched their flocks by night,	*Dum nocte pastores suum*
all seated on the ground,	*custodiunt pecus,*
the angel of the Lord came down,	*circumfulgente gloria*
and glory shone around.	*descendit angelus.*

"Fear not," said he, for mighty dread
had seized their troubled mind;
"Glad tidings of great joy I bring
to you and all mankind.

"Ne timeatis!" inquit is
(nam sunt perterriti)
"Magnum proclamo gaudium
vobis et generi.

"To you, in David's town, this day
is born of David's line
a Saviour, who is Christ the Lord;
and this shall be the sign:

In urbe David hodie
de David stirpe fit
Salvator Christus nomine;
et signum hoc erit:

"The heavenly Babe you there shall find
to human view displayed,
all meanly wrapped in swathing bands,
and in a manger laid."

infantem ibi quaerite
in visu hominum,
vestitum valde viliter,
praesepi creditum."

Thus spake the seraph, and forthwith
appeared a shining throng
of angels praising God, who thus
addressed their joyful song:

Sic ille; cuius comites
nitere visi sunt,
Deum magnificans cohors,
qui sic cecinerunt:

"All glory be to God on high
and on the earth be peace;
good will henceforth from heaven to men
begin and never cease."

"Nunc fiat pax hominibus
et Deo gloria,
et caritas inter duos
esto perpetua."

N. Tate

MM 14—28.12.99

Who are these like stars appearing,
These, before God's throne who stand?
Each a golden crown is wearing:
Who are all this glorious band?
Alleluia, hark! they sing,
Praising loud their heavenly King.

Who are these in dazzling brightness,
Clothed in God's own righteousness,
These, whose robes of purest whiteness
Shall their lustre still possess,
Still untouched by time's rude hand?
Whence came all this glorious band?

These are they who have contended
For their Saviour's honour long,
Wrestling on till life was ended,
Following not the sinful throng;
These, who well the fight sustained,
Triumph by the Lamb have gained.

These are they whose hearts were riven,
Sore with woe and anguish tried,
Who in prayer full oft have striven
With the God they glorified;
Now, their painful conflict o'er,
God has bid them weep no more.

These, the Almighty contemplating,
Did as priests before him stand,
Soul and body always waiting
Day and night at his command:
Now in God's most holy place
Blest they stand before his face.

F.E.Schenck/F.E.Cox

Qui stellariter fulgentes
circumstant Dei thronum,
auri circulos gerentes?
Quae cohors nitentium,
Alleluia qui canunt
Regis et laudes agunt?

Quos iustitiae nitore
Deus ipse vestiit,
quosque vestium candore
nemo spoliaverit
neque tempus invidens?
Unde exercitus nitens?

Salvatori consulentes
hi diu pugnaverunt,
usque ad mortem contendentes:
vulgus haud secuti sunt;
dimicati strenue
Agno vicerunt duce.

Hi sunt valde cruciati
corde aerumnis dedito
et in precibus luctati,
quem colebant, cum Deo;
flere quos diutius
idem iam vetat Deus.

Hi Potentem contemplantes
qui fuere antistites
quod iuberet observantes
nocte sive erat dies,
eius in sanctissimo
ipsum antestant loco.

MM 3—8.3.99

Who can cheer the heart like Jesus,
By his presence all divine?
True and tender, pure and precious,
O how blest to call him mine!
ALL THAT THRILLS MY SOUL IS JESUS:
HE IS MORE THAN LIFE TO ME (TO ME):
AND THE FAIREST OF TEN THOUSAND,
IN MY BLESSED LORD I SEE.

Love of Christ so freely given,
Grace of God beyond degree,
Mercy higher than the heaven,
Deeper than the deepest sea.

What a wonderful redemption!
Never can a mortal know
How my sin, tho' red like crimson,
Can be whiter than the snow.

Ev'ry need his hand supplying,
Ev 'ry good in him I see;
On his strength divine relying,
He is all in all to me.

By the crystal flowing river
With the ransomed I will sing,
And for ever and for ever
Praise and glorify the King.

T.Harris

Quis confortat nos ut Christus
Deus is, et proximus.
Fautor, fidus, carus, castus
is vocatur, et meus.
ILLE MAXIME STUPENDUS
ET QUAM VITA PLUS (MIHI)
OMNIBUSQUE PRAEFERENDUS,
QUOTQUOT ADSINT ALII.

Christi caritas donata,
vasta Dei gratia,
fine lenitas privata,
infra spectes seu supra.

O mirandum Redemptorem!
Culpae quis homo meae
hunc candere scit ruborem
posse purius nive?

Quicquid cupiam proviso
omne bonum est Dei;
eius robore confiso
is est omnia mihi.

Cum redemptis ut cantabo
iuxta flumen limpidum,
sempiternis celebrabo
Regem laudibus meum.

MM 22.2—4.3.02

Who is he, in yonder stall,
At whose feet the shepherds fall?
'TIS THE LORD! O WONDROUS STORY!
'TIS THE LORD, THE KING OF GLORY!
AT HIS FEET WE HUMBLY FALL:
CROWN HIM, CROWN HIM LORD OF ALL.

Adorante rustico
coetu quis in stabulo?
CHRISTUS ILLE PRAEDICANDUS
GLORIAEQUE REX MIRANDUS!
ADORANTES OMNIUM
REDIMITE DOMINUM!

Who is he, in yonder cot,
Bending to his toilsome lot?

Quis manu fabricia
hic laborat in casa?

Who is he, in deep distress,
Fasting in the wilderness?

Quis in solitudine
esurit miserrime?

Who is he that stands and weeps
At the grave where Lazarus sleeps?

Quis sopore conditi
flet sepulchrum Lazari?

Lo, at midnight, who is he
Prays in dark Gethsemane?

Cuius en! Gethsemanes
in tenebris hae preces?

Who is he, in Calvary's throes,
Asks for blessings on his foes?

Quis in Cruce pendulus
orat pro nocentibus?

Who is he that from the grave
Comes to heal and help and save?

Quis, cum post sepultus sit,
nobis opifer venit?

Who is he that from his throne
Rules through all the worlds alone?

Hic quis e throno sedens
unus omne dirigens?

B.R.Hanby

MM 19—26.12.01

Who would true valour see,	*Huc, fortitudinem*
Let him come hither;	*si quis videbit!*
One here will constant be,	*Aestum seu glaciem*
Come wind, come weather;	*hic sustinebit;*
There's no discouragement	*nec ullus efficit*
Shall make him once relent	*ut paenituerit*
His first avowed intent	*quod sponsus sibi sit*
To be a pilgrim.	*Peregrinator.*
Whoso beset him round	*Fabellis horridis*
With dismal stories,	*si forte cingis,*
Do but themselves confound:	*vim eius instruis,*
His strength the more is.	*tuam refringis;*
No lion can him fright;	*terrebit haud leo*
He'll with a giant fight,	*gigasve proelio*
But he will have the right	*quin iure sit suo*
To be a pilgrim.	*Peregrinator.*
No goblin nor foul fiend	*Non is diabolum*
Can daunt his spirit;	*ullum formidat,*
He knows he at the end	*ut qui viventium*
Shall life inherit.	*se fore fidat;*
Then, fancies, fly away;	*fugatis somniis,*
He'll not fear what men say;	*fit, spretis invidis,*
He'll labour night and day	*die seu tenebris*
To be a pilgrim.	*Peregrinator.*

J.Bunyan   *MM 22—26.3.00*

Will your anchor hold in the storms of life,
When the clouds unfold their wings of strife?
When the strong tides lift, and the cables strain,
Will your anchor drift, or firm remain?

Tuane ancora tenet hieme,
ubi nubila lacessunt te?
Aqua cum tollit gemit et rudens,
vaga-ne ancora it, manet an tenens?

WE HAVE AN ANCHOR THAT KEEPS THE SOUL
STEADFAST AND SURE WHILE THE BILLOWS ROLL:
FASTENED TO THE ROCK WHICH CANNOT MOVE,
GROUNDED FIRM AND DEEP IN THE SAVIOUR'S LOVE!

EN! ANCORAM, AQUA CUM TUMET,
QUAE STABILEM ANIMAM TENET,
SAXOQUE ADHAERET IMMOBILI,
TUEATUR QUAM AMOR CHRISTI!

Will your anchor hold in the straits of fear?
When the breakers roar and the reef is near;
While the surges rave and the wild winds blow,
Shall the angry waves then your bark o'erflow?

Satin ancora spretor freti,
reboante unda, prope ut es rupi?
Ubi trux fremet venti fragor,
ratem obruet fluctus furor.

Will your anchor hold in the floods of death,
When the waters cold chill your latest breath?
On the rising tide you can never fail,
While your anchor holds within the veil.

Satin ancora stat, ubi ultimum
aqua frigida premet halitum?
oriente unda teneas locum
quoad ancora stet apud Deum.

Will your eyes behold through the morning light
The city of gold and the harbour bright?
Will you anchor safe by the heavenly shore,
When life's storms are past for evermore?

Tibine apparens erit oppidum
auro nitens tum et ostium?
Tibine otium post maria
perpetuum dabit ancora?

P.J. Owens

MM   25.1—11.2.02

Word supreme, before creation
born of God eternally,
who didst will for our salvation
to be born on earth, and die;
well thy saints have kept their station,
watching till thine hour is nigh.

Now 'tis come and faith espies thee;
like an eaglet in the morn,
one in steadfast worship eyes thee;
thy beloved, thy latest born;
in thy glory he descries thee
reigning from the tree of scorn.

Lo! heaven's doors lift up, revealing
how thy judgments earthward move;
scrolls unfolded, trumpets pealing,
wine-cups from the wrath above,
yet o'er all a soft voice stealing
"Little children, trust and love!"

Thee, the Almighty King eternal,
Father of the eternal word;
thee, the Father's Word supernal,
thee, of both, the Breath adored;
heaven, and earth, and realms infernal
own, one glorious God and Lord.

J. Keble (St John)

Nil est ante te creatum,
te, quem genuit Deus,
Verbum nobis incarnatum
et mactatum haud secus;
bene sanctis vigilatum
est horam manentibus.

Hora adest: fides videt te:
ecce! quidam, acie
aquilari qui notet te
dilectissimusque te
constans veneretur et te
regem noscat in Cruce.

Caelum ecce! reseratur
leges huc mittens tuas;
tuba Liber indicatur
iracundiaeque vas,
parvulisque commendatur
fides atque caritas.

Te potentem atque aeternum
Regem teque Filium
Verbum eiusdem supernum
teque amborum Spiritum
superum, terrestre, infernum
unum laudant Dominum.

MM 4—10.10.00

Worship, honour, glory, blessing,
Lord, we offer to thy name;
Young and old, thy praise expressing,
Join their Saviour to proclaim.
As the saints in heaven adore thee,
we would bow before thy throne;
As thine angels serve before thee,
So on earth thy will be done.

E. Osler.

Nomen tuum rite cunctis
ornamentis colimus;
plauderis, Salvator, iunctis
pueris et senibus.
Aeque nostrum et sanctorum
tibi genu succidat;
more mundus angelorum
totus tibi pareat.

MM 6 Nov 96

Ye holy angels bright,
Who wait at God's right hand,
Or through the realms of light
Fly at your Lord's command,
Assist our song,
For else the theme
Too high doth seem
For mortal tongue.

Ye blessed souls at rest,
Who ran this earthly race,
And now, from sin released,
Behold the Saviour's face,
His praises sound,
As in his light
With sweet delight
Ye do abound.

Ye saints who toil below,
Adore your heavenly King,
And onward as ye go
Some joyful anthem sing;
Take what he gives
And praise him still,
Through good or ill,
Whoever lives.

My soul, bear thou thy part,
Triumph in God above,
And with a well-tuned heart
Sing thou the songs of love.
Let all thy days
Till life shall end,
Whate'er he send,
Be filled with praise.

Baxter/Gurney

Latinised Hymns

Ad Dei dexteram
manentes angeli
quique itis obviam
eiusdem iussui,
canentibus
concinite,
qui neniae
deficimus.

Quīs parta requies
terrestre post onus,
a culpa sospites,
spectatur quīs Deus,
laudate eum,
qui radiis
vestrum suis
fert gaudium.

Quīs durat hic labor,
laudate vos Deum;
dum stet viae tenor,
ciete canticum;
omnes iuvet,
ut in bono
sic in malo,
quod afferet.

Partem cape, anima,
divinitus ovans,
et cum concordia
amorem celebrans;
luces tuas,
dum vixeris,
quicquid det is,
laude impleas.

MM 28.7—1.8.99

Ye servants of God,
your Master proclaim,
and publish abroad
his wonderful Name;
the Name all-victorious
of Jesus extol:
his kingdom is glorious;
he rules over all.

God ruleth on high,
almighty to save;
and still he is nigh:
his presence we have.
The great congregation
his triumph shall sing,
ascribing salvation
to Jesus our King.

Salvation to God
who sits on the throne!
Let all cry aloud,
and honour the Son.
The praises of Jesus
the angels proclaim,
fall down on their faces,
and worship the Lamb.

Then let us adore,
and give him his right:
all glory and power,
all wisdom and might,
all honour and blessing,
with angels above,
and thanks never ceasing
and infinite love.

C. Wesley

Eius famuli laudent Dominum
mirumque Dei vulgent titulum;
Jesum domitorem ubique colant
regnique decorem, cui cuncta cadant.

Supra Deus est et omnipotens,
nobis et adest salvatque regens.
Cantet celebretque, Redemptor, erum
te turba vocetque salutificum.

Salutifici fultique throno
canora Dei sit laus Puero.
Angelicus ante cubat pedibus
Agni venerante choro numerus.

Orandus erit, quod est sapiens,
cui gloria sit, valdeque potens.
Ab angelis aeque sit omnis honor
et gratia neque finitus amor.

MM 12—18.3.99

Ye servants of the Lord,
Each in his office wait,
Observant of his heavenly word,
And watchful at his gate.

Let all your lamps be bright,
And trim the golden flame;
Gird up your loins as in his sight,
For aweful is his name.

Watch! 'tis your Lord's command,
And while we speak, he's near;
Mark the first signal of his hand,
And ready all appear.

O happy servant he
In such a posture found!
He shall his Lord with rapture see,
And be with honour crowned.

Christ shall the banquet spread
With his own royal hand,
And raise that faithful servant's head
Amid the angelic band.

P.Doddridge

Adstate Domini
locis satellites,
gnari caelestis imperi,
ad portam vigiles.

Lucernis aureae
sint flammae. Nam videt;
quo coram vos accingite:
tremendus is cluet.

Hoc Deus imperat,
dum loquimur, prope.
Notate si quid indicat,
promptique attendite.

Beatum famulum
qui sic repertus sit!
Videbit laetus Dominum
coronatusque erit.

Tum, Christe, dans cibum
de manibus tuis,
levabis fidum famulum
et addes angelis.

MM 17—22.3.99

Ye that know the Lord is gracious,
ye for whom a cornerstone
stands, of God elect and precious,
laid that ye may build thereon,
see that on that sure foundation
ye a living temple raise,
towers that may tell forth salvation,
walls that may re-echo praise.

Living stones, by God appointed
each to his allotted place,
kings and priests, by God anointed,
shall ye not declare his grace?
Ye, a royal generation,
tell the tidings of your birth,
tidings of a new creation
to an old and weary earth.

Tell the praise of him who called you
out of darkness into light,
broke the fetters that enthralled you,
gave you freedom, peace and sight:
tell the tale of sins forgiven,
strength renewed and hope restored,
till the earth, in tune with heaven,
praise and magnify the Lord.

C.A. Alington

Vos Deum benignum scitis,
qui locavit, super quem
urbem condere possitis,
angularem lapidem.
Vivum templum, turres, muros
hoc bono fundamine,
gloriam proclamaturos
et salutem, tollite.

Viva saxa vos qui iunxit,
suum cuique dans locum,
reges, sacerdotes unxit,
salutate vos eum,
sancta gens, sciatque mundus
(fessus nam consenuit)
unde vester oriundus
novus ordo venerit.

Is laudetur qui vocavit
prorsum vos e tenebris
quique vincla dissipavit
liberans molestiis.
Novam spem et vim narrate
veniamque scelerum;
vosque, caeli, celebrate
cum tellure Dominum.

MM Oct 96

God save our gracious *Queen
Long live our noble *Queen,
God save the *Queen
Send *her victorious,
Happy and glorious,
Long to reign over us;
God save the *Queen.

O Lord our God, arise,
Scatter our enemies,
And make them fall;
Confound their politics,
Frustrate their knavish tricks;
On thee our hopes we fix:
God save us all.

Thy choicest gifts in store
On *her be pleased to pour,
Long may *she reign.
May *she defend our laws,
and ever give us cause
To sing with heart and voice,
God save the *Queen.

*   King/he/him

ANON

Regina floreat:
eam custodiat
diu Deus.
Diu victoriam,
vitam et gloriam
gubernatoriam
donet Deus.

Exsurge, Domine,
disice et deice
oppositos;
obsta consiliis
illorum et dolis;
ut qui spes una sis,
defende nos.

Quod gremio tenes
ei suppedites;
diu regat
nostris cum legibus:
sic voce nec minus
corde rogabimus
ut floreat.

*   *Rex/eum*

MM 6-9.6.-02